Artificial Intelligence
for Sustainable Applications

Scrivener Publishing
100 Cummings Center, Suite 541J
Beverly, MA 01915-6106

Artificial Intelligence and Soft Computing for Industrial Transformation

Series Editor: S. Balamurugan

Scope: Artificial Intelligence and Soft Computing Techniques play an impeccable role in industrial transformation. The topics to be covered in this book series include Artificial Intelligence, Machine Learning, Deep Learning, Neural Networks, Fuzzy Logic, Genetic Algorithms, Particle Swarm Optimization, Evolutionary Algorithms, Nature Inspired Algorithms, Simulated Annealing, Metaheuristics, Cuckoo Search, Firefly Optimization, Bio-inspired Algorithms, Ant Colony Optimization, Heuristic Search Techniques, Reinforcement Learning, Inductive Learning, Statistical Learning, Supervised and Unsupervised Learning, Association Learning and Clustering, Reasoning, Support Vector Machine, Differential Evolution Algorithms, Expert Systems, Neuro Fuzzy Hybrid Systems, Genetic Neuro Hybrid Systems, Genetic Fuzzy Hybrid Systems and other Hybridized Soft Computing Techniques and their applications for Industrial Transformation. The book series is aimed to provide comprehensive handbooks and reference books for the benefit of scientists, research scholars, students and industry professional working towards next generation industrial transformation.

Publishers at Scrivener
Martin Scrivener (martin@scrivenerpublishing.com)
Phillip Carmical (pcarmical@scrivenerpublishing.com)

Artificial Intelligence for Sustainable Applications

Edited by

K. Umamaheswari,
B. Vinoth Kumar

and

S. K. Somasundaram

Department of Information Technology at PSG College of Technology, Coimbatore, Tamil Nadu, India

Scrivener
Publishing

Wiley Global Headquarters
111 River Street, Hoboken, NJ 07030, USA

For details of our global editorial offices, customer services, and more information about Wiley products visit us at www.wiley.com.

Limit of Liability/Disclaimer of Warranty

Library of Congress Cataloging-in-Publication Data

ISBN 9781394174584

Cover image: Pixabay.Com
Cover design by Russell Richardson

Set in size of 11pt and Minion Pro by Manila Typesetting Company, Makati, Philippines

Printed in the USA

10 9 8 7 6 5 4 3 2 1

Contents

Part II: Data Analytics Applications   127

Part VI: Security Applications   283

Preface

With the advent of recent technologies, the demand for Information and Communication Technology (ICT) based applications such as artificial intelligence (AI), machine learning, Internet of Things (IoT), healthcare, data analytics, augmented reality/virtual reality, cyber-physical systems, and future generation networks has increased drastically. In recent years, artificial intelligence has played a more significant role in everyday activities. While AI creates opportunities, it also presents greater challenges in the sustainable development of engineering applications. Therefore, the association between AI and sustainable applications is an essential field of research. Moreover, the applications of sustainable products have come a long way in the past few decades, driven by social and environmental awareness, and abundant modernization in the pertinent field. New research efforts are inevitable in the ongoing design of sustainable applications, which makes the study of communication between them a promising field to explore.

The book highlights the recent advances in AI and its allied technologies with a special focus on sustainable applications. The content is structured as six different parts focusing on medical, data analytics, e-learning, network, automotive and security applications. The goal of the book is to help researchers and practitioners enrich their knowledge and provide a learning resource for scholars to enhance their latest research ideas and developments. The book covers theoretical background, a hands-on approach, and real-time use cases with experimental and analytical results. A brief introduction to each chapter is as follows:

Chapter 1 discusses the prospect of a predictive machine-learning model for Alzheimer's disease with the help of a minimally invasive blood-based biomarker.

Chapter 2 presents the Bounding Box-based segmentation methods through thresholding, K-Means, and Fuzzy K-Means clustering to segment the COVID-19 chest X-ray images through simple calculations and fast operation.

Chapter 3 describes a model that can anticipate steering angles nearly identical to how a human would manage a car's steering wheel.

Chapter 4 aims to determine the most effective approach to analyzing Single-Nucleotide Polymorphism (SNP) data by combining several Feature Selection (FS) and classification methods. This chapter describes genome-wide prediction analysis to construct methods that predict and diagnose breast cancer dependent on the SNP set.

Chapter 5 discusses the coronavirus spread analysis with the day-to-day ascending behavior analysis by employing trend-check segregation algorithms. Using this approach, the collected COVID-19 data has been analyzed and visualized with respect to the affected cases.

Chapter 6 focuses on analyzing the effectiveness of statewide lockdowns by using Support Vector Regression (SVR) to forecast COVID-19 trends at different intervals, and uses the results generated to understand the effect of these lockdowns on the COVID-19 cases across various states in India.

Chapter 7 presents various existing methodologies for brain tumor detection and segmentation, quality of service, and the improvement of routing paths in Wireless Multimedia Sensor Networks (WMSN), as well as various data fusion methods.

Chapter 8 applies the ensemble method of machine-learning algorithms to predict the air quality and analyze these results in accordance with the comparison of other regression algorithms.

Chapter 9 proposes a new k-means algorithm for huge information grouping that utilizes refined charts in a web-based media organization and information bunching to track down the number of bunches in a set of information.

Chapter 10 provides an up-to-date review of the recent developments in code-smell detection algorithms that employ machine-learning techniques. The chapter covers various aspects, from finding code-smells in Machine-Learning based projects to the detection of code-smells in API documentation.

Chapter 11 explains how to methodically obtain datasets and domain knowledge from consumers and compose corresponding micro-apps for them by using a micro-intelligence application platform capable of classification or regression. This is done while simultaneously guaranteeing that the complexities of ML code, such as model selection and hyperparameter tuning, are abstracted from the client side using AutoML.

Chapter 12 suggests attention estimation techniques to bridge the gap between an online classroom and a traditional offline classroom.

Chapter 13 explores a full-on educational-oriented chatbot, describing various experiences for the users and also precisely answering related questions. The proposed framework provides the student with a specific solution to his or her issue, rather than getting multiple solutions on the internet.

Chapter 14 discusses machine-learning techniques that are suitable for anomaly detection and their challenges based on performance metrics factors. The research issues of various anomaly detection techniques are presented with a brief discussion on certain adaptive algorithms.

Chapter 15 focuses on cryptographic key generation using Elliptic Curve Diffie-Hellman (ECDH) with Deep Convolutional Neural Network (DCNN) and Genetic Algorithm (GA), and how high data confidentiality and data integrity are achieved by preventing unauthorized manipulations and message denial.

Chapter 16 reviews non-recurrent State-of-Charge (SoC) estimation techniques such as Feed-forward Neural Networks (FNNs), Radial Basis Functions (RBF), Extreme Learning Machines (ELM), and Support Vector Machines (SVM). It is recommended that the SoC Estimation Techniques under comparison should share common data sets (both training and testing) and learnable parameters, or else the comparison may be biased.

Chapter 17 introduces a novel system that helps to avoid accidents by selecting two parameters, such as eye and mouth, that help to locate the facial landmarks. Based on that, the eye and mouth aspect ratio are tracked, which helps to identify drowsiness sooner and avoid accidents.

Chapter 18 proposes a smart solution to the security of healthcare IoT-based systems using deep learning-based techniques.

Chapter 19 gives a clear, detailed view of how lattice-based homomorphic encryption works and outlines its uses. In addition, this chapter also aims to discuss the applications that use lattice-based homomorphic encryption and their significance in the recently growing domains of protecting and securing a large amount of data from unauthorized break-ins and destruction.

Chapter 20 focuses on biometric template storage and preservation, and the advantages and challenges of merging blockchain with biometrics. The suggested approach demonstrates that merging biometrics with blockchain improves biometric template protection.

We are grateful to the authors and reviewers for their excellent contributions in making this book possible. Our special thanks go to Mr. Martin Scrivener, Scrivener Publishing, Beverly, MA, for the opportunity to organize this edited book. We are obliged to Dr. S. Balamurugan, Director - Research and Development, Intelligent Research Consultancy Services (iRCS), Coimbatore, Tamilnadu, India for an excellent collaboration.

We hope this book will inspire researchers and practitioners from academia and industry alike, and spur further advances in the field.

Dr. K. Umamaheswari
Dr. B. Vinoth Kumar
Dr. S. K. Somasundaram
July 2023

Part I
MEDICAL APPLICATIONS

Predictive Models of Alzheimer's Disease Using Machine Learning Algorithms – An Analysis

Karpagam G. R.[1*], Swathipriya M.[1], Charanya A. G.[1] and Murali Murugan[2]

[1]Department of Computer Science and Engineering, PSG College of Technology, Coimbatore, Tamil Nadu, India
[2]Director of Engineering, Macy's, Georgia, USA

Abstract

Alzheimer's is a neurodegenerative dementia that occurs in people aged above 65, and there is a rapid growth in the amount of people suffering from it. Almost three out of four AD cases are undiagnosed. This paper comes with the view of identifying a predictive machine learning model for Alzheimer's disease with the help of a minimally invasive blood-based biomarker. By comparing models of different algorithms of machine learning, we conclude that the model following the Random Forest algorithm has the highest efficiency in terms of predicting the positive AD cases with the highest AUC of the ROC curve (0.927).

Keywords: Machine learning, automated machine learning, Alzheimer's disease

1.1 Introduction

In the 1950s many researchers attempted to build models that could interpret the world better than humans do. Then came the term "Machine Learning"-the concept by which the machine can learn and behave in the same way as humans do. Machine learning (ML) saw rapid developments in the late 1990s and in early 2000s and have found its applications across several different domains including healthcare. The introduction of ML in

*Corresponding author: grk@cse.psgtech.ac.in

K. Umamaheswari, B. Vinoth Kumar and S. K. Somasundaram (eds.) Artificial Intelligence for Sustainable Applications, (3–22) © 2023 Scrivener Publishing LLC

healthcare has been a breakthrough in the industry and it is still improving through the advancements in ML. Applications of ML models are used in the healthcare industry in several areas such as diagnosis of diseases, Drug Discovery and Manufacturing, Medical Imaging Diagnosis and Outbreak Predictions etc. [8]. This paper focuses on analyzing the predictive ability of various ML algorithms and their models in the prediction of Alzheimer's disease (AD) [4–6, 9].

AD is the most widely recognized type of neurodegenerative ailment leading to dementia that occurs mostly in individuals beyond the age of 65. A study says that only one out of three cases of AD are diagnosed across the world. As of now, the final diagnosis of Alzheimer's is only done through autopsy. It is one of the diseases whose prediction is difficult at an early stage, because it is often considered as normal symptoms of aging [3]. This difficulty in diagnosis may be the reason for the high ratio of undiagnosed cases to that of the diagnosed cases. So the need for effective and minimally invasive diagnostic models (i.e. diagnosis which doesn't involve severe break through the skin) is very much needed for early diagnosis by which we can avoid severe impairments. In the present study, we utilized the miRNA transcriptomic dataset from the GEO repository and built models using different algorithms in the WEKA platform and came up with the best predictive model by comparing the AUCs of the ROC curves of different models.

1.2   Prediction of Diseases Using Machine Learning

For a while now there have been several applications of artificial intelligence that are prosperous in various fields. AI assisted systems are utilized in healthcare, finance, education and is considered as a boon with enhancement. Being a part of AI machine learning innovations have been able to meet the needs of the people and its growth is unbounded. ML allows software applications to achieve a level of accuracy that can improve the current standards [2]. In the healthcare industry, ML has been utilized to produce accurate predictions of a particular disease. This not only makes the work of healthcare professionals easier but also increases patient outcomes. ML has also been helpful in handling the data and records of patients and in developing new medical procedures. In some ways these applications aim to make things a lot more efficient and easy for people to handle, including cost effectiveness.

However ML typically requires human intervention in various parts. This dependency on humans in order to achieve great performance sometimes becomes a hindrance. Thus to reduce human interventions, save time and increase accuracy in results an enhancement in machine learning technology is necessary. This programmed AI advancement is called Automated Machine Learning – AutoML. Besides the fact that AutoML is an emerging innovative technology, it has been utilized in prediction and analysis of heart diseases, cancer, diabetes, and electronic healthcare (EHR) analysis.

This chapter aims at exploring the ML algorithms and envisioning the best model that could help in predictions of Alzheimer's disease. As of late researchers have been attempting to find biomarkers that indicate the presence of Alzheimer's in patients at an early stage in order to diminish or decline the advancement of the disease. There are various strategies that involve early diagnosis of Alzheimer's disease. Those include brain imaging/neuroimaging , functional imaging, molecular imaging, blood and urine tests, analysis of protein levels (cerebrospinal fluid (CSF) levels of tau and beta-amyloid) and more. During this time with remarkable improvement in the innovative field, the analytic investigation of Alzheimer's has also been improving. We now have reliable technologies in addition to the already existing clinical tests that can provide accurate diagnosis resulting in satisfying patient outcomes. AutoML has been used to successfully identify biomarkers that are minimally invasive [7]. This process promises combined computational efficiency and predictive performance.

1.3 Materials and Methods

Dataset
We used the openly accessible blood-based miRNA transcriptomic dataset from the Gene Expression Omnibus (GEO) repository in the process of building the predictive models. It comprises of data about the miRNA profiles in blood tests of 48 AD patients and 22 sound controls containing 506 features [1].

Tools
The comprehensive, open source ML software WEKA (3.8.5) which lets the users preprocess the dataset, apply diverse ML algorithms on data and analyze various outputs that was used throughout the process of building the models.

1.4 Methods

1. Data pre-processing: The data obtained from the GEO repository is converted into an arff file in the Experimenter application of WEKA and once the arff file is ready, the explorer application in the weka GUI chooser is utilized for the rest of the processes. In this environment we can explore our dataset by first going through the preprocessing process. Initially, the dataset is preprocessed by normalizing and then randomizing it. Since a raw dataset does not contain metrics that can be used for analysis, the values are kept within a scale that is applied for all numeric columns used in the model by normalizing it first. Normalization technique makes sure that our data produces smooth patterns where we can see a significant change in the model performance. It also helps in redundancy. Randomization is a technique that prevents a model from learning the sequence of training. Each point in the data implies independent change on the model without being biased by the same points before them. This is the first and most important step before sending the data to a model [11, 12, 15, 17].

2. Model development: Now that the dataset is preprocessed, it can be used to train a model. Here the method implemented is cross validation 10 folds. It is a most preferred method since the model can train on numerous train test splits offering clear and better signs of how the model will execute. This is done by training the full dataset. Then we use cross validation 10 folds to test the model's ability of making predictions on new data.

3. Visualization: Once the models are ready, the test summary will manifest the performance measures of each model on the dataset. There are several metrics each with its own aim to depict the performance of each model. The area under the ROC curve metric gives the performance for classification models at various thresholds indicating how useful the test is. The higher the value of area under the ROC value, the better a model is at differentiating between patients affected by the disease and the patients without the disease. Similarly each metric has its own way of defining the performance of a model. In addition to these evaluation metrics the visualization tool can also be used to visualize the results [18, 19].

4. Best model prediction: Following the results predicting the best ML algorithm to distinguish between AD and healthy controls becomes easier. Comparing the area under the ROC curve the Random Forest (RF) algorithm produced better results [10, 13, 14, 16].

1.5   ML Algorithm and Their Results

1. J-48 Tree

J48 algorithm is the Java execution of C4.5 decision tree algorithm and C4.5 thusly is an augmentation of Id3 algorithm. In this algorithm, the decision tree is built by splitting the tree from top root to the bottom leaf until it reaches a stage where it cannot be split further. The attribute with which the splitting decision is taken is called the splitting attribute and it is chosen with the help of the information gain ratio. The attribute with the highest gain ratio at that level is chosen to split the tree further. To compute the data gain proportion, we utilize the idea of Information gain and entropy. Entropy indirectly can be defined as how much variance the data has

Information Entropy for a dataset with N classes

$$\text{Information entropy} = c \sum N p\_c \log\_2 (p\_c) \qquad (1.1)$$

Where p_i is the probability of randomly picking an element of class c

Information gain is used to measure how good the split is. Entropy is calculated for the spitted branches separately and the entropy for the split is calculated. The difference between the Entropy before split and after the split is referred to as Information gain. Information gain ratio is the ratio of Information gain to the split entropy.

Information gain ratio = (Information gain)/(Split entropy)

Pseudo code:

1. Check for base cases
2. For each attribute a find the information gain ratio from splitting on A
3. Let A_split be the attribute with the highest information gain ratio.
4. Create a decision node that splits on A_split
5. Repeat the same on the sub lists obtained by splitting on A_split and add those nodes as children of node

The decision tree for our classification is shown in Figure 1.1.a and Analysis via the J48 model produced a high AUC of 0.852 which is shown in Figure 1.1.b.

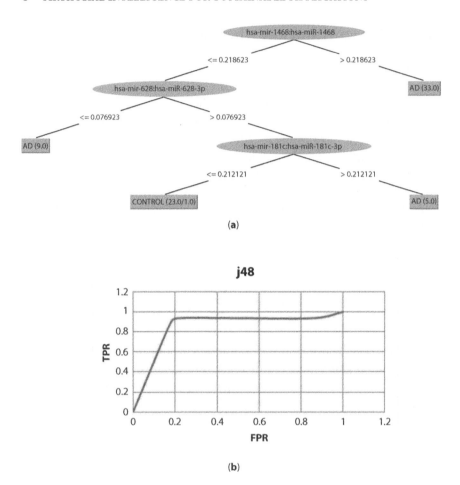

Figure 1.1 (a) Decision tree of j48 algorithm. (b) ROC curve for J48 algorithm.

2. Random Forest

It is a ML technique that is used for solving both classification and regression problems. Among all the ML classification algorithms in use, Random Forest produces the highest accuracy rate. One of the major advantages of using this technique is that it reduces overfitting, eventually increasing the accuracy rate.

Working of Random Forest Algorithm

It resembles the ensemble learning process wherein multiple classifiers are combined to solve complex problems and this increases the accuracy or the performance of the model. The larger the quantity of trees in a forest, the stronger the forest appears to be. Similarly in the RF classifier, the greater the amount of trees, higher will be the accuracy rate or performance of the model. Random Forest classifier contains a reasonable number of decision trees and produces prediction results of various subsets of the given dataset. When a new data point is fed into this phase, then based on the majority or taking the average value of the results, the classifier makes the final prediction.

There are two main advantages of Random Forest algorithm:

a. Since randomly selects subsets of features, the problem of overfitting is prevented.

b. In comparison to decision trees where a set of rules or conditions are laid out once the training dataset is given as input and then prediction is made, Random Forest randomly selects features, builds a number of decision trees and then takes the average or majority prediction result. This gives us a high rate of accuracy.

Explanation for the Pseudocode of the Random Forest Algorithm
This pseudocode works with a precondition that there is a training set S with features F and number of trees as B. A bootstrap sample from the training set S and $S^{(i)}$ denoting the ith bootstrap is selected geor each tree in the forest. Here we use bootstrap sampling technique because sampling is a process of selecting a subset of data from a collection of data and this method involves drawing sample data repeatedly with replacement (since there is a chance that the data point taken from the sample can be repeated in the future also). At each node of the tree, we randomly select some of the features f (a number that is smaller than F) out of F, where F is the set of features. The best split of this f is used to split the nodes. The function RadomizedTreeLearn($S^{(i)}$, F) performs training of a decision tree on the bootstrap sample $S^{(i)}$ selecting F features randomly at each split. By narrowing down the set of features, we accelerate the learning of the tree. The below pseudocode is publicly available and is most commonly used for understanding the working of RF algorithm.

Pseudocode for the Algorithm
Precondition: A training set S: = (x1, y1), . . . ,(xn, yn), features F, and number of trees in forest B.

Analysis via RF model led to an AUC value of 0.927 which is shown in Figure 1.2.b.

```
1 function RandomForest(S , F)

2    H ← ∅

3    for i ∈ 1 , ... , B do

4        S (i) ← A bootstrap sample from S

5        hi ← RandomizedTreeLearn(S(i) , F)

6        H ← H ∪ {hi}

7    end for

8    return H

9 end function

10 function RandomizedTreeLearn(S , F)

11    At each node:

12        f ← very small subset of F

13        Split on best feature in f

14    return the learned tree

15 end function
```

(a)

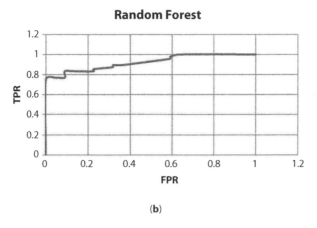

(b)

Figure 1.2 (a) Pseudocode for Random Forest algorithm. (b) ROC curve for Random Forest algorithm.

1.6   Support Vector Machine (SVM)

SVM is likewise one more well-known ML algorithm that can be executed for problems related to both classification and regression. Though it cannot perform well with a large dataset, it is most effective when in high dimensional spaces. This algorithm is widely applied in biological and sciences fields. It can also be used for regression problems as well. Support vector machine is used for extreme cases like identification or classification of datasets and forms a decision boundary also known as the hyperplane surrounded by extreme data points. The data points nearest to the hyperplane are called support vectors and affect the position of the plane. SVM is a frontier which best sorts out two classes. There can be several decision boundaries for a given case, but choosing the best boundary becomes the challenge here for gaining accurate predictions. If there is no optimal decision boundary, there are high chances that new data could be misclassified or it could be incorrectly classified. This is where SVM comes into play. The algorithm basically suggests that only the support vectors are important and all the other training examples are ignorable.

There are two categories of SVM, firstly the support vector regression and the second is the support vector classifier. Here weka executes John C. Platt's Sequential Minimal Optimization (SMO) algorithm for training SVM's. SMO solves a challenge that is generally faced while training a SVM and that is, it abstains from utilizing tedious mathematical Quadratic Programming (QP) optimization problems as solution. Also, it has been proved that SMO is much faster for training a huge size of data.it breaks the huge QP problem into a series of smaller QP problems and then solving it analytically. SMO performs well for large problems and since it uses smallest QP problems which can be settled scientifically, its scaling and computation time is improved significantly.

Analysis via SVM model produced an AUC value of 0.812 which is shown in Figure 1.3.

1.7   Logistic Regression

Logistic regression belongs to supervised ML classification algorithms that support binary classification (true or false). It is usually used when we want to predict the probability of a target value. It is widely used for disease detection.

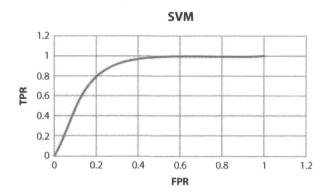

Figure 1.3 ROC curve for SVM algorithm.

Logistic regression fits the data using an s-shaped sigmoid function unlike linear regression where we attempt to fit the data in a line which can be used to predict unknown values. The curve tells the probability of the event.

Logistic regression equation:

$$\log\frac{y}{1-y} = b_0 + b_1x_1 + b_2x_2 + b_3x_3 + \ldots + b_nx_n \qquad (1.2)$$

Only when a decision threshold is taken into account, this regression can be used in classification. There are several factors which affect the threshold value like precision and recall which should be taken into account while deciding upon the threshold value (Table 1.1).

Analysis via RF model produced an AUC value of 0.819 which is shown in Figure 1.4.b.

1.8   K Nearest Neighbor Algorithm (KNN)

The K Nearest Neighbor method is a supervised machine learning approach that is ideal for classification tasks, while it may also be used for regression. It is one of the easiest ML algorithms that utilize a likeness determination strategy. That is, during the training the KNN algorithm technique just gathers and stores data into categories and when new data (test set) is inputted it classifies the new data into a category that is more similar

Table 1.1 Gives the percentage of the total dataset which were correctly and incorrectly classified for different ML algorithms.

Algorithm	Correctly classified (%)	Incorrectly classified (%)
J48	88.5714	11.4286
RF	84.2857	15.7143
SVM	84.2857	15.7143
LOGISTIC	82.8571	17.1429
KNN	91.4286	8.5714
NAIVE BAYES	54.2857	45.7143

to the available categories. In simple words, it classifies a data or feature based on how its neighbors are classified. It is also named as lazy learning and non-parametric algorithm. There is no specific way to determine the K value, that is, the number of neighbors. But usually in a binary classification problem it is best to keep the k value as an odd number. It is also a good practice to use large numbers for K value but not too large otherwise a smaller number of data will be beat by other categories.

The steps to understand KNN algorithm is given below:

a. Initially load the dataset for which prediction is to be made
b. Input a value for K
c. Iterate from 1 to total number of features/data points in the dataset

    (i) Compute the distance between each row of the training set and the test set. The Euclidean distance technique was used to calculate this distance.

    (ii) Furthermore, based on the distance values, the estimated distances are ordered in increasing order.

    (iii) In addition, the top K rows of the sorted array are taken.

    (iv) The most often occurring class from these rows is chosen in this stage.

    (v) Return the anticipated class at the end.

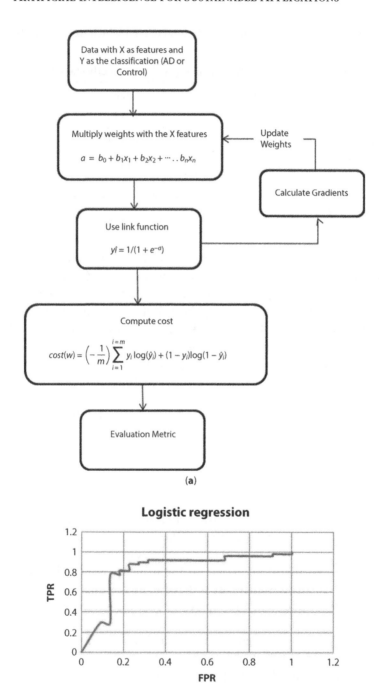

(a)

(b)

Figure 1.4 (a) Workflow for linear regression. (b) ROC curve for logistic regression algorithm.

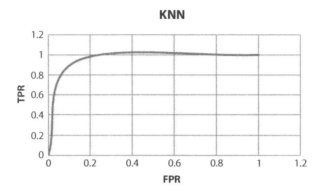

Figure 1.5 ROC curve for Random Forest algorithm.

These are the basic steps for understanding the working of KNN algorithms in machine learning. Analysis via KNN model produced an AUC value of 0.901 which is shown in Figure 1.5.

1.9 Naive Bayes

Naive Bayes machine learning algorithm that is considered as the simplest yet powerful algorithm for classification problems. As the name suggests, the algorithm works based on the Bayes theorem in mathematics which is used for calculating conditional probabilities thus being a probabilistic machine learning algorithm. Thus, it is a given that Naive Bayes work or classify based on an assumption that each feature in a dataset is conditionally independent, that is, each feature is unrelated to each other. Given below is the formula for Bayes theorem

$$P(H|E) = [P(E|H) * P(H)]/P(E) \qquad (1.3)$$

$$P(class|data\ point) = [P(data\ point\ |\ class) * P(class)]/P(data\ point) \qquad (1.4)$$

The above formula calculates the conditional probability of a class. In general, P(H|E) is posterior probability, p(H) is considered as prior probability, p(E/H) as likelihood and P(E) as predictor. Thus the above Bayes formula can also be rewritten as,

Posterior probability = (likelihood * prior)/predictor

In terms of disease prediction, the formula above is used to determine the likelihood that a patient has AD based on whether the test is positive or negative. There are three main measures that give a better understanding of prediction of the disease. This includes base rate, sensitivity, and specificity. The sensitivity measure will reveal the percentage of persons who are genuinely suffering from Alzheimer's disease and have been diagnosed as such. The percentage of those who do not have Alzheimer's disease and are tested to be healthy patients will be used to determine specificity. The percentage of persons with Alzheimer's disease will be represented by the measure's base rate. All these measures could be conveniently calculated using weka's features that includes confusion matrix, test summary and from the threshold curve for AD patients. Thus making the prediction process accurate with given dataset and information. The Bayes theorem is simplified in the Naive Bayes classifier. The Bayes theorem in general assumes that input data is dependent on all other data creating a complexity. Thus in the Naive Bayes classifier, the probability of class for each input data is calculated separately and multiply the resultant values together.

Analysis via Naive Bayes model produced an AUC value of 0.604 which is shown in Figure 1.6.

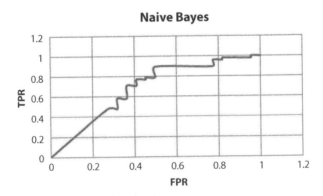

Figure 1.6 ROC curve for Naive Bayes algorithm.

1.10   Finding the Best Algorithm Using Experimenter Application

In order to find the best algorithm with highest accuracy for our dataset, we utilized the experimenter application provided by the weka GUI. It is a powerful tool that is designed to analyze datasets against all the ML algorithms, provided it satisfies the criteria appropriate for that algorithm.

Summarized Table for All Metrics

Table 1.2 The table summarizes the metrics obtained from all the models.

Algorithm	CLASS	TPR	FPR	AUC
	AD	0.938	0.227	0.852
J48	CONTROL	0.773	0.063	0.852
	AD	0.958	0.409	0.927
RF	CONTROL	0.591	0.042	0.927
	AD	0.896	0.273	0.812
SVM	CONTROL	0.727	0.104	0.812
	AD	0.917	0.364	0.819
LOGISTIC	CONTROL	0.636	0.083	0.819
	AD	0.938	0.136	0.901
KNN	CONTROL	0.864	0.063	0.901
	AD	0.479	0.318	0.684
NAÏVE BAYES	CONTROL	0.682	0.521	0.607

Table 1.3 Area under ROC for all the algorithms.

Dataset	J48	RF	KNN	Logistic regression	SVM	Naive Bayes
AD	0.83	0.96	0.89	0.83	0.82	0.72

For example, certain algorithms do not support binary classes like simple linear regression. In such an instance the tool will throw an error and does complete the run analysis process. After making the required changes, weka can now analyze the dataset to see how accurate each algorithm works on our dataset. For this, we set the testbase to ranking and the comparison field to area under ROC curve.

After running the test, we can see that the Random Forest method is the best for our dataset, with the greatest accuracy rate from Table 1.2.

In order to display the values of area under ROC curve we can set the comparison field to Area Under ROC and testbase to any algorithm. Once the test is performed we can evidently see that compared to all the ML algorithms Random Forest produced better performance results. We choose AUC - ROC curve as a factor to decide which algorithm is best and tabulated it in Table 1.3.

AUC–ROC is the best metric when it comes to ranking predictions and also considering both classes equally.

1.11   Conclusion

We evaluated miRNAs from the blood samples of persons with Alzheimer's disease and healthy controls to find the best machine learning algorithm that might be used to diagnose and forecast the disease. Using the same dataset we trained models on various ML algorithms. With machine learning, prediction of diseases has now become a time saving process and promises accurate diagnostic measures. All of these analyses revealed an accuracy rate of 0.812 to 0.927 from Table 1.2, indicating that miRNA biosignatures could be employed as a biomarker for Alzheimer's disease prediction. In the final analysis, we can see that the KNN ML model indicates an excellent area under ROC value of 0.901, which is an acceptable prediction rate for identifying AD disease. Though KNN model's prediction was excellent, analysis via RF model illustrated an outstanding area under ROC

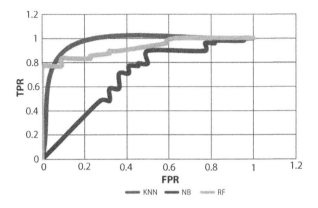

Figure 1.7 ROC curve for KNN, NB, and RF.

value of 0.927. While other algorithms indicated only a fair accuracy rate and Naive Bayes with a poor accuracy rate of 0.684. With additional technological developments, we may be able to forecast Alzheimer's disease at an earlier stage, thereby slowing the course of symptoms and resulting in happier patients. The Figure 1.7 shows the comparison of the algorithms that depicted the best area under ROC value.

1.12   Future Scope

The present study comes with the objective of analyzing how the emerging technology – AutoML (Automated Machine Learning) can be useful in building precise predictive models for identifying diseases using diagnostic clinical data. ML has been infiltrating every facet of our life, and it's good influence has been perplexing. Automated Machine Learning (AutoML) technology can be used to speed up this ML technology and apply it into a variety of real-world settings. In healthcare, AutoML can make the workload of doctors and other healthcare specialists easier. The fundamental goal of AutoML is to make the technology accessible to the general public rather than just a select few. With AutoML technology comes an opportunity to improve healthcare with less human interventions involved (as most of the processes are automated). With this aim we survey relevant ML and AutoML papers and analyze the role it can play in the field of healthcare.

References

1. Leidinger, P., Backes, C., Deutscher, S., Schmitt, K., Mueller, S.C., Frese, K., Haas, J., Ruprecht, K., Paul, F., Stähler, C., Lang, C.J., Meder, B., Bartfai, T., Meese, E., Keller, A., A blood based 12-miRNA signature of Alzheimer disease patients. *Genome Biol.*, 14, 7, R78, 2013, https://doi.org/10.1186/gb-2013-14-7-r78.

2. Truong, A., Walters, A., Goodsitt, J., Hines, K., Bruss, C.B., Farivar, R., Towards automated machine learning: Evaluation and comparison of AutoML approaches and tools. *2019 IEEE 31st International Conference on Tools with Artificial Intelligence (ICTAI)*, pp. 1471–1479, 2019.

3. Uddin, S., Khan, A., Hossain, M. *et al.*, Comparing different supervised machine learning algorithms for disease prediction. *BMC Med. Inform. Decis. Mak.*, 19, 281, 2019, https://doi.org/10.1186/s12911-019-1004-8.

4. Chang, C.H., Lin, C.H., Lane, H.Y., Machine learning and novel biomarkers for the diagnosis of Alzheimer's disease. *Int. J. Mol. Sci.*, 22, 5, 2761, 2021, https://doi.org/10.3390/ijms22052761.

5. Karaglani, M., Gourlia, K., Tsamardinos, I., Chatzaki, E., Accurate blood-based diagnostic biosignatures for Alzheimer's disease via automated machine learning. *J. Clin. Med.*, 9, 9, 3016, 2020, https://doi.org/10.3390/jcm9093016.

6. Dubois, B., Hampel, H., Feldman, H.H., Scheltens, P., Aisen, P., Andrieu, S., Bakardjian, H., Benali, H., Bertram, L., Blennow, K., Broich, K., Cavedo, E., Crutch, S., Dartigues, J.F., Duyckaerts, C., Epelbaum, S., Frisoni, G.B., Gauthier, S., Genthon, R., Gouw, A.A., Proceedings of the Meeting of the International Working Group (IWG) and the American Alzheimer's Association on "The Preclinical State of AD"; July 23, 2015; Washington DC, USA, Preclinical Alzheimer's disease: Definition, natural history, and diagnostic criteria. *Alzheimer's Dement.: The Journal of the Alzheimer's Association*, 12, 3, 292–323, 6, 2016, https://doi.org/10.1016/j.jalz.2016.02.002.

7. Zhao, X., Kang, J., Svetnik, V., Warden, D., Wilcock, G., David Smith, A., Savage, M.J., Laterza, O.F., A machine learning approach to identify a circulating MicroRNA signature for Alzheimer disease. *J. Appl. Lab. Med.*, 5, 1, 15–28, January 2020, https://doi.org/10.1373/jalm.2019.029595.

8. Jackins, V., Vimal, S., Kaliappan, M. *et al.*, AI-based smart prediction of clinical disease using random forest classifier and Naive Bayes. *J. Supercomput.*, 77, 5198–5219, 2021, https://doi.org/10.1007/s11227-020-03481-x.

9. Shigemizu, D., Akiyama, S., Asanomi, Y., Boroevich, K.A., Sharma, A., Tsunoda, T., Matsukuma, K., Ichikawa, M., Sudo, H., Takizawa, S., Sakurai, T., Ozaki, K., Ochiya, T., Niida, S., Risk prediction models for dementia constructed by supervised principal component analysis using miRNA expression data. *Commun. Biol.*, 2, 77, 2019, https://doi.org/10.1038/s42003-019-0324-7.

10. Rong, G., Mendez, A., Assi, E.B., Zhao, B., Sawan, M., Artificial intelligence in healthcare: Review and prediction case studies. *Engineering*, 6, 291–301, 2020, https://doi.org/10.1016/j.eng.2019.08.015.

11. Li, J.P., Haq, A.U., Din, S.U., Khan, J., Khan, A., Saboor, A., Heart disease identification method using machine learning classification in E-healthcare. *IEEE Access*, 8, 107562–107582, 2020.

12. Zvěřová, M., Alzheimer's disease and blood-based biomarkers - potential contexts of use. *Neuropsychiatr. Dis. Treat.*, 14, 1877–1882, 2018, https://doi.org/10.2147/NDT.S172285.

13. Platt, J., Sequential minimal optimization: A fast algorithm for training support vector machines, in: *Advances in Kernel Methods-Support Vector Learning*, p. 208, 1998.

14. Sun, B., Du, J., Gao, T., Study on the improvement of K-nearest-neighbor algorithm. *2009 International Conference on Artificial Intelligence and Computational Intelligence*, pp. 390–393, 2009.

15. Ali, J., Khan, R., Ahmad, N., Maqsood, I., Random forests and decision trees. *Int. J. Comput. Sci. Issues (IJCSI)*, 9, 272–278, 2012.

16. Uma Maheswari, K.M., Pranesh, A., Govindarajan, S., Network anomaly detector using machine learning. *Int. J. Eng. Technol.*, 7, 3.12, 178–179, 2018.

17. Venna, S.R.R., Somayajulu, D., Dani, A., Classification of movie reviews using complemented Naive Bayesian classifier. *Int. J. Intell. Comput. Res.*, 4, 162, 2010.

18. Huang, J., Lu, J., Ling, C.X., Comparing Naive Bayes, decision trees, and SVM with AUC and accuracy. *Third IEEE International Conference on Data Mining*, pp. 553–556, 2003.

19. Bhargava, N., Sharma, S., Purohit, R., Rathore, P.S., Prediction of recurrence cancer using J48 algorithm. *2017 2nd International Conference on Communication and Electronics Systems (ICCES)*, pp. 386–390, 2017.

2

Bounding Box Region-Based Segmentation of COVID-19 X-Ray Images by Thresholding and Clustering

Kavitha S.* and Hannah Inbarani

Department of Computer Science, Periyar University, Salem, India

Abstract

Image segmentation is used to decrease the complication of an image for further processing, analysis and visualization. This work presents the Bounding Box-based segmentation methods through thresholding, K-Means, and Fuzzy K-Means clustering to segment the COVID-19 chest x-ray images as it involves simple calculations and fast operation. Bounding box is generated over the image to locate the object of interest on an image. Before applying these methods the images are histogram equalized using CLAHE to improve the quality of a foggy image with the limited increase in the contrast. The results are evaluated using Intersection over Union (IoU) and Mean Pixel Accuracy (MPA) with the segmented and the ground truth image.

Keywords: Contrast limited adaptive histogram equalization (CLAHE), bounding box, thresholding, K-Means clustering, fuzzy k-means, mean pixel accuracy (MPA), Intersection over Union (IoU)

2.1   Introduction

Corona virus (COVID-19) is one of the most abundantly spread viruses in the world affecting more than 200 countries causing an overwhelming epidemic. As the virus is causing more deaths, it has increased pressure on health organizations to save the affected patients. Hence, it is necessary to detect the virus in a patient as early as possible to provide efficient and

---

Corresponding author: kavitha.chanjhana@gmail.com

K. Umamaheswari, B. Vinoth Kumar and S. K. Somasundaram (eds.) *Artificial Intelligence for Sustainable Applications*, (23–36) © 2023 Scrivener Publishing LLC

accurate treatment. There are many applications of image segmentation such as medical image processing, face recognition, satellite images, etc. [1]. Currently medical imaging such as chest x-rays and chest CT scans can be used to diagnose the decease efficiently. As the manual processing takes lot of time and the dedicated staff to detect the disease from the medical images, it is necessary to create an automated system on medical image techniques to find the decease with higher accuracy and less time [2].

Image segmentation is one of the essential steps in medical image processing for image analysis and recognition. It is used to divide the image into multiple segments from which any useful information such as color, intensity, and texture can be obtained [3]. Though there are several segmentation algorithms used by the several researchers, this paper analyses Region based segmentation such as thresholding and clustering using K-means, Fuzzy K-means on COVID x-ray images for segmentation since these methods involves simple computation and speed. Commonly, the x-ray images are low contrast [4], therefore the image contrast is increased using adaptive histogram equalization before segmentation so that the image is segmented very effectively for further processing [5].

Threshold segmentation is one of the simplest and widely used Region based segmentation method which sets the threshold value. The pixel values falling below or above that threshold can be classified accordingly as an object or the background [6]. The next type of segmentation method called clustering that divides the image into clusters whose elements have similar characteristics in the elements in the same cluster compared to the elements in the different clusters [7]. There are several clustering methods have been proposed and applied in image segmentation. K-Means, proposed by Pengfei Shan [8] is an unsupervised algorithm that divides the image into k clusters to segment the image into different clusters. The main aim of this work is to segment the image using these methods after generating the bounding box and enhancing the contrast. The next section presents the related work. Section 2.3 and section 2.4 explain the data set used for analysis and proposed methodology respectively. Section 2.5 discusses the findings and at the end, the conclusion is presented.

2.2   Literature Review

So for various research works have been done for segmenting the different types of images which are shown in Table 2.1.

Table 2.1 Segmentation of images using various techniques.

Authors	Techniques	Result
Maria Fayez, Soha Safwat *et al.* [9]	K-means and 2D wavelet transform with *K-means* are implemented.	2D wavelet transform with K-means clustering achieved better performance.
Nameirakpam Dhanachandra *et al. [10]*	K -Means and subtractive Clustering	The proposed algorithm has achieved better segmentation.
Alan Jose, S. Ravi and M. Sambath. [11]	K-means and Fuzzy C-Means.	Region of interest and the size of the tumor are found from the resultant segmented image.
Ajala Funmilola A. *et al.* [12]	Fuzzy K-C-means clustering is applied on brain MRI images.	Better time utilization.
Senthilkumaran N. and Vaithegi S. [13]	Local thresholding algorithm (Niblack and Sauvola).	The result of the Niblack algorithm is good compared with the Sauvola algorithm.
M. C. Jobin Christ *et al.* [14]	Silhouette method, Spatial FCM (Fuzzy C-Means), HMRF-FCM.	They concluded that the HMRF-FCM converge fast and gives less error and better accuracy. Silhouette method finds the correct structure and Spatial FCM improves the segmentation results.
H. Kaur and J. Rani [24]	Different Histogram Equalization methods are used.	CLAHE is better than LHE (Local Histogram Equalization) as it consumes more time.
Juntao Wang and Xiaolong Su [8]	K-means and outliers detection method.	It has more accuracy but for large data sets it takes more time.

(Continued)

Table 2.1 Segmentation of images using various techniques. (*Continued*)

Authors	Techniques	Result
G. Yadav *et al.* [17]	CLAHE is used to increase the image quality.	The result of the proposed algorithm shows the better quality video.
Aimi Salihai Abdul *et al.* [20]	Partial contrast stretching and K-Means clustering.	Accuracy – 99.46% F-score – 0.9370
Dhanalakshmi, K., and H. Hannah Inbarani [25]	Fuzzy soft rough K-Means clustering.	Proposed method shows good efficiency.

2.3 Dataset Used

This study uses two COVID images and the associated ground truth images for evaluation. The images are with the size (237, 233, 3) and (227, 239, 3) downloaded from the link https://www.researchgate.net/figure/The-COVID-19-sample-CXR-images-their-corresponding-ground-truth-segment.

2.4 Proposed Method

In this work, we proposed a segmentation model in which CLAHE and the bounding box representation are combined with the Thresholding, K-Means, and Fuzzy K-Means clustering to segment the COVID-19 x-ray images. The proposed model has the following steps and it is represented in Figure 2.1.

    i)   Read the image.

    ii)   Apply the contrast limited histogram equalization.

    iii) Generate bounding box over the histogram equalized image.

    iv) Then, segment the resultant image using threshold-based segmentation and clustering techniques.

    v)   Resultant images of the previous step are compared with the ground truth images through Mean Pixel Accuracy and IoU (Intersection over Union).

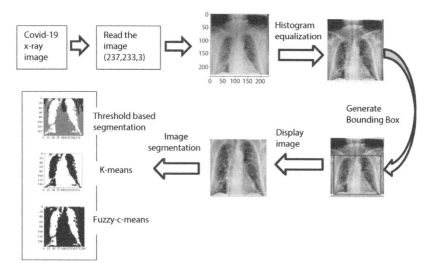

Figure 2.1 Proposed method.

2.4.1   Histogram Equalization

Histogram equalization tries to flatten the histogram to adjust the contrast or brightness of an image to create better quality image. This method helps to produce the better views for x-ray images [15]. The modified part of histogram equalization called Adaptive Histogram Equalization (ADE) performs image enhancement on a particular region and adjust the contrast based on the nearby pixels [16]. CLAHE is an improved method of AHE in which the image enhancement is applied on small regions of an image to improve the contrast [17]. It limits the contrast stretch to avoid over amplification of the contrast. In this work, the sample image is enhanced

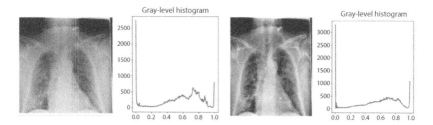

Figure 2.2 Contrast limited adaptive histogram equalization.

through CLAHE with the clip limit value fixed as 0.01 to limit the contrast stretch. It is shown in the Figure 2.2.

2.4.2   Threshold-Based Segmentation

In threshold based segmentation, the pixel values which are under the threshold or the values which are above the threshold is considered as an object or background. It can be stated as:

$$T = T[p,q,s(p,q),f(p,q)] \tag{2.1}$$

In the above equation, the threshold value point T has the co-ordinates p and q, f(p,q) is the gray level and s(x,y) is some local property [18]. The resultant image is obtained as r(p,q) which is stated as:

$$r(x,y) = \begin{cases} 0 & f(p,q) < T \\ 1 & f(p,q) \geq T \end{cases} \tag{2.2}$$

In this work, Local thresholding is used in which multiple threshold vales are set to segment the x-ray image into different classes. The first threshold value is found by calculating the mean of the pixel values of an entire image.

2.4.3   K-Means Clustering

K-Means clustering divides the given data set into K predefined distinct non overlapping clusters. It is an unsupervised machine learning algorithm. Each value from the data set belongs to only one group. For each data point the squared distance is obtained among the data points and the cluster centroid. Based on the distance value the cluster is found for each data point [19]. The steps of K-Means clustering [20] consist of:

  i)   Total number of clusters K and the centroid is specified.
  ii)   For each pixel and the centroid, the Euclidean distance d
        is calculated as:

$$d = ||p(x,y) - c_k|| \tag{2.3}$$

iii) Based on the distance value d, all the pixels are allotted to the nearest cluster.

iv) Calculate the new position of center once all the pixels are assigned by:

$$c_k \frac{1}{k} \sum_{y \in c^k} \sum_{x \in c^k} p(x,y)$$ (2.4)

v) All the above steps are continued till the error value is satisfied.

2.4.4 Fuzzy-K-Means Clustering

Fuzzy K-Means is a widely used soft clustering method for mage segmentation [21]. In fuzzy clustering, the data elements are assigned with membership levels. Based on these levels the data elements are allotted to one or more clusters. This technique is used in the applications where there is no crisp boundary between clusters. The objective function of FCM [22] is represented as:

$$P_{fcm} = \sum_{i=1}^{c} \sum_{n=1}^{N} u_{in}^{m} d_{in}$$ (2.5)

$$U = \{u_{in} \in [0,1], \sum_{i=1}^{c} u_{in} = 1 \forall n, 0 < \sum_{n=1}^{N} u_{in} < N \forall i\}$$ (2.6)

Where U is the membership matrix and u_{in} denotes the degree of membership of pixel in nth position and the ith cluster. d_{in} is the Euclidian distance amongst pixel data and the ith cluster.

2.5 Experimental Analysis

2.5.1 Results of Histogram Equalization

The given two COVID-19 x-ray images are histogram equalized using CLAHE with the clip limit value fixed as 0.01. It is shown in Figure 2.3.

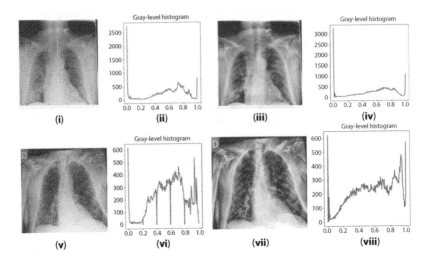

Figure 2.3 (i) Sample image 1. (ii) Histogram of image 1. (iii) Image*1 after histogram equalization. (iv) Histogram of image 1 after histogram equalization. (v) Sample image 2. (vi) Histogram of image 2. (vii) Image 2 after histogram equalization. (viii) Histogram of image 2 after histogram equalization.

From the Figure 2.3, it is shown that the contrast of the given x-ray images are increased and is given as input to the segmentation models for further analysis.

2.5.2   Findings of Bounding Box Segmentation

Figure 2.4 shows the segmented images after applying threshold based segmentation, K-Means and Fuzzy K-Means clustering on the images extracted with Bounding box.

2.5.3   Evaluation Metrics

A) Mean Pixel Accuracy

Pixel accuracy computes the proportion of the number of correctly categorized pixels among the overall pixels. MPA is an enhanced Pixel Accuracy where it calculates the correct pixels per class to find the average of all classes. It is given [23] as:

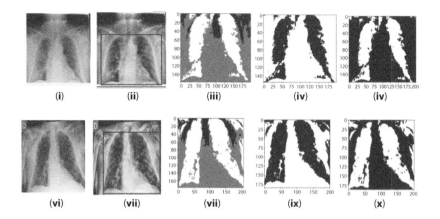

Figure 2.4 Segmented images of image 1 and image*2. (i) Image1. (ii) Image with bounding box. (iii) Thresholding. (iv) K-Means. (v) Fuzzy K-Means. (vi) image 2. (vii) Image 2 with bounding box. (viii) Thresholding. (ix) K-Means. (x) Fuzzy K-Means.

$$MPA = \frac{1}{k+1} \sum_{i=0}^{k} \frac{p_{ii}}{\sum_{j=0}^{k} p_{ij}} \tag{2.7}$$

Where k+1 is the total classes and p_{ii} represents the number of true positives and p_{ij} denotes the false negatives.

B) Intersection Over Union (IoU)

It is an evaluation metric to measure the overlap between the intersection and union of two bounding boxes such as the predicted segmentation and the ground truth. It divides the intersection of predicted and ground truth by the union of predicted and the ground truth image. The lower value of IoU indicates that the prediction is incorrect. It is formulated [23] as:

$$IoU = \frac{1}{k+1} \sum_{i=0}^{k} \frac{p_{ii}}{\sum_{j=0}^{k} p_{ij} + \sum_{j=0}^{k} p_{ji} - p_{ii}} \tag{2.8}$$

C) Accuracy Results of Segmentation Algorithms

All the segmented images which are generated without bounding box are compared with the ground truth images using the metrics such as MPA and IoU for evaluation and the accuracy values are specified in the Table 2.2.

Table 2.3 shows the MPA and IoU score of the segmented images generated for the images with bounding box and the ground truth images.

From the Table 2.2 and Table 2.3, It is shown that the IoU score of all the methods is high for the images generated with bounding box compared to the IoU value of images without bounding box and the threshold based segmentation gives better accuracy than the K-Means and Fuzzy-K-Means method.

Table 2.2 MPA and IoU scores of different segmentation algorithms.

Evaluation metrics	Images without bounding box	Segmentation algorithms		
		Threshold based segmentation	K-Means clustering	Fuzzy K-Means clustering
Mean pixel Accuracy	Image 1	4.7462	2.1037	2.1136
	Image 2	3.9999	4.7042	4.6220
IoU	Image 1	0.4296	0.4448	0.4448
	Image 2	0.2779	0.2675	0.2675

Table 2.3 MPA and IoU scores of different segmentation algorithms.

Evaluation metrics	Images bounding box	Segmentation algorithms		
		Threshold based segmentation	K-Means clustering	Fuzzy K-Means clustering
Mean pixel Accuracy	Image 1	2.9985	1.6290	0.7932
	Image 2	5.2212	2.2371	1.6002
IoU	Image 1	0.6070	0.5674	0.4872
	Image 2	0.4892	0.4654	0.4495

2.6   Conclusion

In this chapter, we have generated bounding box over the images and analyzed the images through the segmentation technique such as Region based segmentation using thresholding, *K-means* and fuzzy *K-means* clustering to segment the COVID x-ray images. The image contrast is increased using CLAHE to create a better quality image before the segmentation. Generating Bounding box over the image helps to locate the object of interest and to reduce the number of features such a way it increases the segmentation accuracy. The results of the segmentation methods are evaluated by matching the segmented image with the ground truth image using MPA and IoU. In the future work, deep learning based segmentation will be applied on the COVID-19 images to obtain the more accurate segmentation.

References

1. Fu, K.-S. and Mui, J.K., A survey on image segmentation. *Pattern Recognit.*, 13, 1, 3–16, 1981.
2. Kekre, H.B., Patankar, A.B., Galiyal, H.R., Segmentation of blast using vector quantization technique. *Int. J. Comput. Appl.*, 72, 20–23, 2013.
3. Khan, W., Image segmentation techniques: A survey. *J. Image Graphics*, 1, 166–170, 2014.
4. Ramani, R.G. *et al.*, The pre-processing techniques for breast cancer detection in mammography images. *Int. J. Image Graph. Signal Process.*, 5, 47–54, 2013.
5. Yadav, G., Maheshwari, S., Agarwal, A., Contrast limited adaptive histogram equalization based enhancement for real time video system. *2014 International Conference on Advances in Computing, Communications and Informatics (ICACCI)*, pp. 2392–2397, 2014.
6. Mohammed, Z.F. and Abdulla, A.A., Thresholding-based white blood cells segmentation from microscopic blood images. *UHD J. Sci. Technol.*, 4, 9–17, 2020.
7. Mota, J.S. and Mascarenhas, M., A review on different methods of image segmentation. *Int. J. Creat. Res. Thoughts (IJCRT)*, 8, 7, 5245–5250, 2020.
8. Shan, P., Image segmentation method based on K-mean algorithm. *EURASIP J. Image Video Process.*, 1, 1–9, 2018.
9. Fayez, M., Safwat, S., Hassanein, E.E., Comparative study of clustering medical images. *2016 SAI Computing Conference (SAI)*, pp. 312–318, 2016.

10. Dhanachandra, N., Manglem, K., Chanu, Y.J., Image segmentation using K-means clustering algorithm and subtractive clustering algorithm. *Proc. Comput. Sci.*, 54, 764–771, 2015.

11. Jose, A., Ravi, S., Sambath, M., Brain tumor segmentation using K-means clustering and fuzzy C-means algorithm and its area calculation. *Int. J. Innov. Res. Comput. Commun. Eng.*, 2, 2, 2320–9801, 2014.

12. Ajala Funmilola, A., Oke, O.A., Adedeji, T.O., Alade, O.M., Adewusi, E.A., Fuzzy k-c-means clustering algorithm for medical image segmentation. *J. Inf. Eng. Appl.*, 2, 6, 21–32, 2012.

13. Senthilkumaran, N. and Vaithegi, S., Image segmentation by using thresholding techniques for medical images. *Comput. Sci. Eng., An International Journal*, 6, 1–13, 2016.

14. Christ, M.C.J. and Parvathi, R.M.S., Fuzzy c-means algorithm for medical image segmentation. *2011 3rd International Conference on Electronics Computer Technology*, vol. 4, pp. 33–36, 2011.

15. Dorothy, R., Joany, R.M., Rathish, J., Prabha, S., Rajendran, S., St Joseph, Image enhancement by Histogram equalization. *Int. J. Nano Corros. Sci. Eng.*, 2, 21–30, 2015.

16. Yoon, I., Kim, S., Kim, D., Hayes, M.H., Paik, J., Adaptive defogging with color correction in the HSV color space for consumer surveillance system. *IEEE Trans. Consum. Electron.*, 58, 1, 111–116, 2012.

17. Yadav, G., Maheshwari, S., Agarwal, A., Contrast limited adaptive histogram equalization based enhancement for real time video system. *2014 International Conference on Advances in Computing, Communications and Informatics (ICACCI)*, pp. 2392–2397, 2014.

18. Gonzalez, R.C. and Woods, R.E., *Digital image processing*, Prentice-Hall, Englewood Cliffs, NJ, 2008.

19. Khan, S.S. and Ahmad, A., Cluster centre initialization algorithm for K-means cluster. *Pattern Recognit. Lett.*, 25, 1293–1302, 2004.

20. Abdul, A.S., Masor, M.Y., Mohamed, Z., Colour image segmentation approach for detection of malaria parasiterusing various colour models and k-means clustering. *WSEAS Trans. Biol. Biomed.*, 10, 1, 41–54, 2013.

21. Ichihashi, H., Miyagishi, K., Honda, K., Fuzzy c-means clustering with regularization by KL information. *The 10th IEEE International Conference on Fuzzy Systems*, vol. 2, pp. 924–927, 2001.

22. Bezdek, J.C., *Pattern recognition with objective fuzzy algorithms*, Plenum Press, New York, 1981.

23. Garcia-Garcia, A., Orts-Escolano, S., Oprea, S., Villena-Martinez, V., Martinez-Gonzalez, P., Garcia-Rodriguez, J., A survey on deep learning techniques for image and video semantic segmentation. *Appl. Soft Comput.*, 70, 41–65, 2018.

24. Kaur, H. and Rani, J., MRI brain image enhancement using Histogram Equalization techniques. *2016 International Conference on Wireless Communications, Signal Processing and Networking (WiSPNET)*, pp. 770–773, 2016.
25. Dhanalakshmi, K. and Inbarani, H.H., Fuzzy soft rough K-Means clustering approach for gene expression data. *Int. J. Sci. Eng. Res.*, 3, 10, 1–7, ArXiv, abs/1212.5359, 2012.

3

Steering Angle Prediction for Autonomous Vehicles Using Deep Learning Model with Optimized Hyperparameters

Bineeshia J.[1]*, Vinoth Kumar B.[2], Karthikeyan T.[3] and Syed Khaja Mohideen[3]

[1]Department of Computer Science and Engineering, PSG College of Technology, Coimbatore, India
[2]Department of Information and Technology, PSG College of Technology, Coimbatore, India
[3]Department of Information Technology, University of Technology and Applied Sciences – Salalah, Oman

Abstract

Autonomous vehicles will optimize our transportation infrastructure and could in the long run improve our lifestyles. Machine Learning has recently advanced, allowing us to get closer to making this technology a reality. The capability of Deep Learning algorithms is used in the proposed study to construct a model that can anticipate steering angles nearly identical to how a human would manage a car's steering wheel. This was accomplished by training a 9-layer deep neural network. Optimization of hyperparameters of neural network models is performed for better results. The model was trained using a small dataset of less than 30 minutes of driving data, resulting in a Root Mean Squared Error of 0.0532 on the testing dataset, far above the benchmark of 0.2068. Finally, this score indicated Deep Learning models' capacity to execute in a human-like manner with only a minimal amount of training.

Keywords: Self-driving cars, deep learning, steering angle, CNN, genetic algorithm

*Corresponding author: bineeshia.joel@gmail.com

K. Umamaheswari, B. Vinoth Kumar and S. K. Somasundaram (eds.) *Artificial Intelligence for Sustainable Applications*, (37–54) © 2023 Scrivener Publishing LLC

3.1   Introduction

One of the most significant technological problems of this decade has been the development of autonomous automobiles which has a significant impact on our society by preventing car accidents, reducing traffic, maximizing fuel efficiency, and lowering vehicle costs. Autonomous automobiles can also save time travelling to work and minimize car ownership costs by moving to an "On-Demand" mode of operation. Due to the deployment of "Deep" Learning algorithms and techniques, such as Convolutional Neural Networks (CNNs), there have been several notable developments in the field of autonomous cars in recent years. Pattern Recognition [1] has been revolutionized by CNNs [2]. Until CNNs became extensively used, most pattern recognition applications had feature extraction stage manually designed which is then preceded by a classifier. CNNs are revolutionary because they automatically learn characteristics from training samples. Applications that require identification of images demand an efficient technique like CNN, as they catch the 2-dimensional element of the image. Furthermore, by scanning a full image with convolution kernels, only a few parameters must be acquired while comparing with the overall tasks. CNNs which possess learnt characteristics, have been widely used for over 2 decades [3], CNN's popularity has skyrocketed over the decades as a result of significant advancements. To begin with, huge, labeled data-sets have been accessible for training, testing and validation. Secondly, to dramatically speed up training and prediction, CNN models are in graphics processing units.

The suggested method displays the capacity to control a car's steering just by processing visual frames acquired using the power of CNNs. Current autonomous steering solutions necessitate an explicit dissection of challenges, like detecting marks in a lane, as shown in Figure 3.1. The main purpose of this research lies in the avoidance of recognition of objects picked by humans like lane dividers, marks in the lane or another car.

This research also focuses on the creation of rules by observing these qualities. The main goal is to leverage data from Udacity to create a framework which determines the angle of a vehicle's steering wheel with a little amount of training (~30 minutes of driving data). The model receives cars' front-view images and produces the angle of the steering wheel. This problem involves predictions of continuous data. End-to-end solutions, in which a single network receives raw input (camera footage) and generates a direct steering order, are seen to be the highlight of current autonomous vehicle technology, and are expected to make up the first wave of

Figure 3.1 Example of lane marking detection.

self-driving automobiles on roads and highways. We can avoid a lot of the complexity that comes with manually selecting features to detect and substantially lower the expense of getting an autonomous vehicle on the road by bypassing LiDAR-based solutions by letting the car figure out how to interpret photos on its own.

The paper is structured as follows. In literature review, several research papers are discussed. In section 3, the proposed system design is illustrated. Its components and working methodologies are also discussed in detail. Section 3.4, is a discussion of the experimental results relating to the proposed system. The paper ends with conclusions and ideas for future work in section 3.5.

3.2 Literature Review

In [1], the standard design of an autonomous system is proposed. Furthermore, an in-depth study of an autonomous system called the Intelligent Autonomous Robotics Automobile is also presented. A number of platforms which do research on autonomous vehicles were developed by many technology firms and are proposed and published as well. In [2], a self-driving car prototype which is based on monocular vision and employs Neural Networks on Raspberry Pi is proposed. In recent years, it has been demonstrated that Convolutional Neural Networks (CNNs) outperform other techniques in a variety of perception and control tasks. The capability of learning thousands of characteristics from a big volume of labeled information is one of the core aspects behind these amazing outcomes. In [2], a deep neural network is used to find an approach that inputs raw data and outputs steering wheel angle prediction. [3] proposed a study to see if low-utilization rural public transportation lines may be substituted with autonomy systems on demand. A cost and service level comparison was made between current transit systems and potential transit systems that are available on demand. Another analysis, focusing on operational considerations, is proposed, employing a simulated technique wherein the robot taxis are controlled in a road system, considering congestion impacts. The findings show that for rural locations, a central controlled transit system that is available on demand will be an appealing choice. An algorithm that is exclusively reliant on visual or camera input is proposed by [4]. A powerful lane recognition technique for autonomous cars is presented utilizing modern computer vision techniques. Simulation results in various scenarios are shown to prove the efficiency of the suggested line detecting technique when compared to the standard techniques. In real-world driving video simulations, YOLO which stands for You Only Look Once is a CNN algorithm used for detecting objects [5]. The computations are performed by the NVIDIA GTX 1070 which has a RAM of 8 GB. The paper demonstrates the strategies proposed for lane guidance and autonomous vehicle environment. [6] proposed a caching technique in autonomous cars, which is dependent on passenger characteristics gathered through deep learning. The following suggestions were also made. At first, deep learning models for content prediction must be cached. Secondly, a communication technique is required for collecting and caching infotainment content. An approach for Light Detection and Ranging (LiDAR) and camera fusion is presented by [7], which could be suited for executing with time constraints in self-driving cars. This approach is based on the clustering algorithm. [8] proposed a way for using reinforcement learning(RL) under two conditions: (i) RL works in combination with a baseline rule-based driving policy, and (ii) Only when the rule-based method appears to be failing and the RL policy's confidence is high, the RL gets involved. Their motivation was to apply an inadequately trained RL policy to improve (Audio-Visual) AV performance consistently. The suggested strategy outperforms both the pure RL policy and the baseline rule-based policy in simulations. [9] proposed the following aspects: a view on autonomous vehicles with an emphasis on perception, how self-driving cars will be affected technically and commercially by government policy, and how cloud infrastructure will perform an important role in development. [10] also proposed a learning strategy for calculating the best steering angle for keeping the car in its lane. With the human driving data as input the model can steer the automobile and stays in its lane after training. [11] explores a tracking system for trajectories. The steering angle of the vehicle's front wheel is computed using a predictive controller with tire cornering angle and road traction limitations. The objective of [12] is to use a broad survey to act as a bridge between Neural networks and autonomous cars. Feudal Steering, the method proposed by [13] is based on current Hierarchical Learning (HRL) work and consists of a manager and a worker network. The networks function on separate temporal scales. The task is divided into management and worker sub-networks via feudal learning. In driving, temporal abstraction allows for more complicated primitives than a single time instance of the steering angle. Quantitative arguments and Qualitative arguments of how cameras can reliably predict the angle of the steering wheel even when traditional cameras fail is proposed in [14], for example: During fast motion and difficult lighting circumstances. Finally, the benefits of utilizing transfer learning from conventional to event-based vision are highlighted, and it is demonstrated.

3.3 Methodology

3.3.1 Architecture

Three main cameras one at the left, one at the right and one at the center record the surroundings and the output is sent to the random shift and rotation part where in the images are randomly rotated in clockwise direction by a given number of degrees after which the output is passed to the hyper parameter tuning section where an optimal combination of hyperparameters are selected for the learning algorithm. The next stage involves the CNN which takes the input image and predicts the steering wheel angle as shown in Figure 3.2.

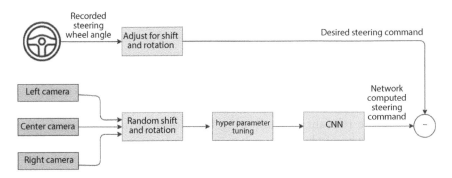

Figure 3.2 System design.

3.3.2   Data

Udacity's Challenge #2 Dataset was used to train this model, which is based on driving data from San Mateo, CA to Half Moon Bay, CA (curvy and highway driving). This collection contains image frames collected by a set of on-board cameras, each of which is linked to a certain steering angle and timestamp. Udacity excluded stationary segments and lane shifts from the dataset. Only the middle images were chosen, despite the fact that the imagery originated from three distinct cameras (left, center, and right). There are six pieces to the Challenge #2 Dataset. As needed by Udacity's Challenge #2, parts 1, 2, 5, and 6 were used for training, while parts 4 and 3 were utilized for validation and testing respectively.

3.3.3   Data Pre-Processing

The objective of data pre-processing stage is to process data from raw input video into an understandable format. A pre-processing phase [7] is performed on data used for training and inference, in which various inputs are scaled to the same dimensions and stacked into batches. Although inputting non-pre-processed video and allowing the neural network to learn features is applicable, but emphasizing on processed video will accelerate the process of training. Hence, video processing is performed first. Video processing is the process of breaking down a video into individual frames. The following are the pre-processing steps that were used:

1. The 640 × 480 pixels' raw images in the dataset are scaled to 256 × 192 pixels.
2. Because the RGB colors on the images do not provide relevant information to help estimate steering angles, the images were converted to grayscale.
3. Two successive difference images were used and computed lag 1 differences between image frames. For example, at time t, $[(t)-x(t-1),x(t-1)-x(t-2)]$ is given as an input, where x denotes the grayscale image. To anticipate the current steering angle, no future frames were used. All of these stages contribute to reducing the size of the data and magnifying more relevant data, allowing the model to run faster and more precisely. Every image in the training, validation, and test subsets was subjected to data pre-processing. Figure 3.3, depicts an image after it has been pre-processed. As can be

Figure 3.3 Sample of a pre-processed image.

seen, RGB colors have been eliminated, leaving only the borders visible. These edges aid in the model's recognition of patterns such as street lanes and other cars.

3.3.4   Hyperparameter Optimization

In any deep learning algorithm, the hyper parameters affect certain elements such as, are batch size, filter size and learning rate as shown in Figure 3.4, which in turn affects the accuracy of the algorithm. These elements are either established by external influence or by a developer's background experience. Rather than using conventional methods and probabilities, genetic algorithms are the ideal choice for optimizing hyper parameters.

The following steps are performed in order to solve the issue of hyperparameter.

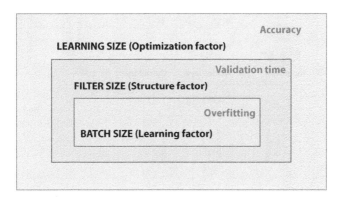

Figure 3.4 Affected elements for each hyperparameter.

- Generate a population of numerous NN's.
- Allocate hyper-parameters to each NN at random (within a range).
- For a certain number of iterations, the following steps are performed:

  1. Training all the NNs at the same time or one at a time.
  2. Compute their training costs once the training is completed.
  3. Determine each NN's "fitness" based on its cost.
  4. Determine the maximum fitness of the population (essential for step 5).
  5. Choose two NNs based on their fitness as determined by a probability scheme.
  6. Crossover is performed over the genes of the two NNs. The obtained child NN will have properties of both NN's.
  7. Mutation is performed over the genes of the child NN to introduce some randomness to the algorithm.
  8. For the number of NN's of the population, repeat steps 5-7. Save the obtained children in a new population and allocate the obtained population to the old population's variable.

After performing all of the processes above, the algorithm will produce a population comprising a NN with the optimal hyper-parameters. Of all

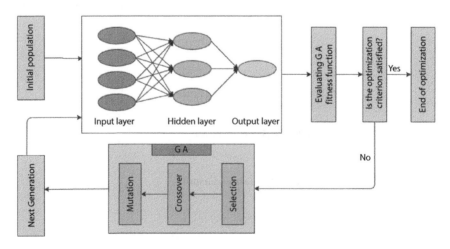

Figure 3.5 Iterative process to fine-tune hyperparameters.

the population the obtained population will have the fittest NN. Figure 3.5, depicts the iterative process to fine-tune hyper-parameters using genetic algorithms. The hyper parameters: batch size, epoch size, filter size and learning rate are considered. [100, 30, 5, 0.001,] are the hyper parameters obtained after optimization by the genetic algorithm.

3.3.5 Neural Network

Deep Learning refers to the use of Neural Networks for machine learning because of its ability to extract "deeper" information patterns from provided data by replicating how real neurons behave. CNN has proved its efficiency in classification and recognition of images. CNNs are used to extract features from images by lowering their dimensionality. Through a succession of convolutions, the CNN design decreases the dimensionality of an input image until it provides a single output at the end. Convolutional Layers operate by filtering over small sections of an image. A convolutional layer requires two primary parameters to do this: Kernel and Stride. The kernel is the size (in pixels) through which each convolution will filter, while the stride is the amount of pixels that are shifted each time our filter is moved. The result is nearly alike as the input size when stride is set to 1. It is about half the size with a stride of 2.

The architecture of the network as depicted in Figure 3.6 has nine layers, comprising of five convolutional and four fully connected layers. The convolutional layers were chosen based on the results of a series of trials having each layer configured differently.

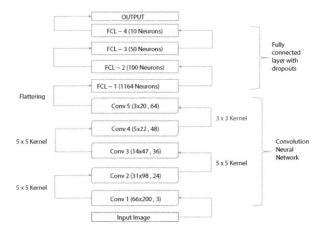

Figure 3.6 Convolution neural network.

In the network, the first three layers, utilized a 2x2 stride with a kernel size of 5x5 kernel. The remaining layers are non-strided and use a kernel of size 3x3. Three fully connected layers follow the network's five convolutional layers, leading to an output control value that is the inverse turning radius.

3.3.6 Training

In order to reduce the difference between the values of the input (human driven command) and output (the steering wheel angle prediction), the weights of a neural network must be trained. Epochs are used to train deep neural networks. Each epoch trains the model's weights by passing batches of pre-processed images through it, as well as providing values for training and validation loss. Following training, the weights with the lowest validation loss are fed into the model, which predicts the test dataset's output. The dataset consists of a 30-frame-per-second, which is a 25-minute video of an actual car driving (around 45,000 images). The weights were trained in order to reduce the mean squared error (MSE) between the input and output. The dataset is split in two halves in a temporal order, with the first 80 percent used for training and the second 20 percent for testing.

3.4 Experiment and Results

The structure of this model comprises nine layers with a total of 444,819 parameters, which implies that there are over 400 thousand parameters that can be tweaked for each image that travels through the neural network in order to forecast steering angle. Curves, street lanes, cars, and other components may be identified using some of these parameters. Image augmentation was used to pre-process all of the input data, allowing the model to perform better and have an RMSE of less than 0.10. The data that Machine Learning models are fed is one of the most essential factors. We went a step further in this example, cleaning the dataset by deleting segments that remained constant for extended periods of time. Because of the filtering, the model was able to overfit more slowly, resulting in more accurate predictions and an RMSE of less than 0.06. Because of this, the model was able to achieve a validation loss of 0.00154 during training, resulting in a final RMSE of 0.0532. As a result, the model accurately predicted steering angles with an RMSE of 0.0532.

3.4.1   Benchmark

Udacity provides a benchmark for researchers to measure their model's performance in order to make the review process easier. For comparison, an example file with an RMSE of 0.2067 has 0 for every steering forecast.

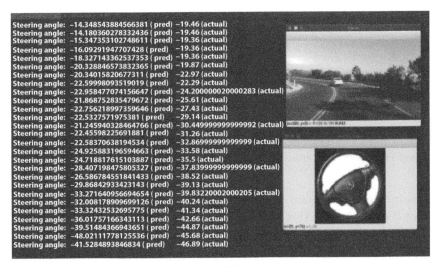

(a) when the road is curvy

(b) when the road is straight

Figure 3.7 Steering angle predictions.

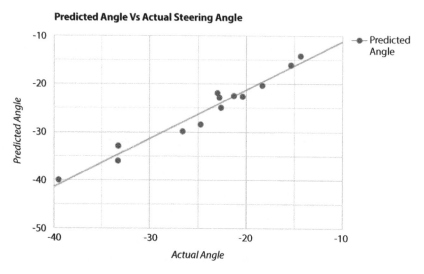

Figure 3.8 Tendency of predicted angles.

This implies that a good prediction model should have an RMSE of less than 0.2068. An RMSE of 0.2067 is used as a benchmark for this problem. Although the model does not forecast angles perfectly, its RMSE of 0.0532 indicates that it performs admirably with a very small difference when compared to human-controlled steering. Figure 3.7, shows how the

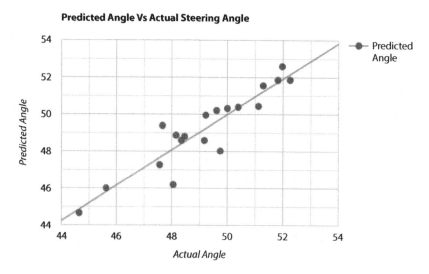

Figure 3.9 Tendency of errors.

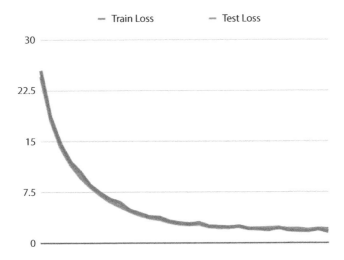

Figure 3.10 Comparison of train loss vs. test loss.

steering angle predictions can be visualized in a simulator-like format in a video.

Figures 3.8 and 3.9 show the patterns for both our model's predictions and the errors resulting from those predictions, providing a more detailed picture of the findings. Figure 3.8 illustrates a positive trend in the predictions, indicating that if the real angles increase, the anticipated angles will increase as well, and vice versa. Figure 3.9 depicts an almost-neutral tendency for errors between predictions and real angles, implying that the error rate remains roughly constant regardless of whether the real angles grow or decrease. Figure 3.10 depicts a comparison of train loss (blue) vs. test loss (green). The forecasts can be observed to be very close to the real angles, with only a minor variance on larger angles. Table 3.1 illustrates the comparison of predicted vs. actual steering angle predictions.

Table 3.1 Comparison of predicted angle vs. actual steering angle.

Predicted angle	Actual steering angle
-14.3485438	-19.46
-14.18038028	-19.46
-15.3473531	-19.36

(Continued)

Table 3.1 Comparison of predicted angle vs. actual steering angle. (*Continued*)

Predicted angle	Actual steering angle
-16.09291948	-19.36
-18.30714386	-19.36
-20.32804657	-19.87
-20.34015821	-20.97
-22.59998094	-22.29
-22.95847707	-24.2
-21.86875284	-25.61
-22.7562181	-27.43
-22.8327572	-29.14
-21.24594033	-30.449
-22.45598006	-31.26
-22.5837063	-32.069
-24.9250832	-33.58
-24.71001762	-35.5
-28.40719048	-37.009
-26.58678455	-38.52
-29.86042933	-39.13
-33.27164096	-39.83
-32.88017891	-40.24
-33.30432683	-41.34
-36.01757166	-42.66
-39.51484367	-44.07
-40.02111778	-45.68
-41.5284893	-46.89

3.5   Conclusion

This model shows that CNNs have the capability to learn the road without manual decomposition. The best results were achieved when the hyper parameters of CNN were optimized using genetic algorithms. With a minimal size of driving data (~30 minutes) the model learnt to steer a car like a human. From a sparse training signal (steering alone), the CNN is able to learn relevant road features. During training, for example, the system learnt to discern the road layouts without using tagged labels. Even while this model works well, there are several modifications that can be made to make it even better. Further work is required to enhance the network's reliability for affirmation, and improve the visualization of the network's internal processing stages by including depth features and information from LiDAR. Training using a variety of road conditions, such as road type and weather, may enable the model to learn to drive over a wider range of terrains. The model may be able to reduce the error for big steering angles if it is trained on a larger dataset with a wider range of curves.

References

1. Do, T.D., Duong, M.T., Dang, Q.V., Le, M.H., Real-time self-driving car navigation using deep neural network. *4th International Conference on Green Technology and Sustainable Development (GTSD)*, pp. 7–12, 2018.
2. Badue, C., Guidolini, R., Carneiro, R.V., Azevedo, P., Cardoso, V.B., Forechi, A., Jesus, L., Berriel, R., Paixão, T.M., Mutz, F., Veronese, L.P., Oliveira-Santos, T., De Souza, A.F., Self-driving cars: A survey. *Expert Syst. Appl.*, 165, 1–31, 2021, https://doi.org/10.1016/j.eswa.2020.113816.
3. Sieber, L., Ruch, C., Hörl, S., Axhausen, K.W., Frazzolia, E., Improved public transportation in rural areas with self-driving cars: A study on the operation of Swiss train lines. *Transp. Res. Part A: Policy Pract.*, 134, 35–51, April 2020, https://doi.org/10.1016/j.tra.2020.01.020.
4. Muthalagu, R., Bolimera, A., Kalaichelvi, V., Lane detection technique based on perspective transformation and histogram analysis for self-driving cars. *Comput. Electr. Eng.*, 85, 1–16, July 2020, https://doi.org/10.1016/j.compeleceng.2020.106653.
5. Nugraha, B.T., Su, S.F., Fahmizal, Towards self-driving car using convolutional neural network and road lane detector. *2nd International Conference on Automation, Cognitive Science, Optics, Micro Electro-Mechanical System, and Information Technology (ICACOMIT)*, pp. 65–69, July 2020.

6. Ndikumana, A., Tran, N.H., Kim, D.H., Kim, K.T., Hong, C.S., Deep learning based caching for self-driving cars in multi-access edge computing. *IEEE Trans. Intell. Transp. Syst.*, 22, 2862–2877, July 2020.

7. Verucchi, M., Bartoli, L., Bagni, F., Gatti, F., Burgio, P., Bertogna, M., Real-time clustering and LiDAR-camera fusion on embedded platforms for self-driving cars. *Fourth IEEE International Conference on Robotic Computing (IRC)*, pp. 398–405, 2020.

8. Cao, Z., Xu, S., Peng, H., Yang, D., Zidek, R., Confidence-aware reinforcement learning for self-driving cars. *IEEE Trans. Intell. Transp. Syst.*, 23, 7419–7430, 06 April 2021.

9. Daily, M., Medasani, S., Behringer, R., Trivedi, M., Self-driving cars. *Computer*, 50, 12, 18–23, 06 April 2021.

10. Chen, Z. and Huang, X., End-to-end learning for lane keeping of self-driving cars. *IEEE Intelligent Vehicles Symposium (IV)*, 2017.

11. Chen, T., Cai, Y., Chen, L., Xu, X., Sun, X., Trajectory tracking control of steer-by-wire autonomous ground vehicle considering the complete failure of vehicle steering motor. *Simul. Modell. Pract. Theory*, 109, 1856–1860, May 2021, https://doi.org/10.1016/j.simpat.2020.102235.

12. Gupta, A., Anpalagan, A., Guan, L., Khwaja, A.S., Deep learning for object detection and scene perception in self-driving cars: Survey, challenges, and open issues. *Array*, 10, 1–74, July 2021, https://doi.org/10.1016/j.array.2021.100057.

13. Johnson, F. and Dana, K., Feudal steering: Hierarchical learning for steering angle prediction. *IEEE/CVF Conference on Computer Vision and Pattern Recognition Workshops (CVPRW)*, vol. 1, pp. 4316–4325, 2020.

14. Maqueda, A.I., Loquercio, A., Gallego, G., Garcia, N., Scaramuzza, D., Event-based vision meets deep learning on steering prediction for self-driving cars. *IEEE/CVF Conference on Computer Vision and Pattern Recognition (CVPR)*, vol. 1, pp. 5419–5427, 2018.

15. Liang, X., Wang, T., Yang, L., Xing, E., CIRL: Controllable imitative reinforcement learning for vision-based self-driving. *Proceedings of the European Conference on Computer Vision (ECCV)*, pp. 604–620, 2018.

16. Kim, J. and Canny, J., Interpretable learning for self-driving cars by visualizing causal attention. *Proceedings of the IEEE International Conference on Computer Vision*, vol. 1, pp. 2961–2969, 2017.

17. Xu, H., Gao, Y., Yu, F., Darrell, T., End-to-end learning of driving models from large-scale video datasets. *Proceedings of the IEEE Conference on Computer Vision and Pattern Recognition (CVPR)*, vol. 1, pp. 3530–3538, 2017.

18. He, S., Kangin, D., Mi, Y., Pugeault, N., Aggregated sparse attention for steering angle prediction. *24th International Conference on Pattern Recognition (ICPR) IEEE*, pp. 2398–2403, 2018.

19. Chen, J., Wang, Z., Tomizuka, M., Deep hierarchical reinforcement learning for autonomous driving with distinct behaviors. *IEEE Intelligent Vehicles Symposium (IV)*, pp. 1239–1244, 2018.

20. Ferdowsi, A., Challita, U., Saad, W., Deep learning for reliable mobile edge analytics in intelligent transportation systems: An overview. *IEEE Veh. Technol. Mag.*, 14, 1–7, March 2019, https://doi.org/10.1016/j.jksuci.2021.07.020.

21. Yuan, Q., Zhou, H., Li, J., Liu, Z., Yang, F., Shen, X.S., Toward efficient content delivery for automated driving services: An edge computing solution. *IEEE Network*, 32, 80–86, 2018.

22. Liang, L., Ye, H., Li, G.Y., Toward intelligent vehicular networks: A machine learning framework. *IEEE Internet Things J.*, 6, 124–135, Feb. 2019.

23. Atallah, R.F., Assi, C.M., Khabbaz, M.J., Scheduling the operation of a connected vehicular network using deep reinforcement learning. *IEEE Trans. Intell. Transp. Syst.*, 20, 1669–1682, May 2018.

24. Paul, N., Chung, C.J., Timmis, I., Teaching vehicles to steer themselves with deep learning. *IEEE International Conference on Electro Information Technology (EIT)*, pp. 419–421, 2021.

25. Kim, J. and Bansal, M., Towards an interpretable deep driving network by attentional bottleneck. *IEEE Rob. Autom. Lett.*, 6, 7349–7356, 2021.

26. Newman, J., Sun, Z., Lee, D.J., Self-driving cars: A platform for learning and research. *Intermountain Engineering, Technology and Computing (IETC)*, pp. 1–5, 2020.

27. Lade, S., Shrivastav, P., Waghmare, S., Hon, S., Waghmode, S., Teli, S., Simulation of self driving car using deep learning. *2021 International Conference on Emerging Smart Computing and Informatics (ESCI)*, pp. 175–180, 2021.

28. Mobahi, M. and Sadati, S.H., An improved deep learning solution for object detection in self-driving cars. *28th Iranian Conference on Electrical Engineering (ICEE)*, pp. 1–5, 2020.

29. Sotelo, M.A., Advanced motion prediction for self-driving cars. *IEEE International Conference on Autonomous Robot Systems and Competitions (ICARSC)*, pp. 1–2, 2021.

30. Lin, G.H., Chang, C.H., Chung, M.C., Fan, Y.C., Self-driving deep learning system based on depth image based rendering and LiDAR point cloud. *IEEE International Conference on Consumer Electronics - Taiwan (ICCE-Taiwan)*, pp. 1–2, 2020.

31. Muenster, M., Lehner, M., Rixen, D., Requirement derivation of vehicle steering using mechanical four-poles in the presence of nonlinearities. *Mech. Syst. Signal Process.*, 155, 1–18, 16 June 2021, https://doi.org/10.1016/j.ymssp.2020.107484.

4

Review of Classification and Feature Selection Methods for Genome-Wide Association SNP for Breast Cancer

L.R. Sujithra[1]* and A. Kuntha[2]†

[1]CSE Dr. N. G. P. Institute of Technology, Coimbatore, India
[2]Coimbatore Institute of Technology, Coimbatore, India

Abstract

Cancer is a complicated disease with many molecular changes driven by hereditary, environmental, and lifestyle factors. Cancer cells develop abnormalities that alter the cells normal development, proliferation, and death cycle. Breast cancer remains the commonest analyzed cancer among women and the main cause of cancer-related deaths. Selection and identification of Single-Nucleotide Polymorphisms (SNPs) remain most significant assessment for Genome-Wide Association Studies (GWAS) related to breast cancer. Nevertheless, at the domain to detecting SNP and classification of healthy-patient, several significant challenges remain. The greatest difficulty is the problem of dimensionality as, the total amount of observations is significantly less than the total amount of SNPs and the healthy-patient data quantity also differ. Because of these difficulties, selecting and classifying features is extremely challenging. Machine Learning (ML) is a revolutionary method that is ideally situated to uncover the unseen biological interactions used for enhanced breast cancer finding and diagnosis. This review goal is to determine the best effective approach of analyzing SNP data by combining several Feature Selection (FS) and classification methods. This paper describes Genome-Wide prediction analysis to construct methods that predict whether or not by a latest proceeding, can diagnose the breast cancer dependent on the SNP set. It also gives an overview of FS and techniques of machine learning used to predict breast cancer. Latest FS and machine learning application advancements are highlighted, with descriptions of how these techniques can lead to enhanced

*Corresponding author: sujianu52@gmail.com
†Corresponding author: kunthavai@cit.edu.in

K. Umamaheswari, B. Vinoth Kumar and S. K. Somasundaram (eds.) *Artificial Intelligence for Sustainable Applications*, (55–78) © 2023 Scrivener Publishing LLC

disease identification and the incorporation of genetic features into future customized healthcare.

Keywords: Single nucleotide polymorphisms (SNPs), deoxyribonucleic acid (DNA), genome-wide association studies (GWAS)

4.1 Introduction

Complex diseases frequently lack a clear biological inheritance pattern at the level of population. Specific elements can't cause for disease to appear. Natural life, scientific experimentation, and research collections can all be used to build a biological data knowledge base. Where species-specific information is available, classical organism collections are useful, as it aids in new discoveries [1]. Numerous biological research investigations have been piloted, resulting in enormous genetic data resources. These information sources, it is frequently stated, are not yet properly exploited [2]. These sources of data also provide statistical issues; for example, the Family-Wise Error Rate (FWER) shows at least single incorrect discovery in several test, which is known as to generate major false positive issues [3]. FWER rises as the number of marker candidates grows. From the growth exposed that, issue of computing slant is substantial in genomic data, therefore, the size of input file is the same, but the processing time for variant calling is quite differs. A variant in a single nucleotide that resides at an exact locus at the genome that is appear in a population of a residence to a significant degree [4–6]. It is necessary on the way to examine disease-associated SNPs used to help expose the genetic basis of complex hereditary disease using genome-wide genotyping of SNPs in genome of humans [7]. Single nucleotide polymorphism differences in base pairs of DNA and SNP profiles have remain known for Genome-Wide Association Studies (GWAS) area to define a wide range of disorders in it. The quantity of SNP is generally higher than quantity of things, which are the common issue. SNPs distinguish one person from others and aid in the detection of genetic diversity in a population [8]. The major factor affecting an individual's link to pupils is genomic variant. From the research, a number of approaches for assessing SNP susceptibility in GWAS have been presented; each one examines every SNP separately. Nevertheless, only a minimum percentage of SNPs are significantly reflected on complex disease features, and the majority of SNPs have low individual penetrance [9]. Several common human disorders, instead, have been linked to complex interactions between numerous SNPs. This is termed as multi locus interactions.

Main goals of SNP analysis are to create a model that can classifying the trials as match to a well or affected individual [10]. The huge number of

SNPs, on the other hand, makes it difficult to construct accurate prediction systems. Nonetheless, for lowering time complexity and enhancing accuracy, selecting a subcategory of descriptive and significant SNPs is critical [11]. As a result, to improve the efficiency in order to be classifiers and to minimize period requirements, the first phase of SNP data analysis ought to remain the choice of the furthermost discriminative and informative subcategory of SNPs. For this goal, feature selection approaches have been utilized, although they have typically only been used to a limited number of particular genes related with human disease, with only a rare study applying feature selection techniques across the entire genome. A machine learning-based system's successful testing on the selection of an appropriate feature selection strategy. The method of drastically lowering the dimensional of space in feature while keeping the exact depiction are unique data's is known as feature selection (FS) [12]. Increased performance in classification, decreased speed in learning, data interpretation are simple, and better prediction generalization capabilities are the key benefits. FS techniques, on the other hand, have a higher computational complexity and require parameter modification to find best feature subsets. Wrapper and filter techniques are the two most common types on Feature selection methods. Depending on the classifiers Wrapper methods chosen, filter methods of filter are independent of the classification algorithm [13]. During training phase, wrapper methods utilize a classifier to choose a best subcategory of features. Specific classifier is utilized in the feature selection process, both techniques provide very competitive performance. Nevertheless, they are computationally costly and over-fitting to prone. Approaches in Wrapper are frequently inapplicable to SNP data due to the long calculation times required owing to the excessive dimensionality of the data. Filter methods, unlike wrapper methods, are not dependent on classifiers. They use a variety of metrics to assess the discriminatory potential of characteristics, including symmetrical uncertainty, mutual information, and fisher score [14]. When contrasted with other FS approaches, filter methods are quicker, more mountable, highly effective and be a strong generality capability. Methods involved in filter, on the other hand is typically underperform wrapper methods. Numerous feature selection methods have recently been created that combine the benefits of filter and wrapper techniques, generally by using filter methods first and then wrapper techniques. This research looked at a variety of machine-learning approaches with various properties [15].

Building accurate predictive models based on ML for complex disease offers a difficulty in dimensionality associated to SNP data that is larger size of feature compared to trial size [16]. Integrating several ML methods is one technique to get around the obscenity of dimensionality problem.

The major focus is how to use a feature selection algorithm on data set at earlier employing ML-based classification algorithms to classify samples. For instance, SVM, coupled with NB and DTs, remains to detect cases related to breast cancer utilizing SNP chosen by material gain. Additionally, mean variance calculations and kNN (K-Nearest Neighbor) have been used to evaluate SNP importance and do classification tasks on the breast cancer database [17]. The primary objectives of cancer prediction and prognosis differ from those of cancer detection and diagnosis. The prediction of cancer susceptibility (that is risk analysis), cancer recurrence, and cancer survivability are the three predictive foci in cancer prediction/prognosis [18]. In first scenario, one is attempting to predict the chance of developing a specific type of cancer before it occurs. In the second example, one is attempting to estimate the chance of cancer recurrence after disease appears to have resolved [19]. In the third situation, after the disease has been diagnosed, one attempts to forecast an outcome (life expectancy, survival, progression, tumor-drug sensitivity). The effectiveness of the prognostic prediction in latter two cases is certainly dependent, in part, on the effectiveness or quality of diagnosis [20]. The major aim in this research remains to determine the best real approach of analyzing SNP data by combining several Feature Selection (FS) and classification methods. In this paper describes about a genome-wide prediction analysis to construct models that predict whether or not a novel subject resolves the breast cancer issues depending on their SNP profile implementation. It also includes a summary of FS and techniques utilize machine learning used to forecast breast cancer.

Remaining of this study is to set as follows: The second section examines recent approaches and their implementations. The third section discusses the problems with current system. The empirical findings are discussed in Section 4.4, and the conclusion with future work is discussed Section 4.5.

4.2   Literature Analysis

Since the significance of predictive medicine and the increasing reliance on machine learning to make predictions, authors thought it would be useful to carry out a detailed review of published surveys using machine learning approaches in conjunction with SNP selection in cancer prediction and prognosis in this segment. The goal is to find out various ML techniques are used, for a training in particular data actually integrated, what are the categories involve in endpoint SNP predictions are being made, what types of cancers are being researched, and how well these techniques perform in predicting cancer susceptibility or patient outcomes. Surprisingly, when it related to cancer prognosis and prediction, the majority of research was focused on three subsections: 1) a discussion of SNP gene selection techniques; 2) a discussion of SNP classifiers; and 3) a discussion of SNP DL (Deep Learning) classifiers.

4.2.1   Review of Gene Selection Methods in SNP

Boutorh and Guessoum [21] introduced a novel hybrid intelligent method for breast cancer diagnosis formed on Neural Networks (NN) and Association Rule Mining (ARM) that utilizes a dimensionality issue in Evolutionary Algorithm (EA) to deal with it. To choose decrease dimensionality and most informative features by identifying connections between SNP, ARM optimized by Grammatical Evolution (GE) is flexible to employ, whereas NN is active to get effective classification. Therefore, suggested NN-GEARM method was tested on a breast cancer SNP database acquired from Gene Expression Omnibus (GEO) website as National Center for Biotechnology Information. The algorithm that was developed has a 90% accuracy rate.

Li and Cao [22] utilized k-center method for dimensionality in data, and uncertainty in symmetric was included in the distance measurement at the k-center approach to link the imbalance among SNPs data. In the hospital, an enhanced k-center method, the k-MSU method, is suggested to offer experimental findings the clinical test data showing that k-MSU method in SNP choice had better organization accuracy and an improved effects.

Alzubi *et al.* [23] suggested an approach for determining the most enlightening SNPs and choose an appropriate SNP subcategory using an exact hybrid feature selection algorithm. This suggested technique is based on combination of filter approaches with wrapper approach, namely the Support Vector Machine Recursive Feature Elimination (SVM-RFE) and Conditional Mutual Information Maximization (CMIM) technique. At Autism Spectrum Disorder (ASD) SNP data source acquired from National Center for Biotechnology Information, the suggested approach was compared to three modern methods for FS methods:

- Minimum Redundancy Maximum Relevancy (mRMR)
- CMIM
- Relief

With the mention classification models: SVM, NB, LDA, and k-NN. The experimental findings show that adopted feature selection method performs well compared to all other feature extraction methods and achieves up to 89% classification accuracy for the database employed.

Prathibha and Chandran [24] suggested a feature selection method based on genetics. Heuristic search on GA replicates the procedure for natural selection. Heuristic in this is frequently employed for finding a practical solution for search challenges and in optimization. Problem in grouping is clustering a collection of objects so that those are similar group are extra similar than in other groups. A population-based search method is the Bee Colony Optimization (BCO) technique. It imitates honey bee colonies' food foraging behavior. The technique conducts at a neighborhood search is kind of pair with worldwide search in its simplest form, and it may be utilized for combinatorial and continuous optimization. The FS method Genetic clustering with BCO is easily adapted to the databases from Leukemia cancer in this research. The FS method results in decreased of 80% in the number of features. The important gene/SNP set, the accuracy and specificity were 70% and 82%, correspondingly. The number of features has been significantly decreased, while knowledge quality has improved.

Boutorh and Guessoum [25] developed a novel hybrid intelligent system that utilizes Evolutionary Algorithms (EA) is grind with issues in dimensionality, formed on Association Rule Mining (ARM) and Neural Networks (NN). Conversely, ARM optimized by Grammatical Evolution (GE) is utilized toward choose the furthermost informative features and decrease dimensionality in two different databases of case and control specimens via parallel extraction of associations among SNP. Alternatively, NN is employed to make effective classification as a supplement to the prior work. The parameters of the two combined approaches are set using the GA. Four separate SNP databases from NCBI Gene Expression Omnibus (GEO) website were used to test the suggested GA-NN-GEARM method. When integrated with other classifiers, the resulting model had countless classification accuracy, reaching 100% in circumstances, and outperformed several FS methods.

For feature selection, Rathasamuth and Pasupa [26] employed gain information to conjunction at technique of binary flower pollination, and a cut-off-point-finding threshold for setting at 0 or 1 values for a solution vector in the position and a GA bit-flip mutation operator. They had termed Modified-BFPA. SVM is used as the classification model. When compared to some other FS methods, the blend of methods is very least competitive. It has chosen only 1.765% of very important SNP out of a total of 10,210 SNPs. It chooses SNPs that had a classification accuracy of 95.12%. It was also rapid: iterations of average 1.60 with association of

SVM were used for selecting a set of SNPs which are best with maximum classification accuracy.

To examine these interactions, Jiang *et al.* [27] presented a unique boosting-based ensemble technique. For feature selection, a Gini impurity-based importance score technique was developed. Here on genotyping data of SNPs obtained by South eastern University of China, researchers assessed its effectiveness and compared it to NB, SVM, and Rf. The experimental findings indicate its validity and effectiveness in identifying SNP interactions. Furthermore, their strategy offered a significant advantage in terms of processing time and resources.

Zhao *et al.* [28] suggested a computational method that includes ML methods for identifying phenotypic subgroups associated with discriminant genotype markers by comparing genotype data with phenotype data. The suggested discriminant SNP identifier model is empirically tested using a simplex sample of Autism Spectrum Disorder (ASD). Choosing six phenotype markers to sample the cluster into a yield of five multidimensional subgroups formed on phenotype markers' extremities with hexagonal lattice. Determine which SNP sets were discriminant between these subgroups, the selection model in SNP include selection of random subspace for SNPs combined with FS techniques. Using SVM prediction model, this resulted in a SNPs sets with a total ROC act of 95%. SNPs biological analysis related to genes diagonally subcategories is introduced toward assess their importance in clinical data.

Cong *et al.* [29] suggested a component analysis-based method principal aimed at minimizing the data dimension in gene so that SNP sites can be clustered in a low-dimensional space. In addition, a tagSNPs selection procedure based on oriented graph theory is developed. At last, depending on the real-world 1000 Genomes Project database, we can obtain lesser tag SNPs than conventional techniques by initiating the entire process of constructed SNP classification model.

4.2.2   Review of Classification Methods in SNP

Cai and Jiang [30] created a unique Artificial Neural Network (ANN) approach for applications involved in biomedical that rely on Matrix Pseudo-Inversion (MPI). The MPI-ANN in a three-layer feed-forward NN (input layer, hidden layer, and output layers) and the linking the hidden and output layers based on weights are generated straight depending on MPI and not depending on a long learning cycle. For comparison, the LASSO technique is also provided. Through fivefold cross validation, the MPI-ANN technique's performance is validated using single nucleotide polymorphism (SNP) replicated an actual breast cancer data. Test results reveal that the created MPI-ANN is effective for illness classification and prediction, with higher accuracy (that is, rate of correct predictions) than LASSO. The MPI-ANN outperforms other ML approaches, including SVM, LR, and an iterative ANN, according to the findings based on actual breast cancer data. Furthermore, tests display the MPI-ANN may be employed to choose biomarkers as well.

In genetic epidemiology research, Uppu *et al.* [31] presented a multifactor dimensionality reduction based associative classifier to identifying SNPs connections. By changing minor allele frequency, heritability, sample size, and case-control ratios the methods are tested up to one to six loci models. When compared to earlier techniques, the test findings exposed significant gains to detect single nucleotide polymorphisms (SNPs) interaction based on accuracy the complex diseases are detected. Furthermore, employing sporadic breast cancer data, the method was effectively assessed. The findings reveal interactions between five variants in three estrogen-metabolism genes.

Wang *et al.* [32] developed and applied the SNP combination factor from previous knowledge, as well as emotional neural networks (ENN) for analyze illness vulnerability. Researchers obtained a superior susceptibility classification outcome by submitting the data to ENN and engaging particle swarm optimization with hierarchical structure (PSO HS) to train the parameters. The experimental findings on a real database demonstrate that using emotional neural networks to know risk/protect factors improves the performance of disease susceptibility assessment.

Anekboon *et al.* [33] presented a novel method based on genetic material of various measurements, a new cross-over strategy, major order FS and novel mutation procedures. From this approach identify a chromosome that is in suitable length and has the valuable features. The efficiency of the suggested methodology was demonstrated using Crohn's disease data obtained from association studies depend on case–control. The suggested SNP prediction approach outperformed earlier proposed methods such as the i) optimum random forest (ORF), ii) univariate marginal distribution algorithm, iii) support vector machine (SVM), iv) complementary greedy search-based prediction algorithm (CGSP), v) combinatorial search-based prediction algorithm (CSP), and vi) discretized network flow (DNF) with respect to prediction accuracy. When evaluated in contradiction of this genuine data sets with a cross-validation of 5-fold, the approach had exactness of 90.4%, sensitive of 87.5%, and specific of 92.2%.

López *et al.* [34] utilized the Random Forest (RF) approach to find the most key features (SNPs) associated to diabetes, assigning every attribute a weight (importance degree) ranging from 0 to 1. SVMs and LR were also employed because they are two additional well-known machine learning approaches in the medical field. Their results were compared to those obtained by RF. Additionally, the RF-derived relevance of the attributes was utilized to conduct predictions using the k-NN technique, which weighted attributes in the similarity measure as per their RF-derived relevance. Six hundred and seventy-seven people are tested. The SNPs' significance is until 0.897 area with in the ROC curve in relate to risk prediction, owing to RF's ability to manage the difficulty of feature overfitting, interactions and unknown attribute values with esteem to prediction accuracy stand with the constancy of the estimated significance of the features, RF outperforms all other ML approaches evaluated.

Budiarto *et al.* [35] developed a technique for estimating ancestry from SNP genotyping data that included K Means clustering with PCA estimation. In terms of clustering quality and computing time, this approach was compared to a baseline model termed fast STRUCTURE. The developed framework and the baseline model are trained and evaluated using public data from the 1000 Genome Project. The suggested model is capable of generating clusters with more precision than rapid STRUCTURE (91.02% over 90.39%). More significantly, it can reduce calculation time by up to 100 times compared to fast STRUCTURE (from 490 seconds to 4.86 seconds).

Elsebakhi *et al.* [36] suggested functional networks to formed a tendency score and Newton Raphson-maximum-likelihood optimizations as a new large-scale machine learning method to improve its performance in highlighting dimensionality, with imbalanced distribution, and sparse attributes challenges in huge biomedical data. Various cases are circumstances formed on combined phenotypic and genomics; huge biomedical data is suggested as: i) real-life biomedical data, ii) optimal design of cancer chemotherapy; iii) recognize inpatient-admission of individuals with primary diagnosis of cancer; iv) recognize severe asthma exacerbation children via integrated phenotypic and SNP repository data; and v) mixture models simulation studies. The performance of developed paradigm was compared to the current modern data mining, machine learning, and statistics schemes in comparative studies. On the four benchmark datasets, the findings of the new classifier's performance against the most frequent classifiers have been reported as graphs and tables. Then find a new classifier to exceed current modern statistical ML techniques in terms related to reliability and efficiency. Novel predictive modeling classifier reduces computational time and provides consistent results, with the potential to be extended to cope with high-performance computing systems blended to next-generation sequencing data in future.

Sun *et al.* [37] introduced epiACO, an ant colony optimization algorithm-reflect the approach to identify interactions in epistatic. The new functions with fitness Svalue, a memory-based strategy, are all strengths of epiACO and path selection techniques. To excellently and efficiently quantify connections among SNP mixtures and the phenotype, the Svalue takes benefits of both Bayesian network and mutual information. To guide adaptively ant behaviors of exploration and exploitation, two path selection techniques are offered: probabilistic and stochastic path selection method. The memory-based technique is meant to keep track of candidate solutions from past to current iteration and compare the results for produce novel candidate solutions, resulting in more exact method of epistasis detection.

The Clonal Heterogeneity Investigation Tool was introduced by Li and Li [38], that calculates fraction related to cellular for both mutations and sCNAs to employ their circulations to notify macroscopic clonal architecture. More than half of the group of 700 breast cancer tumors seem to have numerous identifiable aneuploid tumor clones and most of them demonstrate subtype-exact variations in clonality for known cancer genes.

4.2.3   Review of Deep Learning Classification Methods in SNP

Uppu *et al.* [39] proposed a deep multi-layered feed forward neural network for predicting two-locus polymorphisms in genome-wide data owing to interactions. By changing the parameters of the models under various circumstances, validate the performance of the trained multilayer neural network alone. Additionally, through assessing on an actual dataset, the prior method's discoveries are validated in this study. The experimental results on a real dataset indicate a substantial improvement in prediction accuracy over previous methods. The findings reveal two-locus polymorphisms with highly ranked to interact them may be lead to breast cancer susceptibility.

Based on deep learning methods, Li *et al.* [40] presented a three-stage framework comprising prediction, clustering, and epistasis detection to handle both heterogeneity and epistasis of complex diseases. The epistasis recognition step employs an optimized multi-objective approach get identify numerous potential epistatic SNP sets that contribute to various subtypes of complicated diseases. The case group's subtypes are then defined using a K-means clustering technique. Lastly, a DL model based on graphics processing unit (GPU) has been developed for disease prediction. Experiments on pure and heterogeneous databases suggest that this technique has the potential to be helpful and might be used instead of other methods. As a result, when epistasis and heterogeneity coexist, the technique is particularly well suited to the identification of complicated diseases.

Kotlarz et al. [41] proposed a deep learning approach for classifying next-generation sequencing based SNPs hooked on right and inappropriate calls based on array-based genotype information. The deep learning methods were created using Python. Numerous methods is tested: 1) the basic, nave classifier, 2) the naïve method improved by different weights on pre-imposing inappropriate and right SNP class in computing injury measure, 3) and 4) the naïve method modify the random re-sampling (with replacement) of the improper SNPs to match 30%/60%/100% of the number of exact SNPs. The training data set consists of 2,227,995 right (97.94%) and 46,920 inappropriate SNPs from three bulls, whereas the validation database comprised of 749,506 right (98.05%) and 14,908 inappropriate SNPs from one bull. From the study, reveal that maximum parsimonious nave model and weighting of model with SNP class provides better result for classifying the valid data set for an infrequent event classification issue, such as inappropriate SNP detection in NGS data. Both methods classify 19.1% of the truly inappropriate SNP as inappropriate and 99% of the truly right SNP as correct, yielding an F1 score of 0.21, which was the greatest one among the methods evaluated.

Alakwaa et al. [42] created a deep learning technique for metabolomics-based breast cancer ER state classification that had greatest forecast accuracy (AUC = 0.93) and revealed more disease. Promote the uses of for classifying metabolomics research community based on feed-forward networks-based deep learning methods.

DeepSEA, an DL–based algorithmic system created by Zhou et al. [43], straight learns from large-scale chromatin-profiling data to regulate a sequence code, allowing single-nucleotide sensitivity to sequence changes from the change predict the chromatin effects. This capacity was also utilized to increase the prioritizing of functional variations, such as disease-associated variants and expression quantitative trait loci (eQTLs).

Sun et al. [44] created and deployed a multilayer deep neural network (DNN) survival typical to abstract information, generate accurate an understandable prediction. The forecast evaluation of DNN existence model is compared to numerous ML-based survival algorithms in a series of simulated tests. At last, researchers demonstrated that DNN existence model not lone outperforms numerous conventional existence predictions model with respect to prediction accuracy (e.g., c-index =0.765), and similarly finds clinical risk mean top subgroups successfully through effective learning process the difficult structures between genetic variant, utilizing GWAS data from two large-scale randomize clinical trials in AMD over 7800 samples. Additionally, using DNN survival model, extract a subject explicit significance quantity for every predictor, which gives significant visions into modified primary prevention of clinical management for the disease.

Montaez *et al.* [45] reported an association study in which data from genome-wide association studies (GWAS) are coupled with the deep learning method to evaluate prediction potential of statistically significant single nucleotide polymorphisms (SNPs) linked to obesity phenotype. This method illustrates how deep learning may be used as a strong framework for GWAS research, capturing information about SNPs and their significant relationships. The assessment of genetic SNPs data from population-based genome-wide research has been explored using basic statistical techniques and methodologies. Static association testing among separate SNP and obesity was carried out using LR in an additive model.

Pirmoradi *et al.* [46] presented a technique for identifying important SNPs and classifying healthy and unhealthy patient samples that was both fast and accurate. To begin, the nominal SNP data is converted to numeric by using Mean Encoding technique, which is an intelligent approach. Then, for feature selection, a two-step filter approach is utilized to eliminate redundant and irrelevant features. Lastly, the suggested deep autoencoder is used to categorize data so that it could automatically create its outline depending on the source data. To test the method, researchers utilized five distinct SNP datasets from Gene Expression Omnibus (GEO) database, comprising thyroid cancer, mental retardation, breast cancer, colorectal cancer, and autism. The suggested technique has prospered in feature selection and classification, allowing it to accurately classify healthy and patient samples in thyroid cancer, mental retardation, breast cancer, colorectal cancer, and autism based on selected features with 100%, 94.4%, 100% and 99.1% accuracy, correspondingly. In comparison to previous published efforts, the findings demonstrate that it was highly effective.

4.3 Comparison Analysis

Table 4.1 illustrates the benefits and drawbacks of current SNP-based risk prediction models, in addition to the performance of SNP-based risk prediction models.

Table 4.1 Benefits and drawbacks of current SNP-based risk.

Author name	Title	Merits	Demerits
Boutorh, A. and Guessoum, A. [21]	Classification of SNPs for breast cancer diagnosis using neural-network-based association rules.	The system has achieved a level of accuracy of up to 90%.	Complexity of time.
Rathasamuth, W. and Pasupa, K., [26]	A Modified Binary Flower Pollination Algorithm: A Fast and Effective Combination of Feature Selection Techniques for SNP Classification.	It chooses only 1.76% of the most important SNPs out of a total of 10,210 SNPs.	Other types of diseases are not covered by this plan.
Jiang, L., Zhang, B., [27]	Prediction of SNP sequences via gini impurity based gradient boosting method.	This method had a significant benefit in terms of computational time and resources.	A huge dataset is required.
Cong, T., Wang [29]	Big Data Driven Oriented Graph Theory Aided tag SNPs Selection for Genetic Precision Therapy.	To cluster SNP sites, this technique lowers the gene data dimension.	The suggested approach has not been tested on other datasets.
Cai, B. and Jiang, X., [30]	A novel artificial neural network method for biomedical prediction based on matrix pseudo-inversion.	It provides substantially higher accuracy.	The computational efficiency is quite low.
Uppu, S., Krishna, A., [31]	A multifactor dimensionality reduction based associative classification for detecting SNP interactions.	Effective in the classification of all kinds of cancer.	It hasn't been tested with real-time data.

(Continued)

Table 4.1 Benefits and drawbacks of current SNP-based risk. (*Continued*)

Author name	Title	Merits	Demerits
Anekboon, K., Lursinsap [33]	Extracting predictive SNPs in Crohn's disease using a vacillating genetic algorithm and a neural classifier in case–control association studies.	Increases the performance of classification.	There is no dimensionality reduction.
López, B., Torrent-Fontbona, F., [34]	Single Nucleotide Polymorphism relevance learning with Random Forests for Type 2 diabetes risk prediction.	With respect to risk prediction, it gives an area with in the ROC curve of up to 0.89 for SNPs.	Increases the complexity of time.
Elsebakhi, E., Lee, F., Schendel, E., [36]	Large-scale machine learning based on functional networks for biomedical big data with high performance computing platforms.	The new predictive modeling classifier reduces computing time while providing reliable result.	Does not detect the disease-gene-drug relationship.
Sun, Y., Shang, J., [37]	epiACO-a method for identifying epistasis based on ant Colony optimization algorithm.	Accomplishes better results in terms of accuracy.	Memory requirements are high.
Li, B. and Li, J.Z., [38]	A general framework for analyzing tumor subclonality using SNP array and DNA sequencing data.	For known cancer genes, this approach reveals subtype-specific variations in clonality.	The risk prediction tool has a difficult architecture to create.

Table 4.1 Benefits and drawbacks of current SNP-based risk. (*Continued*)

Author name	Title	Merits	Demerits
Kotlarz, K., Mielczarek, M., Suchocki [41]	The application of deep learning for the classification of correct and incorrect SNP genotypes from whole-genome DNA sequencing pipelines.	It presents 99% of exactly correct SNPs as correct and resulting in F1 score of 0.21 — the greatest along compared techniques.	There has not been any testing on a large dataset.
Alakwaa, F. M., Chaudhary, K., & Garmire, L. X. [42]	Deep learning accurately predicts estrogen receptor status in breast cancer metabolomics data.	Best prediction accuracy (AUC = 0.93) and improved disease biology revealed.	Use of a dimensionality reduction model is required.
Sun, T., Wei, Y., [44]	Genome-wide association study-based deep learning for survival prediction.	It needs the least amount of training time.	For complex structure, there is less efficiency.
Pirmoradi, S., Teshnehlab, M., [46]	A Self-organizing Deep Auto-Encoder approach for Classification of Complex Diseases using SNP Genomics Data.	For thyroid cancer, mental retardation, breast cancer, colorectal cancer, and autism, it can categorized healthy and patient samples based on selected features with 100%, 94.4%, 100%, 96%, and 99.1% accuracy, correspondingly.	The provided data requires additional time to train.

According to the results of the preceding research, SNP-based risk information is potential to have an exact value in the breast cancer risk prediction.

4.4   Issues of the Existing Works

Traditional machine learning techniques stand gradually being utilized in present era as genetic epidemiology to identify the underlying architecture of complicated diseases. This study presents Genome Wide Predictive Studies (GWPSs), that take source value as a GWAS (SNP arrays for a certain group of objects, each categorized as a circumstance or a control) but produce a classify method that can be utilized to find the classes category of an undiagnosed person based on their SNP profile. ML techniques comprise a large variety of static, probabilistic and optimization approaches to make computers to train on such classifiers from categorized patient information. Many fields of biology and medicine have effectively used machine learning to develop useful predictions. The researchers looked at finding a gene [47], eukaryote promoter recognition [48], protein structure prediction [49], pattern recognition in microarrays [50], gene regulatory response prediction [51], protein/gene identification in text [52], and gene expression microarray-based cancer prognosis and diagnosis. Unfortunately, none of the models have fully clarified challenge of identifying and classify patterns in genetic data. Deep learning is an evolving field that enables machines to understand information by presenting it in hierarchical abstractions. The present research suggests using deep learning to discover SNP connections linked to a complicated disease. They allow computer models to use general-purpose learning techniques to find the representations needed for classification. By delivering excellent prediction accuracy in a variety of scenarios, these deep structured learning models offer stability, generalization, and scalability to huge data. Nevertheless, due to the intrinsic mathematical and computational complexity of the topic, identifying these SNP connections remains one of the most difficult tasks [53]. The curse of dimensionality, genetic variability, computational complexity, missing heritability, and the nonappearance of marginal effects are only a few of the problems. There is no one approach that can properly detect and interact SNPs by exposing their links to disease manifestations.

4.5   Experimental Results

This section compares and contrasts available machining learning approaches in order to investigate the relationship between SNP interactions and progress a model for breast cancer in early detection. To measure prediction of the classifiers, performance measures are required.

Although accuracy is a widely used statistic, it might produce mislead-
ing findings when data has an uneven class distribution. Even in the event
of class imbalance, evaluation measures like as F-measure and Matthews
Correlation Coefficient may be used to assess how effectively a classifier
can discriminate between various classes. The confusion matrix in Table
4.2 represents the accurately and inaccurately classified cases per class for
a binary classification. True positive (tp), false positive (fp), false negative
(fn), and true negative (tn) counts are represented as a confusion matrix by
tp, fp, fn, and tn, correspondingly. F-Measure is calculated based on these
counts:

$$Precision = \frac{tp}{tp + fp} \tag{4.1}$$

$$recall = \frac{tp}{tp + fn} \tag{4.2}$$

$$F - measure = \frac{2 * precision * recall}{precision + recall} \tag{4.3}$$

Another statistic for assessing the accuracy of binary classifications is
the Matthews Correlation Coefficient (MCC). MCC mean a balanced measure that may be employed even if the class distribution is uneven since it
takes into account tp, fp, fn, and tn counts. MCC is an associated coefficient that has a value between -1 and +1 and is used for compare actual
and predicted events. A score of +1 denotes a correct prediction, whereas
a value of -1 denotes a mismatch between the predicted and actual labels.

Figure 4.1 shows how the processing time for the amount of datasets
within allocated datasets is contrasted in the graph above. This graph
shows that, when compared to current methods, the recommended SNP-
DAE takes the least amount of time to process. As a result, the SNP-DAE

Table 4.2 Two-class classification confusion matrix.

Actual/Predicted as	Positive	Negative
POSITIVE	Tp	Fn
NEGATIVE	Fp	tn

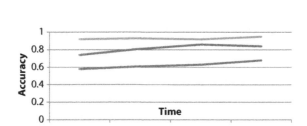

Figure 4.1 Accuracy comparison results of different techniques.

method outperforms all other methods because it produces optimal results in SNP interactions while maintaining a high rate of accuracy.

Figure 4.2 shows how the precisions of the amount of data within defined datasets were compared. As the number of datasets increased, so did the value of accuracy. This graph shows that, when compared to previous approaches, the recommended methods of SNP-DAE provide higher accuracy, resulting in better outcomes.

The memory comparison results of the various techniques for cancer disease prediction are given in Figure 4.3. Figure 4.3 displays how recall the number of datasets within assigned datasets compared to the suggested and current techniques. As the quantity of datasets increased, the recall value increased as well.

When compared to the current techniques, the recommended SNP-DAE approach gives a higher f-measure, as displayed in Figure 4.4. As an outcome, the SNP-DAE algorithm is likely to produce optimal results in

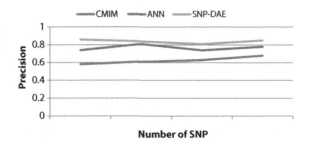

Figure 4.2 Precision comparison results of different techniques.

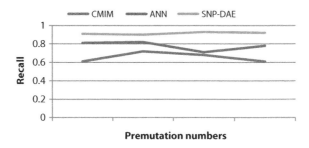

Figure 4.3 Recall comparison results of different techniques.

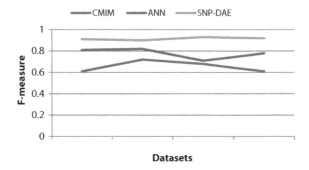

Figure 4.4 F-measure comparison results of different techniques.

SNP interactions. When compared to previous methods, the SNP-DAE method has a high f-measure.

4.6   Conclusion and Future Work

This chapter shows thorough investigation analysis the previously published cancer diagnostic approaches. The findings from the prior research works employing the simulated datasets are validated by assessing the models on real data. The approaches revealed that the top fifteen SNP interactions are strongly linked to sporadic breast cancer. The performances of the approaches are evaluated based on validation, training, and testing. Thorough analyzes remain carried out through varying the model parameters to obtain the optimal results from the existing techniques. It is clearly observed from the survey that only SNP interactions are currently being investigated. Thus, there is still research to be done for exploring the higher-order interactions in high- dimensional data [54, 55]. The exploitation of deep learning techniques in cancer diagnosis is a recent trend for research framework [56]. Future research work is to investigate other recent approaches for pre-processing, feature selection and classification.

References

1. Sobrino, B., Brión, M., Carracedo, A., SNPs in forensic genetics: A review on SNP typing methodologies. *Forensic Sci. Int.*, *154*, 2-3, 181–194, 2005.
2. Chen, C.C., Schwender, H., Keith, J., Nunkesser, R., Mengersen, K., Macrossan, P., Methods for identifying SNP interactions: A review on variations of logic regression, random forest and bayesian logistic regression. *IEEE/ACM Trans. Comput. Biol. Bioinf.*, *8*, 6, 1580–1591, 2011.
3. Terada, A., Yamada, R., Tsuda, K., Sese, J., Genetics and population analysis LAMPLINK: Detection of statistically significant SNP combinations from GWAS data. *Bioinformatics*, *32*, 3513–3515, 2016.
4. Deng, L., Huang, G., Zhuang, Y., Wei, J., Sam, S.A.M., HiGene: A high-performance platform for genomic data analysis, in: *Proceedings of the 2016 IEEE Int. Conference on Bioinformatics and Biomedicine*, Shenzhen, China, 15–18 December 2016, pp. 576–583.
5. Chen, G. and Xie, X., A light weight SNP detection algorithm for the breast cancer targeted sequencing data. *Biomed. Res.*, *28*, 3574–3579, 2017.
6. Bayerl, H., Kraus, R.H.S., Nowak, C., Foerster, D.W., Fickel, J., Kuehn, R., Fast and cost-effective single nucleotide polymorphism (SNP) detection in the absence of a reference genome using semideep next-generation Random Amplicon Sequencing (RAMseq). *Mol. Biol. Resour.*, *18*, 107–117, 2018.
7. Kobayashi, M., Ohyanagi, H., Takanashi, H., Asano, S., Kudo, T., Kajiya-Kanegae, H., Nagano, A.J., Tainaka, H., Tokunaga, T., Sazuka, T. *et al.*, Heap: A highly sensitive and accurate SNP detection tool for low-coverage high-throughput sequencing data. *DNA Res.*, *24*, 397–405, 2017.
8. Hajiloo, M., Damavandi, B., HooshSadat, M., Sangi, F., Mackey, J.R., Cass, C.E., Damaraju, S., Breast cancer prediction using genome wide single nucleotide polymorphism data. *BMC Bioinf.*, *14*, 13, 1–10, 2013.
9. Ferreira, M.A., Gamazon, E.R., Al-Ejeh, F., Aittomäki, K., Andrulis, I.L., Anton-Culver, H., Parsons, M.T., Genome-wide association and transcriptome studies identify target genes and risk loci for breast cancer. *Nat. Commun.*, *10*, 1, 1–18, 2019.
10. Nguyen, T.T., Huang, J.Z., Wu, Q., Nguyen, T.T., Li, M.J., Genome-wide association data classification and SNPs selection using two-stage quality-based

random forests. *BMC Genomics*, 16, 2, 1–11, 2015, December. BioMed Central.

11. Soumare, H., Rezgui, S., Gmati, N., Benkahla, A., New neural network classification method for individuals ancestry prediction from SNPs data. *Biodata Min.*, *14*, 1, 1–14, 2021.

12. Tahir, M. and Sardaraz, M., A fast and scalable workflow for SNPs detection in genome sequences using hadoop map-reduce. *Genes*, *11*, 2, 166, 2020.

13. Wu, Q., Ye, Y., Liu, Y., Ng, M.K., SNP selection and classification of genome-wide SNP data using stratified sampling random forests. *IEEE Trans. Nanobiosci.*, *11*, 3, 216–227, 2012.

14. Ho, D.S.W., Schierding, W., Wake, M., Saffery, R., O'Sullivan, J., Machine learning SNP based prediction for precision medicine. *Front. Genet.*, *10*, 267, 2019.

15. Saenko, V.A. and Rogounovitch, T.I., Genetic polymorphism predisposing to differentiated thyroid cancer: A review of major findings of the genome-wide association studies. *Endocrinol. Metab.*, *33*, 2, 164–174, 2018.

16. Chatterjee, N., Shi, J., García-Closas, M., Developing and evaluating polygenic risk prediction models for stratified disease prevention. *Nat. Rev. Genet.*, *17*, 7, 392–406, 2016.

17. Dite, G.S., MacInnis, R.J., Bickerstaffe, A., Dowty, J.G., Allman, R., Apicella, C., Hopper, J.L., Breast cancer risk prediction using clinical models and 77 independent risk-associated SNPs for women aged under 50 years: Australian breast cancer family registry. *Cancer Epidemiol. Prev. Biomarkers*, *25*, 2, 359–365, 2016.

18. Wray, N.R., Yang, J., Hayes, B.J., Price, A.L., Goddard, M.E., Visscher, P.M., Pitfalls of predicting complex traits from SNPs. *Nat. Rev. Genet.*, *14*, 7, 507–515, 2013.

19. Katsaouni, N., Tashkandi, A., Wiese, L., Schulz, M.H., Machine learning based disease prediction from genotype data. *Biol. Chem.*, *402*, 8, 871–885, 2021.

20. Matukumalli, L.K., Grefenstette, J.J., Hyten, D.L., Choi, I.Y., Cregan, P.B., Van Tassell, C.P., Application of machine learning in SNP discovery. *BMC Bioinf.*, *7*, 1, 1–9, 2006.

21. Boutorh, A. and Guessoum, A., Classication of SNPs for breast cancer diagnosis using neural-network-based association rules, in: *2015 12th International Symposium on Programming and Systems (ISPS)*, pp. 1–9, IEEE, 2015 April.

22. Li, L. and Cao, L., SNP selection based on k-center algorithm, in: *2019 6th International Conference on Systems and Informatics (ICSAI)*, pp. 1449–1454, IEEE, 2019 November.

23. Alzubi, R., Ramzan, N., Alzoubi, H., Hybrid feature selection method for autism spectrum disorder SNPs, in: *2017 IEEE Conference on Computational Intelligence in Bioinformatics and Computational Biology (CIBCB)*, pp. 1–7, IEEE, 2017 August.

24. Prathibha, P.H. and Chandran, C.P., Feature selection for mining SNP from Leukaemia cancer using Genetic Algorithm with BCO, in: *2016 International Conference on Data Mining and Advanced Computing (SAPIENCE)*, pp. 57–63, IEEE, 2016 March.

25. Boutorh, A. and Guessoum, A., Complex diseases SNP selection and classification by hybrid association rule mining and artificial neural network—Based evolutionary algorithms. *Eng. Appl. Artif. Intell.*, 51, 58–70, 2016.

26. Rathasamuth, W. and Pasupa, K., A modified binary flower pollination algorithm: A fast and effective combination of feature selection techniques for SNP classification, in: *2019 11th International Conference on Information Technology and Electrical Engineering (ICITEE)*, pp. 1–6, IEEE, 2019 October.

27. Jiang, L., Zhang, B., Ni, Q., Sun, X., Dong, P., Prediction of snp sequences via gini impurity based gradient boosting method. *IEEE Access*, 7, 12647–12657, 2019.

28. Zhao, J., Nguyen, T., Kopel, J., Koob, P.B., Adieroh, D.A., Obafemi-Ajayi, T., Genotype combinations linked to phenotype subgroups in autism spectrum disorders, in: *2019 IEEE Conference on Computational Intelligence in Bioinformatics and Computational Biology (CIBCB)*, pp. 1–8, IEEE, July 2019.

29. Cong, T., Wang, J., Guan, S., Mu, Y., Bai, T., Ren, Y., Big data driven oriented graph theory aided tagsnps selection for genetic precision therapy. *IEEE Access*, 7, 3746–3754, 2018.

30. Cai, B. and Jiang, X., A novel artificial neural network method for biomedical prediction based on matrix pseudo-inversion. *J. Biomed. Inf.*, 48, 114–121, 2014.

31. Uppu, S., Krishna, A., Gopalan, R.P., A multifactor dimensionality reduction based associative classification for detecting SNP interactions, in: *International Conference on Neural Information Processing*, 2015, November, Springer, Cham, pp. 328–336.

32. Wang, X., Peng, Q., Zhong, T., Analysis of disease association and susceptibility for SNP data using emotional neural networks, in: *2014 International Joint Conference on Neural Networks (IJCNN)*, pp. 2901–2905, IEEE, 2014 July.

33. Anekboon, K., Lursinsap, C., Phimoltares, S., Fucharoen, S., Tongsima, S., Extracting predictive SNPs in Crohn's disease using a vacillating genetic algorithm and a neural classifier in case–control association studies. *Comput. Biol. Med.*, 44, 57–65, 2014.

34. López, B., Torrent-Fontbona, F., Viñas, R., Fernández-Real, J.M., Single nucleotide polymorphism relevance learning with random forests for type 2 diabetes risk prediction. *Artif. Intell. Med.*, 85, 43–49, 2018.

35. Budiarto, A., Mahesworo, B., Baurley, J., Suparyanto, T., Pardamean, B., Fast and effective clustering method for ancestry estimation. *Proc. Comput. Sci.*, 157, 306–312, 2019.

36. Elsebakhi, E., Lee, F., Schendel, E., Haque, A., Kathireason, N., Pathare, T., Syed, N., Al-Ali, R., Large-scale machine learning based on functional

networks for biomedical big data with high performance computing platforms. *J. Comput. Sci.*, 11, 9–81, 2015.

37. Sun, Y., Shang, J., Liu, J.X., Li, S., Zheng, C.H., epiACO-a method for identifying epistasis based on ant Colony optimization algorithm. *Biodata Min.*, *10*, 1, 1–17, 2017.

38. Li, B. and Li, J.Z., A general framework for analyzing tumor subclonality using SNP array and DNA sequencing data. *Genome Biol.*, *15*, 9, 1–23, 2014.

39. Uppu, S., Krishna, A., Gopalan, R.P., A deep learning approach to detect SNP interactions. *J. Software*, *11*, 10, 965–975, 2016.

40. Li, X., Liu, L., Zhou, J., Wang, C., Heterogeneity analysis and diagnosis of complex diseases based on deep learning method. *Sci. Rep.*, *8*, 1, 1–8, 2018.

41. Kotlarz, K., Mielczarek, M., Suchocki, T., Czech, B., Guldbrandtsen, B., Szyda, J., The application of deep learning for the classification of correct and incorrect SNP genotypes from whole-genome DNA sequencing pipelines. *J. Appl. Genet.*, *61*, 4, 607–616, 2020.

42. Alakwaa, F.M., Chaudhary, K., Garmire, L.X., Deep learning accurately predicts estrogen receptor status in breast cancer metabolomics data. *J. Proteome Res.*, *17*, 1, 337–347, 2018.

43. Zhou, J. and Troyanskaya, O.G., Predicting effects of noncoding variants with deep learning–based sequence model. *Nat. Methods*, *12*, 10, 931–934, 2015.

44. Sun, T., Wei, Y., Chen, W., Ding, Y., Genome-wide association study-based deep learning for survival prediction. *Stat. Med.*, *39*, 30, 4605–4620, 2020.

45. Montaez, C.A.C., Fergus, P., Montaez, A.C., Hussain, A., Al-Jumeily, D., Chalmers, C., Deep learning classification of polygenic obesity using genome wide association study SNPs, in: *2018 International Joint Conference on Neural Networks (IJCNN)*, pp. 1–8, IEEE, 2018 July.

46. Pirmoradi, S., Teshnehlab, M., Zarghami, N., Sharifi, A., A self-organizing deep auto-encoder approach for classification of complex diseases using SNP genomics data. *Appl. Soft Comput.*, *97*, 106718, 2020.

47. Baldi, P., Brunak, S., Bach, F., *Bioinformatics: The machine learning approach*, MIT Press, 2001.

48. Larranaga, P., Calvo, B., Santana, R., Bielza, C., Galdiano, J., Inza, I., Robles, V., Machine learning in bioinformatics. *Briefings Bioinf.*, *7*, 1, 86–112, 2006.

49. Tarca, A.L., Carey, V.J., Chen, X.W., Romero, R., Drăghici, S., Machine learning and its applications to biology. *PLoS Comput. Biol.*, *3*, 6, e116, 2007.

50. Cruz, J.A. and Wishart, D.S., Applications of machine learning in cancer prediction and prognosis. *Cancer Inf.*, *2*, 2006. 117693510600200030.

51. Mathé, C., Sagot, M.F., Schiex, T., Rouzé, P., Current methods of gene prediction, their strengths and weaknesses. *Nucleic Acids Res.*, *30*, 19, 4103–4117, 2002.

52. Won, K.J., Prügel-Bennett, A., Krogh, A., Training HMM structure with genetic algorithm for biological sequence analysis. *Bioinformatics*, *20*, 18, 3613–3619, 2004.

53. Yi, T.M. and Lander, E.S., Protein secondary structure prediction using nearest-neighbor methods. *J. Mol. Biol.*, *232*, 4, 1117–1129, 1993.

54. Pirooznia, M., Yang, J.Y., Yang, M.Q., Deng, Y., A comparative study of different machine learning methods on microarray gene expression data. *BMC Genomics*, *9*, 1, 1–13, 2008.

55. Middendorf, M., Kundaje, A., Wiggins, C., Freund, Y., Leslie, C., Predicting genetic regulatory response using classification. *Bioinformatics*, *20*, suppl_1, i232–i240, 2004.

56. Zhou, G., Shen, D., Zhang, J., Su, J., Tan, S., Recognition of protein/gene names from text using an ensemble of classifiers. *BMC Bioinf.*, *6*, 1, 1–7, 2005.

COVID-19 Data Analysis Using the Trend Check Data Analysis Approaches

Alamelu M.[1]*, M. Naveena[2], Rakshitha M.[3] and M. Hari Prasanth[4]

[1]Kumaraguru College of Technology, Coimbatore, India
[2]MUSIGMA, Bangalore, India
[3]TCS, Bangalore, India
[4]Quinbay, Bangalore, India

Abstract

The coronavirus produces a worldwide threat to the human population after 2019. In overall the globe has endeavoring to the spread of this virus and affected the market expenditure in the field of economy, data sources, life thread, and all other resources. With the present scenario analysis, the proposed COVID-19 trend check analysis approach the paper will discuss about the virus spread analysis with the day-to-day ascending behavior analysis using the trend check segregation algorithms. Using this approach, the collected COVID-19 data analysis has been analyzed and visualized with respect to the affected cases with the selective country wise.

Keywords: Trend check segregation 1 algorithm, trend check segregation 2 algorithm, trend check analysis system

5.1 Introduction

COVID-19 is a virus spread by the family of the newly discovered corona virus. The symptoms it may cause is of the cold, cough, and the fever. The disease can be recovered with the people immunity power and health. Considering with the old age people having the health issues like cardio-vascular disease, cancer, diabetics patients and relevant to other health

---

*Corresponding author: alamelu.m.it@kct.ac.in

K. Umamaheswari, B. Vinoth Kumar and S. K. Somasundaram (eds.) *Artificial Intelligence for Sustainable Applications*, (79–88) © 2023 Scrivener Publishing LLC

disease may hardly affected with this virus. Currently, many of the people in the world have been affected with the disease and many of them recovered and many of them have died with the disease [6].

The many existing analysis has been analyzed and worked out to make the prediction analysis. From the proposed COVID-19 research study analysis the work has been analyzed and executed with the positive affected cases and the recovered cases [7]. The study analysis has been executed with the COVID-19 Data segmentation analysis using the trend check approaches. In this approach the state wise COVID-19 data analysis has been taken and tested with the COVID-19 Data segmentation analysis using the trend check approaches. Using this approach, the COIVD affected issue has been analyzed with respect to the parameters of affected cases, recovered cases, and country level segregated analysis [10].

5.2 Literature Survey

Amir Ahmad, Sunita Garhwal *et al.* [2020] have made the analysis of the COVID-19 with the different taxonomies. Where the different machine learning approaches have been analyzed and detailed with the view of the COVID-19 analysis. The taxonomy has been analyzed with the machine learning, deep learning regression, network, and social media search query-based analysis [1].

R. Sujat, Jyotir Moy Chatterjee *et al.* [2020] defined the machine learning forecasting model for COVID-19. The author discusses about the machine learning models specifically of the linear regression, multilayer perception and auto regression analysis has been taken for the COVID-19 analysis in India. The forecasting analysis can also be analyzed for the future based statistical data [2].

Vasilis, Pantelis and Sotiris *et al.*, make the comparative study analysis of the COVID-19 active cases in a population. The six different time series have been taken and analyzed with the two different set of databases. The time series models such as ARIMA (Auto Regressive Integrated Moving Average), HWAAS (Holt Winters Additive Model), TBAT, prophet has been taken for the analysis and provided as the comparison for the COVID-19 analysis [3].

Vikas and Saurabh [3] proposed the application of machine learning time series analysis for prediction COVID-19 pandemic. The approach discussed about the dataset collected from the World Health Organization. They have done research on total number of deaths, recovered cases of virus for a particular timestamp of 5 months. Depending on this result the author have predicted the spread of virus and used seven methods for comparing among them by using RMSE values and ARIMA model for predicting the worldwide death cases. Data preprocessing has been done for training and testing data for modeling [4].

Akib Mohi Ud Din Khanday, Syed Tanzeel Rabani *et al.* [2020], have classified the textual clinical medical reports using the AI based analysis tools. In this case, the traditional machine learning algorithms are used to predict the analysis. The feature engineering can be incorporated with the frequency, bag of words and report length [5].

5.3   COVID-19 Data Segregation Analysis Using the Trend Check Approaches

The proposed system shows the flow of execution of the COVID-19 data analysis. The flow of execution starts with the data set COVID-19 analysis data collection and from that the set of COVID-19 affected cases can be filtered with the affected positive cases, trend check analysis with respect to the countries. The collected data set can be first input into the system. The collected data have the statewise COVID-19 confirmed and the recovered cases. Also, it have the trend check analysis data that have the country wise analysis status that has to been defined for the test data classification for the analyzing of the COVID-19 cases [9].

The generated data has been input to the proposed algorithm called the trend check analyzing algorithm. In this algorithm it can classify the segregation of the data with the trend check analysis data algorithm.

Trend check analysis data segmentation algorithm:

The algorithm will be executed with the analysis of the

5.3.1   Trend Check Analysis Segregation 1 Algorithm

1. The input data can be segregated with the present data (P) and the expected data (O) P,O
2. With the case of the analysis the differentiation of the present and the expected data can be differentiated with the parameters of the number of positive cases (PS), recovered cases (RC) and the number of months (M).
3. Present can be taken for the minimum of 5 months and with the selected parameters.

$$\Sigma \, 5M \, ^* \, (P)$$

4. With respect to that the expected data is calculated with the predictive and average summation analysis.

Total Prediction $P = \Sigma \, p1, p2...p5/$mean value

5.3.2   Trend Check Analysis Segregation 2 Algorithm

The algorithm can be executed for the next 15 days analysis from the report of the trend check analysis segregation 1 analysis.

1. The trend segmentation can be analyzed with respect to the set of input data received from the trend check analysis segmentation.
2. In the received data the segmentation can be divided with the present (RP) and the expected data (RE).

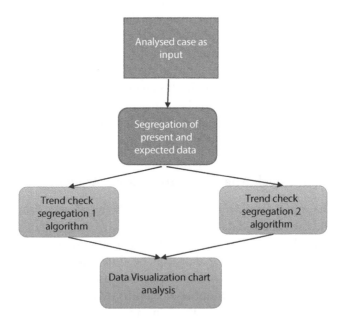

Figure 5.1 Track check analysis system.

3. A weightage has been fixed for the present data and used to calculate the average mean analysis.

4. With respect to the present weight analysis calculate the expected data.

Total expected data = $\sum$ wp1,wp2...wp5/average mean value analysis

The following Figure 5.1 will show the execution process of the trend check analysis approach.

Figure 5.1 represents the trend check analysis execution system. The execution can be start up from the COVID case analysis inputs and the data can be segregated as the present and the expected data. With respect to the present and the expected data the two sets of algorithms can be classified further as trend check segregation 1 and trend check segregation 2 algorithm.

5.4 Results and Discussion

The results and discussion discuss the proposed track check analysis system model that displays the resultant graphs. Graph 5.1 shows the analysis of the COVID confirm cases from the year of 2020 to 2021. X axis shows the year of increasing cases with the COVID affected analysis and the

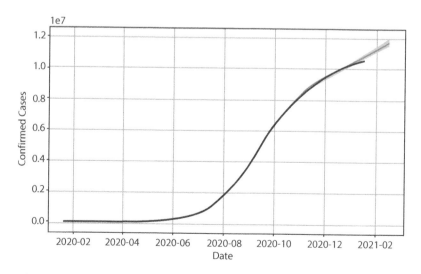

Graph 5.1 Track check segregation analysis 1.

y axis shows the confirmed cases. With respect to the trend check segmentation check1 algorithm the present and the expected data can be segregated with the predictive summation analysis [8].

Graph 5.2 depicted the representation of the graph implies the view of the trend check segmentation 2 algorithm with respect to the total number of cases affected with the affected cases with the confirmed cases with the country wise. In this case, the weightage analysis can be taken and implied for the test analysis. From the graph the x-axis shows the dates and y axis shows the total number of cases affected. The increasing blue curve will depict the predicted analysis of the test analysis cases.

The below diagram shows the doughnut chart visualizes the recovered, active, and deceased cases of world COVID-19 cases. In the Scatter plot, the X Label depicts the Death Rate per Million and Y Label depicts the 10 hotspot countries and India. Comparison of Hotspot countries by total number of cases with respect to dates has been done where the cases are low in the month of March 2020 and tends to be increasing eventually till January 2021.

The Graph 5.3 represents the comparison studies of the different hot spot countries taken for the analysis. The countries like India, USA, Italy, and South Korea has been taken for the analysis and taken for the COVID case analysis. The multiple color of variations has been taken and put forward for the trend check analysis. The variation of the increasing curve can represent the COVID affected cases with respective the country wise.

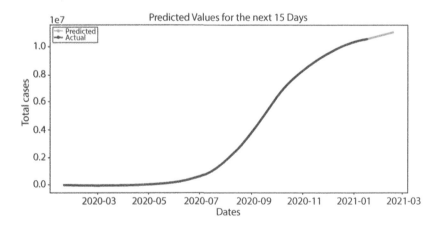

Graph 5.2 Trend check analysis 2.

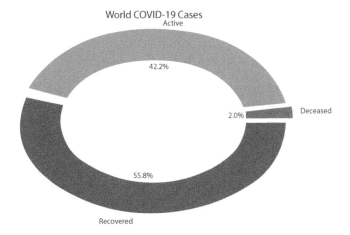

Graph 5.3 Visualization chart of world COVID cases.

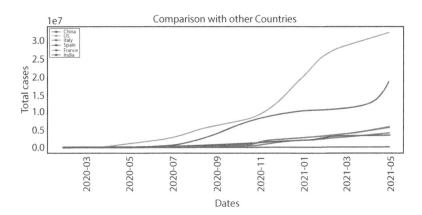

Graph 5.4 Comparison of cases in hotspot countries.

In Graphs 5.4 and 5.5 shows the flow graph execution of the hotspot countries specified. In the graph can show the death rate of the COVID affected cases in the country wise.

From the country wise it will show the affected cases.

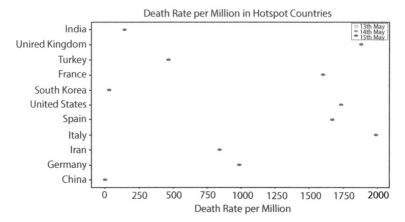

Graph 5.5 Death rate per million hotspot countries.

5.5 Conclusion

The proposed approach COVID-19 trend check analysis approach may use to analyze the COVID-19 test cases with respect to the positive affected cases with respect to the selective countries. The proposed approach can be analyzed with the two-approach algorithm of track check analysis 1 and track check analysis 2 algorithms. From this algorithm it used to predict the analysis of the COVID affected positive cases with the selected country wise and used to predict the analysis with the next 15 days disease prediction. Using this analysis, the test data can be analyzed and make to visualize the data analysis.

References

1. Ahmad, A., Garhwal, S., Ray, S.K., Kumar, G., Malebary, S.J., Barukab, O.M., The number of confrmed cases of COVID-19 by using machine learning: Methods and challenges. *Arch. Comput. Methods Eng.*, 28, 4, 2645–2653, 2020.
2. Sujath, R., Chatterjee, J.M., Hassanien, A.E., A machine learning forecasting model for COVID-19 pandemic in India. *Stochastic Environ. Res. Risk Assess.*, 34, 7, 959–972, 2020.
3. Chaurasia, V. and Pal, S., Application of machine learning time series analysis for prediction COVID-19 pandemic. *Res. Biomed. Eng.*, Springer, 39, 35–47, 2020.

4. Papastefanopoulos, V., Linardatos, P., Kotsiantis, S., OVID-19: A comparison of time series methods to forecast percentage of active cases per population. *Appl. Sci.*, 10, 11, 3880, 2020.

5. Khanday, A.M.U.D., Rabani, S.T., Khan, Q.R., Rouf, N., Mohi Ud Din, M., Machine learning based approaches for detecting COVID-19 using clinical text data. *Int. J. Inf. Technol.*, 12, 3, 731–739, 2020.

6. Gupta, A., Gupta, H.P., Biswas, B., Dutta, T., Approaches and applications of early classification of time series: A review. *IEEE Trans. Artif. Intell.*, 1, 1, 47–61, 2020.

7. Latif, S., Usman, M., Manzoor, S., Iqbal, W., Qadir, J., Tyson, G., Castro, I., Razi, A., Kamel Boulos, M.N., Weller, A., Crowcroft, J., Leveraging data science to combat COVID-19: A comprehensive review. *IEEE Trans. Artif. Intell.*, 1, 1, 85–103, 2020.

8. Kalita, I. and Roy, M., Deep neural network-based heterogeneous domain adaptation using ensemble decision making in land cover classification, in: *IEEE Transactions on Artificial Intelligence*, vol. 1, issue 3, pp. 167–180, 2020.

9. Sadamoto, T. and Chakrabortty, A., Fast real-time reinforcement learning for partially-observable large-scale systems, in: *IEEE Transactions on Artificial Intelligence*, vol. 1, issue 3, pp. 206–218, 2020.

10. Jia, Z., Cai, X., Zheng, G., Wang, J., Lin, Y., SleepPrintNet: A multivariate multimodal neural network based on physiological time-series for automatic sleep staging, in: *IEEE Transactions on Artificial Intelligence*, vol. 1, issue 3, pp. 248–257, 2020.

6

Analyzing Statewise COVID-19 Lockdowns Using Support Vector Regression

Karpagam G. R.[1][*], Keerthna M.[1], Naresh K.[1], Sairam Vaidya M.[1], Karthikeyan T.[2] and Syed Khaja Mohideen[2]

[1]Department of Computer Science and Engineering, PSG College of Technology, Coimbatore, Tamil Nadu, India
[2]Department of Information Technology, University of Technology and Applied Sciences - Salalah Thumrait Rd Thumrayt Street, Oman, Salalah, Dhofar

Abstract

Since the advent of the COVID-19 pandemic, the Indian Government has resorted to various strategies to contain the spread of this virus. One of these was the introduction and implementation of the nation-wide lockdown. Initially, the nation-wide lockdowns were instrumental in containing the spread, but during the first quarter of 2021 the second wave caused major problems across different states, which led to the introduction of state-wise lockdowns with different time spans based on the severity of the virus. This paper focuses on analyzing the effectiveness of the aforesaid state-wise lockdowns by using support vector regression (SVR) to forecast COVID-19 trends at different intervals, and to use the results generated to understand the effect of these state-wise lockdowns on the COVID-19 cases across various states. SVR is simple to update, has strong generalization capacity, and a high prediction accuracy, making it an appropriate solution for forecasting COVID-19 cases that fluctuate daily and require a high level of accuracy due to the severity of the problem. The suggested method makes use of graphical analysis to easily understand the effectiveness of a lockdown and looks deeper into the results to explain its success, or failure.

Keywords: Forecasting, SVR, COVID-19, lockdown, machine learning

---

[*]Corresponding author: grk.cse@psgtech.ac.in

K. Umamaheswari, B. Vinoth Kumar and S. K. Somasundaram (eds.) Artificial Intelligence for Sustainable Applications, (89–116) © 2023 Scrivener Publishing LLC

6.1 Introduction

In the 1950s, researchers began to explore various paths towards mechanizing intelligence. They started programming computers to get them to accomplish some of the cognitive activities that only humans could - including but not limited to playing checkers, shape and pattern recognition, and binary pattern detection. Artificial intelligence (AI) technology has matured remarkably since then, and now comes with a diverse set of sophisticated computational tools. Because of the increasing power of relatively inexpensive computers, the availability of big databases, and the advent of the World Wide Web, they may be implemented very effectively. Many human cognitive talents can be approximated by modern programs, which can automate some of them entirely and even outperform humans in others.

On December 31, 2019, the World Health Organization reported a wave of pneumonia cases in Wuhan, China, with an unclear etiology. Eventually, the previously unknown new virus was discovered and coined as COVID-19. This belonged to the family of coronaviruses that predominantly caused respiratory problems in human beings. There was an outbreak of the virus across different parts of the world, and it had severe impacts on the economy, and lifestyle of the population. Eventually, WHO declared COVID-19 to be a pandemic.

The devastating pandemic spread fast and was difficult to contain, which resulted in the loss of countless lives. India being a vast country with the second highest population in the world added on to the difficulty of containing the virus. Hence, the government resorted to slowing down the spread by ordering a nation-wide lockdown. This solution came along with a lot of problems, with the major one being the economic impact on a large portion of the population.

This led to the eventual relaxation of restrictions once the virus was contained to an extent. However, in the first quarter of 2021, the second wave once again caused major problems across various states in India. The cases were rising at an alarming rate, and even the reinforcement of state-wide lockdowns proved ineffective in few states, doing nothing to contain the virus.

The power that Machine Learning (ML) currently possesses makes it an ideal approach for forecasting and analyzing. This paper utilizes support vector regression to create a model and analyze the effectiveness of the state-wide lockdowns enforced. Furthermore, we look deeper into the results to see the reasons as to why some lockdowns that sounded good in principle produced unsatisfactory results.

6.2   Background

ML is a subfield of artificial intelligence that focuses on the technology's learning aspect by developing algorithms that best represent a data set. In contrast to traditional programming, where an algorithm can be explicitly coded to operate on a data set to produce the intended output, in ML, the data set is not explicitly coded to produce the desired output; a computer is supplied with a dataset [5, 6] and associated outputs to create a program. ML generates an algorithm from subsets of data, which may use innovative or varied combinations of features and weights that are generated from basic principles. All four primary learning approaches are utilized to accomplish diverse tasks: supervised, unsupervised, semi-supervised, and reinforcement learning.

Supervised ML is used when all the observations in the dataset [7] are labeled. Unsupervised ML is used when all the observations in the dataset are unlabeled, that is, it does not require inherent labels. Semi-supervised ML is used when some of the observations of the dataset are labeled and the remaining (generally the majority) are usually unlabeled. Reinforcement ML is a feedback-based ML technique in an agent learns how to behave in each environment by executing actions and watching the outcomes of those actions. Since the COVID-19 data set is supervised, the discriminative modelling subset of supervised ML was considered as the ideal approach for regression analysis forecasting. Several regression models were tested (explained in section 6.4), and SVR was selected as the optimal regression technique to be applied on the dataset to analyze the effectiveness of various state-wide lockdowns across India.

6.2.1   Comprehensive Survey – Applications in Healthcare Industry

ML is speeding up the speed of logical revelation across fields, and medication is no exemption. From language handling devices that speed up exploration to prescient calculations that ready clinical staff for a looming respiratory failure, AI supplements human understanding [27] and practice across clinical controls [28].

Be that as it may, with all the "solutionism" around ML and its advancements, medical services suppliers are naturally wary about how it will truly help patients and welcome a profit from the venture. Numerous ML arrangements available for medical care designs are customized to take care of an unmistakable issue, for example, recognizing the danger of creating sepsis, or diagnosing bosom malignancy. Organizations find it unfeasible to change their approaches and capitalize on their initiative because of these out-of-the-box ML configurations. Using the most recent ML break-throughs, such as sound and visual data handling, and open-source data science allows the medical care companies to alter models to solve a variety of problems. Data scientists are able to build unique applications that fit healthcare [2] IT's tight standards and improve patient care in a range of situations using open-source tools, thereby separating a business from its competition.

According to research published last year in the New England Journal of Medicine, medical burnout [17] is an issue in 83 percent of organizations. Half of them believe that "offloading managerial chores", will help fix the problem and allow doctors to spend more time with patients. Updating electronic health records and reviewing them are big components of these management responsibilities (EHRs). Almost all hospitals and clinics in the United States employ an EHR system. Most people believe that improv-ing the efficiency of the HCE update is the most important thing they can do. This is where natural language processing (NLP) techniques come in handy. Clinicians can dictate notes directly to the EHR using Natural Language Processing (NLP) tools, which use algorithms to recognize and classify words and phrases. Instead of reading notes and test data, phy-sicians and patients can watch charts and summaries created using NLP technologies to gain a better understanding of the patient's overall health. Clinicians can spend more time with patients if they spend less time main-taining EHR.

Anomaly detection algorithms are being used by healthcare providers all around the world to anticipate heart attacks, strokes, sepsis, and other cata-strophic problems using machine learning techniques. El Camino Hospital is one such case. Their researchers developed a technique for forecasting patient falls using electronic health records, bed alarm data, and nurse call data. This innovative gadget notifies personnel when a patient is at high danger of falling, allowing them to take preventative measures. They were able to reduce falls by 39%. A fall-related in-patient injury adds 6.3 days to a hospital stay and costs $14,000, according to the Joint Commission for Transforming Healthcare. The Sepsis Sniffer Algorithm (SSA) devel-oped by the Mayo Clinic is another example. When the danger of acquiring sepsis grows, the algorithm analyses vital sign measurements and demo-graphic data to trigger an alert and cutting down the screening time by 72%. This frees up doctors and nurses to focus on the ailments that brought people to them in the first place.

To stay up with developments in certain fields of medical research, scientists and clinicians would have to read and evaluate a massive number of papers and studies. Between 2007 and 2016, scientists published almost 342,000 articles on medication evaluation and analysis alone.

In the coming years, medical researchers will benefit from using NLP techniques and neural networks to parse literature. The workload of radiologists has increased dramatically in recent years. According to research, an average radiologist must interpret an image once every 3-4 seconds to keep up with the present demand. ML applications, on the other hand, can accurately diagnose breast cancer from mammograms. The Houston Methodist Research Institute has created an early breast cancer [24] detection program that reads mammograms with an accuracy of 99% and is 30 times faster than a human at providing diagnostic information. These tools also reduce the necessity for biopsies. Most radiologists think that these tools assist them in providing better patient care. They improve their skills, but they do not replace them. Several researchers utilized several tools like scikit-learn, keras, TensorFlow, and various other open-source tools to construct ML models for the diagnosis of skin cancer [3] with an accuracy of 87–95%. Dermatologists, on the other hand, can detect melanomas with an accuracy of 65–85%. Several medical organizations including the Mayo Clinic, and the Boston Children's Hospital have collaborated on an open-source NLP project called cTAKES to develop a tool [1] that can parse the unstructured data in EHRs to extract various insights. The comprehensive survey is summarized in Table 6.1, Table 6.2, and Table 6.3.

6.2.2   Comparison of Various Models for Forecasting

There are various regression methods available for forecasting, of which few that were considered for the purpose of this paper are compared below in Table 6.4. From the techniques considered, linear regression is not suitable for real world problems due to its poor performance in the presence of outliers. Decision tree performs poorly for regression due to its slow speed caused due to splitting of the nodes, and the time taken for training and testing. In random forest regression, an increasing number of trees brings down the overall performance of the model which makes it inefficient for real-time predictions. Hence, for the purpose of this paper Support Vector Regression was considered the ideal regression technique to obtain highly accurate predictions in real time, and to obtain the necessary results.

Table 6.1 Comprehensive survey of ML applications.

Purpose/Goal	References	Remarks
Machine learning methodologies, techniques, algorithms, and applications in medical diagnostics are discussed.	J. Jeba Praba, J.H. Kamdar, John J. Georrge [8]	Deep learning, an advanced AI technology, has sparked a boom in AI and significant changes of diagnostic medical imaging systems, pathology, and dermatology are to be brought about soon.
This paper is a discussion of the analysis of publicly available data sets about biomedical and clinical trial, which is considered to be real-world evidence.	Shah, P., Kendall, F., Khozin [22]	This Journal's aim is to engage and inform the readers on the value of emerging technologies like AI/ML in facing major adversities in the modernization of the existing clinical development process.
This research proposes an accurate diabetics prediction algorithm.	Duaa Enteesha Mhawi, Ikhlas Watan Ghindawi, Mustafa S. Kadhm [14]	For removing the unwanted data, the proposed system uses the K-nearest neighbor technique. The proposed system was able to attain a high classification result of 98.7%.

Table 6.2 Comprehensive survey of ML/DL algorithms.

Purpose/Goal	References	Remarks
A variety of supervised learning algorithms are discussed for classifying the patients who have been diagnosed with lung cancer, on the basis of their survival rate.	Alexandra R.de Carlo, Behnaz Abdollahi, Chip M. Lynch, Hermann B. Frieboes, Joshua D. Fuqua, James *et al.* [4]	The results reveal that the projected values for low to intermediate survival periods agree with real values, which leads to the suggestion that these supervised learning approaches to data could be useful in estimating patient survival times.
The aim of this research is to describe a decision-making system that uses machine learning classifiers to anticipate decisions in contrast to actual doctor decisions.	Muhammad Zain Amin, Amir Ali Mountain View, California [13]	This approach aids in predicting when surgery should be used. This case study has a 95.00 percent accuracy rate.
The goal is to forecast cancer using the Naive Bayes, j48, and k-nearest neighbor methods.	Helal Ahmed, Romana Rahman Ema, Md. Rafsun Jony Mollick, Shanjida Khan, *et al.* [24]	The accuracy was measured using 10-fold cross-validation in the Weka tool. The accuracy of the Naive Bayes method was found to be 98.2%, that of the k-nearest neighbor method is 98.8%, and that of the j48 method is 98.5%.
The goal is to introduce Feature Correlated Nave Bayes, a novel COVID-19 diagnosis strategy (FCNB).	Badawy, M., Mansour, N.A., Saleh, A.I., *et al.* [12]	The findings demonstrate the efficacy of the FCNB method, which delivers the highest detection accuracy (99 percent).
The major trends in the use of supervised ML algorithms for illness risk prediction is discussed in this paper.	Arif Khan, Shahadat Uddin, Md Ekramul Hossain and Mohammad Ali [23]	The Support Vector Machine algorithm is used the most, followed by the Nave Bayes algorithm. The Random Forest (RF) algorithm, however, is more accurate.

Table 6.3 Comprehensive survey of COVID-19 ML/DL.

Purpose/Goal	References	Remarks
The purpose of this paper is to create a ML approach for diagnosing COVID-19 quickly and effectively.	Deri-Rozov, S. Shomron, N., and Zoabi, Y. [30]	With only eight features, the model can accurately predict COVID-19 test outcomes.
The goal of this paper is to develop an automated ML model that can aid in the identification of the COVID-19 infection in the chest using high-resolution X-ray imaging technology.	Heidari, M., Shariati, S.A. and Zargari Khuzani, A. [29]	This program develops a set of ideal features from CXR images in order to build a ML classifier that can accurately and correctly separate the COVID-19 instances from non-COVID-19 instances.
The goal of this paper is to develop a ML technique to predict whether a patient with the Covid-19 infection will survive or not.	Armando Torres-Gomez, Mario A., Quiroz-Juarez, *et al.* [21]	The suggested application uses a neural network and Bayesian inference to quickly identify high-risk individuals, with an accuracy up to 93.5%, specificity up to 90.9%, and sensitivity up to 96.1%.
This goal of this paper is to conduct an initial assessment of patients who are likely to be diagnosed and to provide assistance to them, so that they can receive timely treatment and quarantine recommendations.	Chongxiang Tong, Jiangpeng Wu, Junfeng Li, Liting Zhang, Pengyi Zhang, Wenbo Meng, *et al.* [9]	The gadget is a new technique that can detect COVID-19. The random forest approach was applied, yielding a precision of 0.9167.

Table 6.4 Comparison of various regression techniques.

Model	Description	Merits	Demerits
Linear Regression	Linear regression is a supervised learning algorithm that predicts the dependent variable by finding a linear relationship with the independent variable.	It is simple to implement, and less complex than other algorithms.	Any outliers affect the algorithm badly and it over-simplifies real world problems.
Decision Tree Regression	The goal of the decision tree method is to create a training model that can predict the target variable's class or value based on fundamental rules learned from the training data.	It is easy to understand, implement and requires little data preprocessing.	It tends to overload, resulting in instability when a little change in the data generates a large change in the tree structure.
Random Forest Regression	Random forest is a supervised learning system that solves regression and classification issues using ensemble methods.	It offers a method for estimating missing data that works well and retains accuracy even when a considerable amount of the data is missing.	For real-time predictions, the algorithm may be too sluggish and unsuccessful due to the enormous number of trees.
Support Vector Regression	SVR is a supervised learning method that uses the same ideas as SVM to predict discrete values. The primary assumption of SVR is to find the best-fitting line.	The decision model is simple to update and offers a high prediction accuracy and generalization capacity.	When there is a lot of noise in the data set, the decision model does not perform effectively.

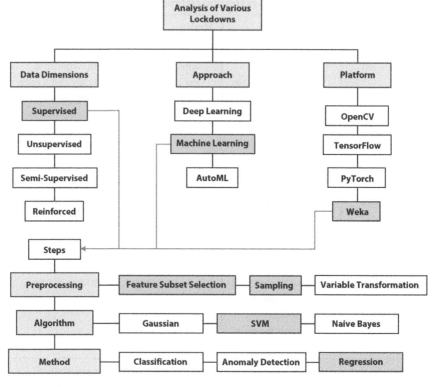

Figure 6.1 Context of the work.

6.2.3   Context of the Work

The context of the work done in this paper is described in Figure 6.1.

6.3   Proposed Work

As a precautionary measure against COVID-19, the entire 1.38 billion population of India was subjected to a statewide lockdown on the evening of March 24, 2020. Eventually, these restrictions were relaxed and a general decline in the spread of COVID-19 was seen. However, during the second wave, there was an imbalance in the spread of COVID-19. Few states were adversely affected, while few did not. This led to state wise lockdowns, sometimes consecutive ones to contain the spread of the virus. This paper aims to analyze various state wise lockdowns to determine if the lockdowns were effective, and if they were not, then to identify the reasons.

For working on this problem, a COVID-19 data set was selected that had records of daily cases since the inception of COVID-19 in India, across all states and their respective state-wide lockdowns, shown in Appendix A.

A model using SVR was built on Python and WEKA to forecast the trends of the virus at various intervals, across various lockdowns to determine their efficiency. This model was based upon the MVC model to obtain an effective and functional model. MVC is an architectural paradigm that divides an application into three logical components: Model, View, and Controller. Every component is made to deal with a certain aspect of application development. The components' responsibilities are given below, and their interaction is displayed in Figure 6.2.

a) Model – It is the lowest level of the architecture, and it oversees data maintenance. Because the model is linked to the database, adding, retrieving, and other operations are performed in the model component. As a result, the model serves as the backend, which houses all the data logic.

b) View – The view component oversees data representation. It is responsible for creating the user interface for the user. The data acquired by the model is used to construct the views. As a result, the view serves as the frontend, or graphical user interface (GUI).

c) Controller – The controller is an important part of the design because it acts as a middleman between the view and the model, allowing them to communicate. As a result, the controller is the application's brain, controlling how the data is displayed.

The MVC components are implemented in section 6.1. to get a solid foundation for the conceptual architecture.

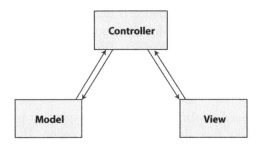

Figure 6.2 The MVC architecture.

6.3.1   Conceptual Architecture

The proposed system has five layers, and they are:

1. Application Layer – The Application Layer consists of the user interface of the application and has two layers - the Input Interface Layer is required for getting the input from the COVID-19 dataset, and the Output Interface Layer is required for displaying the results obtained graphically. It is the View of conceptual architecture.
2. Communication Layer – The Communication Layer contains all the business-related logics and handles incoming requests and serves as a link between the Model and the View. It is the Controller of conceptual architecture.
3. Preprocessing Layer – The Preprocessing Layer cleans, formats, and organizes raw data so that machine learning models can use it. It makes up a part of the Model of conceptual architecture. It consists of seven steps,
    1. Obtain the data set
    2. Add all the necessary libraries to your system.
    3. Import the data set
    4. Recognizing and dealing with missing values
    5. Categorical data encoding
    6. Data set segmentation
    7. Feature scaling
4. Processing Layer – The Processing Layer is concerned with the now usable raw data, and is used to apply SVR, the required mathematical modelling and statistical knowledge. It makes up another part of the Model of conceptual architecture.
5. Storage Layer – The Storage Layer is where the model and/ or the results are stored - in this paper a cloud database is used where the information is stored online on a cloud. It is the final part of the Model of conceptual architecture. The representation of the layers is displayed in Figure 6.3.

6.3.2   Procedure

SVM is a supervised machine learning technique that is frequently used for classification but may also be used for regression. This approach plots all data items as points on a graph, with the value of a specific attribute

Application Layer Input Interface Layer Output Interface Layer	
Preprocessing Layer Obtain the data set Add all the necessary Import the dataset Recognizing and dealing withmissing values Categorical data encoding Data set segmentation Feature scaling	**Communication Layer**
Processing Layer Machine learning algorithm Mathematical modelling Statistical knowledge	
Storage Layer Cloud database	

Figure 6.3 The conceptual architecture.

serving as the coordinate, and then determines a hyperplane (a line in a 2-D graph) that effectively distinguishes the various classes. Support Vector Regression (SVR), a regression model based on SVM, is utilized here. SVR is implemented in this paper using the SMOreg algorithm. Based on a collection of training samples, we must find a mapping between a particular input domain and real numbers in regression. The decision boundary is set at an arbitrary distance, considered to be ε (maximum error allowed), w_i is a constant, and x_i is a feature of the dataset. We choose data points that lie in between the decision boundaries and the hyper-plane.

Let the equation of the hyper-plane be,

$$y = mx + c \qquad (6.1)$$

Then the equation of the decision boundaries become,

$$mx + c = \varepsilon, \text{ and} \qquad (6.2)$$

$$mx + c = -\varepsilon \qquad (6.3)$$

Hence and hyper-plane should satisfy the following condition,

$$-\varepsilon < y - (mx + c) < \varepsilon \qquad (6.4)$$

This allows us to take only points within the decision boundary, and those which have least error rate, and those which are within the range of tolerance set. There are several steps to be implemented when performing SVR, which are:

1. Collect the set of data for training.
    The appropriate dataset is fetched, and the various libraries required to create a model are imported if needed, though all libraries need not be imported at the same time.
2. Choose a subset of this data, a kernel, and the different parameters.
    The required features are filtered from the dataset, and all necessary cleaning and preprocessing is done to make sure only the needed features are present in the kernel.
3. Form a correlation matrix.
    A correlation matrix is a table that shows the correlation between the different features in our kernel, which is important for predictions as predictions are made based on the other features present and the data from the matrix can be easily represented as a scatterplot.
    The equation for the correlation matrix is,

$$K_{ij} = \exp \left(\Sigma_k \, \theta_k \mid x_k^{\,i} - y_k^{\,j} \mid^2 \right) \qquad (6.5)$$

    Any certain value can be added to the point values (x and y), as a regularizer.
    This is important as it summarizes the data and allows for more advanced analysis methods.
4. Train the model with the dataset chosen.
    A portion of data is given as input into the model and the prediction made by the model is checked against the actual value, (i.e.) the model is fit with the training data, this is known as supervised learning, which gives rise to an efficient and accurate model by altering the bias of the dataset.
    Let K be the correlation matrix and hence a major part of the algorithm is,

$$K \, \hat{a} = \hat{y} \qquad (6.6)$$

    Where $\hat{a}$ is the unknown which is to be found to be able to make the estimator, while $\hat{y}$ is the vector value of the training dataset chosen.
5. Use the results to create the estimator, which is used to forecast here.

The estimator is an object that fits a model with a set of training data and then can find patterns in the data to predict or forecast a certain feature.

Using equation (6.6) from the previous section, the value of â can be obtained, and produce the estimator with the value, as,

$$\hat{a} - 1 = K - 1\,\hat{y} \tag{6.7}$$

Now to estimate an unknown value, let z represent the unknown value, then â and K is needed to calculate the estimate, using the equation,

$$\hat{z} = K\,\hat{a} \tag{6.8}$$

Finally, the coefficient matrix is calculated using the following equation,

$$Ki = \exp\left(\sum_{k} \theta_k \,|\, x_k^{\,i} - x_k^{\,*}\,|^2\right) \tag{6.9}$$

The value provided by the estimator is the final estimate predicted by the model. With all the calculated values we can perform SVR, for the given dataset. Figure 6.4 shows what SVR looks visually on a graph, where ε is the maximum error tolerance, $z_i k_i + \varepsilon$ and $z_i k_i - \varepsilon$ represents the decision boundaries, while $z_i k_i$ represents the Hyper-plane. The SMOreg algorithm is being used to implement SVR here.

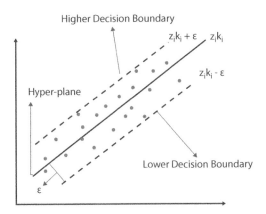

Figure 6.4 Illustration of SVR.

6.4 Experimental Results

The experimental data set is a COVID-19 data set, which defines several indicators for all Indian states and union territories. For this forecasting, the only metrics considered were the date, name of the state/union territory, cumulative confirmed COVID-19 cases, and the duration of the various lockdowns. The preprocessing was done on Python 3.9.0, the forecasting was performed using WEKA 3.8.5 and the results generated were graphically displayed using Tableau. The cumulative cases have been normalized for a better comparison. The tables used for the experiment are Tables 6.5–6.9, and the graphs obtained through the experiment are displayed as Figures 6.5–6.14.

Table 6.5 Duration of state-wide lockdowns in Maharashtra.

Lockdown	Start	End
Lockdown 1	22/04/2021	30/05/2021
Lockdown 2	06/06/2021	15/06/2021

Table 6.6 Duration of state-wide lockdowns in Tamil Nadu.

Lockdown	Start	End
Lockdown 1	10/05/2021	23/05/2021
Lockdown 2	24/05/2021	31/05/2021

Table 6.7 Duration of state-wide lockdowns in Odisha.

Lockdown	Start	End
Lockdown 1	10/05/2021	19/05/2021
Lockdown 2	01/06/2021	17/06/2021

Table 6.8 Duration of state-wide lockdowns in Punjab.

Lockdown	Start	End
Lockdown 1	10/05/2021	19/05/2021
Lockdown 2	01/06/2021	17/06/2021

Table 6.9 Population density and confirmed COVID-19 cases of the selected states.

State	Population density (km²) [18]	Confirmed Cases (as of 29/07/21)
Maharashtra	365	6,276,057
Tamil Nadu	555	2,552,049
Odisha	269	970,814
Punjab	551	598,882

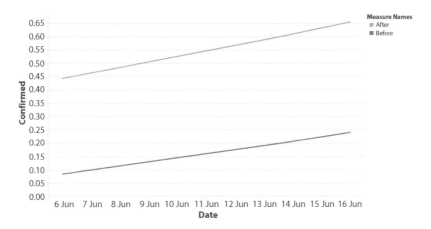

Figure 6.5 The predicted cases before and after Lockdown 1 in Maharashtra.

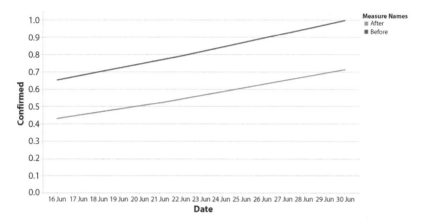

Figure 6.6 The predicted cases before and after Lockdown 2 in Maharashtra.

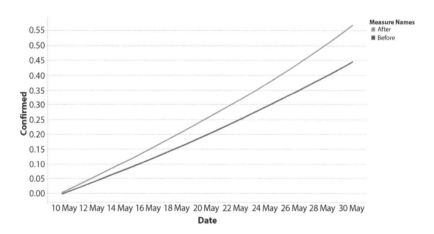

Figure 6.7 The predicted cases before and after Lockdown 1 in Tamil Nadu.

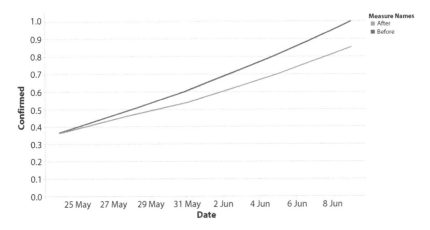

Figure 6.8 The predicted cases before and after Lockdown 2 in Tamil Nadu.

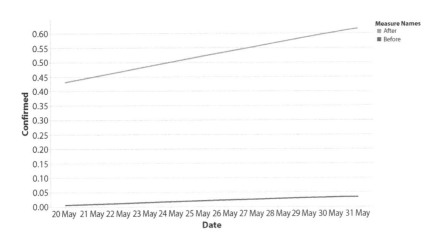

Figure 6.9 The predicted cases before and after Lockdown 1 in Odisha.

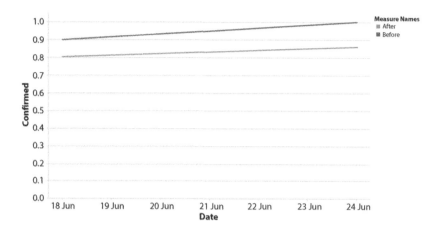

Figure 6.10 The predicted cases before and after Lockdown 2 in Odisha.

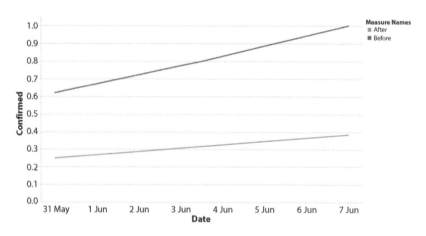

Figure 6.11 The predicted cases before and after Lockdown 1 in Punjab.

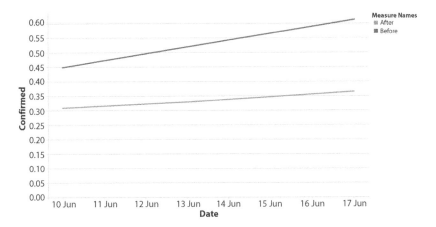

Figure 6.12 The predicted cases before and after Lockdown 2 in Punjab.

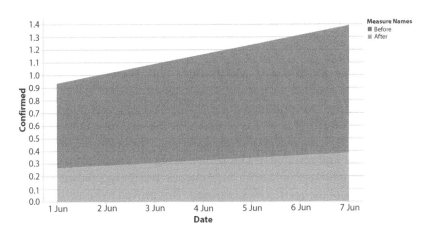

Figure 6.13 Area chart to show the predicted cases before and after Lockdown 1 in Punjab.

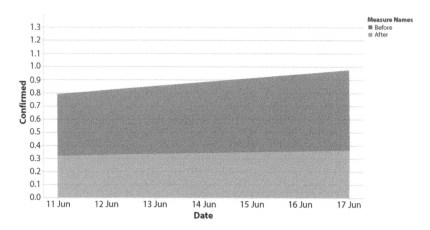

Figure 6.14 Area chart to show the predicted cases before and after Lockdown 2 in Punjab.

6.5   Discussion and Conclusion

1.   Maharashtra

During the first lockdown in Maharashtra [10], there was a significant increase in the number of instances. Maharashtra's COVID-19 caseload had surpassed the four million mark with 67,468 people testing positive for the virus on 21 April 2021 which proved to be the last straw for the government. This was the highest ever single spike since the beginning of the pandemic last year and resulted in a lockdown being imposed in two days. This caused chaos among people, with large queues to buy essentials, and a poor understanding of the restrictions imposed. This proved to be an unsuccessful lockdown and was unable to contain the virus as seen in Figure 6.3, and hence a second lockdown [11] was required. However, by the time of the second lockdown the situation improved slightly as seen in Figure 6.4, but given Maharashtra's higher population density, and a poor implementation of the initial lockdown, the virus was not contained properly resulting in over six million people being infected by 29 July 2021. Overall, there was a slight improvement over the due course of the lockdown but there was much left to be desired.

2.   Tamil Nadu

Tamil Nadu bolsters a very high population density and containing the spread of the virus was an enormous task. During the first quarter of 2021, Tamil Nadu did a good job in containing the virus, however a significant rise in the COVID-19 cases was observed during the second week of May, which resulted in the enforcement of a lockdown. This sudden increase was a result of the elections that were conducted during the first week of May. The incubation period of the virus being 3–4 days, the increase in the spread during the lockdown was obvious. From Figure 6.5, the first lockdown [25] proved to be unsuccessful which led to the inevitable enforcement of the second lockdown [26]. Like Maharashtra, the second lockdown produced better results and ended up being successful in containing the virus. This was partially due to the first lockdown preventing any mass gatherings - such as the elections, which led to the second lockdown being efficient and successful.

3. Odisha

Odisha has a moderate population density, and the virus was statistically handled well during the first quarter of 2021. However, during the first week of May, a significant increase in the reported cases was observed. This was rumored to be due to the previous underreporting of COVID-19 cases by the government, and due to an outbreak in various rural regions in Odisha. A state-wide lockdown [15] was enforced to contain the spread, and like the previous states, it proved to be ineffective as seen in Figure 6.7. Eventually, the government decided to enforce a partial lockdown [16] after the end of the first one from May 19, 2021, to June 1, 2021, with relaxed restrictions. This did not produce meaningful results, and hence a second lockdown was enforced. Similarly, the second lockdown proved to be effective and brought about a significant decrease in expected COVID-19 cases as shown in Figure 6.8, which led to the second lockdown being the effective, and successful lockdown once again.

4. Punjab

Punjab has a very high population density, one of the highest in India and containing the virus was never going to be an easy task. However, Punjab produced impressive results and managed to contain the virus very well, given its circumstances. Before enforcing complete lockdowns, Punjab imposed several partial ones during the month of April which helped people to get accustomed to lockdowns. So, when the first complete lockdown [19] was enforced in May, the results were very effective and it helped in bringing down the expected cases by a lot, as shown in Figure 6.9. This encouraged the government to enforce a second lockdown [20] due to a slight increase in cases at the start of June, which also produced really good results and contained the virus, as shown in Figure 6.10. This led to both the lockdowns being successful and containing the virus very well, and the difference in their effectiveness was marginal as seen in Figures 6.11–6.12. Hence, the implementation of both the lockdowns was done very well by Punjab, and a huge success.

The purpose of the paper was to identify and study the relationship between the trends in COVID-19 cases and the various lockdowns of a state. From Figure 6.3 to Figure 6.12, a common trend is noticed between the first and the second lockdown that the second lockdown is generally more efficient than the first, and it is mostly successful in comparison to its counterpart. This behavior is caused due to a variety of reasons such as people panic buying before the first lockdown, being unfamiliar with the lockdown restrictions, which they eventually get familiarized with by the second lockdown. Hence, a second consecutive lockdown (or) an extended first lockdown produces better results in containing the spread than an individual lockdown over a short duration.

6.5.1   Future Scope

AutoML, or Automated Machine Learning, is concerned with providing ML solutions to data scientists without requiring them to conduct extensive research into hyper-parameters, selection and compression of models, and preparation of data parameters is ongoing. AutoML also assists data scientists with data visualization, model intelligibility, model deployment, and other tasks. As a result, it is more user-friendly than hand-coded algorithms and frequently produces faster, more accurate results. As a result, enterprises without a specialized data scientist or an ML expert can use the AutoML software platforms to access ML. AutoML is built to complete mechanical jobs quickly and accurately, allowing people to focus on more complicated or unique activities. Things like monitoring, analysis, and problem identification that AutoML automates are mechanical operations that are faster when automated. However, because AutoML is such a new topic, most of the tools aren't fully developed. In the future, when AutoML tools are fully developed, they would be able to replace ML in different places. When the user is inexperienced on which is the optimal algorithm for a given dataset, he wastes a lot of time in trying different algorithms and researching them, whereas AutoML would select the most optimal algorithm on its own. Especially, modern datasets are getting larger day by day and preprocessing and algorithm selection are crucial, and by running an incorrect algorithm a lot of time is wasted. For example, the COVID-19 epidemic generates a large amount of data every day, all over the world - in cities, states, countries, and continents. By using AutoML to analyze the data, we would be able to generate results in a shorter time, and this would allow the scientists to do greater work with the data analysis in a lesser time frame. So, AutoML will help in significantly reducing the time taken for the aforesaid in the future.

References

1. Apache cTAKES™, natural language processing system for extraction of information from electronic medical record clinical free text, 2021, http://ctakes.apache.org/index.html Accessed 02 June 2021.
2. Barnes, Missouri, Fairview, Kaiser Permanente, Wentworth-Douglass, The Joint Commission Center for Transforming Healthcare, 2021, https://www.centerfortransforminghealthcare.org/en/improvement-topics/preventing-falls Accessed 05 June 2021.
3. Brinker, T.J., Hekler, A., Utikal, J.S., Grabe, N., Schadendorf, D., Klode, J., Berking, C., Steeb, T., Enk, A.H., von Kalle, C., Skin cancer classification using convolutional neural networks: Systematic review. *J. Med. Internet Res.*, 20, 10, e11936, 2018, https://doi.org/10.2196/11936.
4. Lynch, C.M., Abdollahi, B., Fuqua, J.D., de Carlo, A.R., Bartholomai, J.A., Balgemann, R.N., van Berkel, V.H., Frieboes, H.B., Prediction of lung cancer patient survival via supervised machine learning classification techniques. *Int. J. Med. Inf.*, 108, 1–8, 1386–5056, 2017, https://doi.org/10.1016/j.ijmedinf.2017.09.013.
5. Raj Kumar, S., Dataset on novel coronavirus disease in India, 2021, https://www.kaggle.com/sudalairajkumar/covid19-in-india.
6. National Informatics Centre, India's COVID 19 statewise status, 2021, https://www.mygov.in/corona-data/covid19-statewise-status/.
7. National Informatics Centre, India's COVID 19 statewise status, 2022, https://www.mygov.in/corona-data/covid19-statewise-status/.
8. Kamdar, J.H., Jeba Praba, J., Georrge, J.J., Artificial intelligence in medical diagnosis: Methods, algorithms and applications, in: *Machine Learning with Healthcare Perspective. Learning and Analytics in Intelligent Systems*, vol. 13, V. Jain and J. Chatterjee (Eds.), pp. 27–37, Springer, Cham, 2020, https://doi.org/10.1007/978-3-030-40850-3_2.
9. Wu, J., Zhang, P., Zhang, L., Meng, W., Li, J., Tong, C., Li, Y., Cai, J., Yang, Z., Zhu, J., Zhao, M., Huang, H., Xie, X., Li, S., Rapid and accurate identification of COVID-19 infection through machine learning based on clinical available blood test results. *medRxiv*, 20051136(1–11), 2020, https://doi.org/10.1101/2020.04.02.20051136.
10. Maharashtra lockdown 1 guidelines, 2021, https://www.maharashtra.gov.in/Site/Upload/Government%20Resolutions/English/202104051005324619.pdf Accessed 07 July 2021.

11. Maharashtra lockdown 2 guidelines, 2021, https://www.maharashtra.gov.in/Site/Upload/Government%20Resolutions/English/202005311030217319.pdf Accessed 08 July 2021.

12. Mansour, N.A., Saleh, A.I., Ali, M., Hesham, A., Accurate detection of COVID-19 patients based on Feature Correlated Naïve Bayes (FCNB) classification strategy. *J. Ambient Intell. Hum. Comput.*, 1868-5145, 1–33, Badawy2020, https://doi.org/10.1007/s12652-020-02883-2.

13. Amin, M.Z. and Ali, A., Performance evaluation of supervised machine learning classifiers for predicting healthcare operational decisions, pp. 1–7, 2021, https://www.researchgate.net/profile/Muhammad-Amin-40/publication/329515048_Performance_Evaluation_of_Supervised_Machine_Learning_Classifiers_for_Predicting_Healthcare_Operational_Decisions/links/5c0c277aa6fdcc494fe4a3a6/Performance-Evaluation-of-Supervised-Machine-Learning-Classifiers-for-Predicting-Healthcare-Operational-Decisions.pdf.

14. Kadhm, M.S., Ghindawi, I.W., Mhawi, D.E., An accurate diabetes prediction system based on k-means clustering and proposed classification approach. *Int. J. Appl. Eng. Res.*, 13, 6, 0973–4562, 2018, https://www.researchgate.net/publication/323945877_An_Accurate_Diabetes_Prediction_System_Based_on_K-means_Clustering_and_Proposed_Classification_Approach.

15. Odisha lockdown 1 guidelines, 2021, https://health.odisha.gov.in/pdf/Lockdown-guideline-State-Odisha-from-5th-May-2021-19th-May-2021.PDF Accessed 10 July 2021.

16. Odisha lockdown 2 guidelines, 2021, https://health.odisha.gov.in/pdf/Guidelines-extension-lockdown-till-17062021-30052021.pdf Accessed 10 July 2021.

17. Physician burnout is a problem at 83% of healthcare organization, 2018, https://ehrintelligence.com/news/physician-burnout-is-a-problem-at-83-of-healthcare-organizations Accessed 13 June 2021.

18. Population census of India, 2011, https://www.censusindia.gov.in/2011census/PCA/PCA_Highlights/pca_highlights_file/India/Chapter-1.pdf Accessed 11 July 2021.

19. Punjab lockdown 1 guidelines, 2021, https://cdn.s3waas.gov.in/s3c5ab0b-c60ac7929182aadd08703f1ec6/uploads/2021/05/2021052489.pdf Accessed 14 July 2021.

20. Punjab lockdown guidelines, 2021, https://cdn.s3waas.gov.in/s3e2c0be245 60d78c5e599c2a9c9d0bbd2/uploads/2021/06/2021060245.pdf Accessed 18 July 2021.

21. Quiroz-Juarez, M., Torres-Gomez, A., Hoyo-Ulloa, I., León-Montiel, R., de, J., U'Ren, A., Identification of high-risk COVID-19 patients using machine learning, medRxiv: Cold Spring Harbor Laboratory Press, pp. 1–9, 2021, http://dx.doi.org/10.1101/2021.02.10.21251510.

22. Shah, P., Kendall, F., Khozin, S., Artificial intelligence and machine learning in clinical development: A translational perspective. *NPJ Digit. Med.*, 2, 69, 1–5, 2019, https://doi.org/10.1038/s41746-019-0148-3.

23. Uddin, S., Khan, A., Hossain, M., Comparing different supervised machine learning algorithms for disease prediction. *BMC Med. Inform. Decis. Mak.*, 19, 281, 1–16, 2019, https://doi.org/10.1186/s12911-019-1004-8.

24. Maliha, S.K., Ema, R.R., Ghosh, S.K., Ahmed, H., Mollick, M.R.J., Islam, T., Cancer disease prediction using naive bayes,k-nearest neighbor and J48 algorithm. *2019 10th International Conference on Computing, Communication and Networking Technologies (ICCCNT)*, pp. 1–7, 2019, https://doi.org/10.1109/ICCCNT45670.2019.8944686.

25. Tamil Nadu lockdown 1 guidelines, 2021, https://cms.tn.gov.in/sites/default/files/go/rev_e_371_2021.pdf Accessed 06 July 2021.

26. Tamil Nadu lockdown 2 guidelines, 2021, https://cms.tn.gov.in/sites/default/files/go/revenue_e_386_2021.pdf Accessed 07 July 2021.

27. Williams, T., AI in healthcare: Identifying risks & saving money, Techopedia, 2020, https://bit.ly/2PqJo3y. Accessed 16 June 2021.

28. The AI software diagnoses cancer risk 30 times faster than a human doctor with 99 percent accuracy, 2016, https://www.wired.co.uk/article/cancer-risk-ai-mammograms Accessed 17 June 2021.

29. Zargari Khuzani, A., Heidari, M., Shariati, S.A., COVID-classifier: An automated machine learning model to assist in the diagnosis of COVID-19 infection in chest X-ray images. *Sci. Rep.*, 11, 9887(1–6), 2021, https://doi.org/10.1038/s41598-021-88807-2.

30. Zoabi, Y., Deri-Rozov, S., Shomron, N., Machine learning-based prediction of COVID-19 diagnosis based on symptoms. *NPJ Digit. Med.*, 4, 1, 3, 2021, https://doi.org/10.1038/s41746-020-00372-6.

A Systematic Review for Medical Data Fusion Over Wireless Multimedia Sensor Networks

John Nisha Anita* and Sujatha Kumaran

*Sathyabama Institute of Science and Technology Chennai,
Tamil Nadu, India*

Abstract

Modern healthcare applications require fast detection of human diseases which saves the human life on time. In order to achieve this, the detection or identification of such diseases and their current severity levels should be transferred to the physician who is in remote area primary health centers. In this article, brain tumors are detected and the status of the segmented tumor regions is transmitted to the remote locations through number of sensor nodes which requires low energy consumption. This article presents various existing methodologies for brain tumor detection and segmentation, quality of service and routing path improvement in Wireless Multimedia Sensor Networks (WMSN) and various data fusion methods. The conventional methodologies are explained with their proposed algorithm and also their limitations under different experimental or simulation environmental conditions are discussed in this article.

Keywords: Brain tumors, fusion, WMSN, quality of service, path selection

Corresponding author: nishusuban@gmail.com

K. Umamaheswari, B. Vinoth Kumar and S. K. Somasundaram (eds.) Artificial Intelligence for Sustainable Applications, (117–126) © 2023 Scrivener Publishing LLC

7.1   Introduction

Enhancing contemporary medical principles, medical imaging technology is playing a progressively significant role in everyday medical diagnosis and medical research [1]. The tumor represents uncontrolled cancer cell growth in any part of the body, while a tumor in the brain is an abandoned brain cell growth Benign or malignant may be a brain tumor [6]. In detection of brain tumor in low accuracy is the major problem for physicians, to overcome these various techniques [18, 20–25] were reviewed in this paper. The survey is studied on the following topics.

7.1.1   Survey on Brain Tumor Detection Methods

In this examination, different methods of detection and segmentation of brain tumors are detailed [9, 10]. Most conventional methods used machine learning and deep learning methods to spot and segment tumor regions in MRI images of the brain.

7.1.2   Survey on WMSN

In this review, the various conventional protocols and routing procedure in WMSN are discussed with their main limitations.

7.1.3   Survey on Data Fusion

This section elaborates various conventional data fusion methods [19] which are used in WMSN. The limitations of the conventional methods are also discussed in this section.

7.2   Literature Survey Based on Brain Tumor Detection Methods

Ming Li *et al.* [1], the authors developed a three-dimensional multimodal information fusion using Convolutional Neural Network (CNN). To increase the rapidity of the network and evade overfitting problem a normalization layer is added in between convolution and pooling layer [1]. The author has improved the function of weight loss for the detection of brain tumors in the non-focal area. The experimental results for single modal and multi modal compared and better results obtained in multi-CNN. open access dataset is used for the comparison with existing methods and the author acquire sensitivity 99.8%, specificity 92.8% and dice 92.7 which improves the detection of brain tumor in 3D-CNN.

Khairul Islam *et al.* the authors proposed template-based K-means algorithm and Principal Component Analysis (PCA) which reduce computation time for detection of brain tumor [2]. Super pixels and PCA are combined to obtain the features to increase the precision. The investigational results were proved that the proposed technique obtained the better performance in terms of accuracy, sensitivity, specificity are 95%, 97.36%, and 100%. The main disadvantage of this method is applied on insignificant dataset and deep learning system to improve the detection rate.

Nilesh Bhaskarrao Bahadure *et al.* used Berkeley Wavelet Transform (BWT) for transforming the pixel relating with spatial were converted into multi oriented relating pixels [3]. Then, non-linear Support Vector Machine (SVM) kernels were applied to identify the tumor pixels and the segmented tumor pixels were compared with the gold standard images. The authors compared their proposed BWT based brain tumor detection algorithm with other state of art approaches to validate the efficiency of the performance. The authors obtained 92.9% of precision rate and 94.1% of Recall rate of the proposed method which used the proposed BWT based SVM classification algorithm. The main limitation of this work was that this work was tested on limited brain MRI image sample resources and hence there is no robust behavior of this proposed method. Table 7.1 contains the comparisons of the existing methods for brain tumor detection with their limitations.

Jalali *et al.* developed non-linear self-organizing map for identifying the tumor regions in source brain MRI images [4]. The authors combined different soft computing methods such as Artificial Neural Networks (ANN) and Deep Belief Network (DBN) to form the hybrid classification algorithm. This developed algorithm was tested on open access dataset brain MRI images. The authors validated their developed algorithm using cross validation algorithms and the experimental results were highlighted that this proposed method achieved significant improvement in brain tumor segmentation approach. The authors obtained 89.1% of precision rate and 91.6% of Recall rate of the proposed method which used ANN classification algorithm. The authors obtained 91.6% of precision rate and 93.7% of Recall rate of the proposed method which used DBN classification algorithm. From these experimental results with respect to classification approaches, DBN algorithm provided optimum tumor segmentation results when compared with the investigational results of the proposed method using ANN classification approach.

Table 7.1 Comparisons of the existing methods for brain tumor detection with their limitations.

Author details	Year	Methodology	Dataset	Specificity (%)	Sensitivity (%)	Accuracy (%)	Limitations of the conventional method
Ming Li et al. [1]	2019	Multi-CNN	BRATS2018	92.8	99.8	NA	Low performance analysis results.
Md Khairul Islam et al. [2]	2021	Template based K-means Algorithm with PCA	Kaggle.com (2018)	100	97.36	95	It has to be implemented using large dataset in order to improve the accuracy.
Nilesh Bhaskarrao Bahadure et al. [3]	2017	BWT-SVM classification approach	DICOM, Brainweb Dataset	94.2	97.72	96.5	To improve the accuracy more than one classifier has to be used.
Sharif et al. [5]	2021	HWF and YOLOv2 deep learning architecture	BRATS2018,BRATS 2019, BRATS 2020	NA	99	99	High detection time.
Jia et al. [7]	2020	SVM based FAHS segmentation algorithm	BRATS	NA	NA	98.51	Overall segmentation process takes more time. FAHS-SVM needs more number of iterations to obtain high accuracy.

Abbreviations: HWF, Homomorphic wavelet filter; PCA, Principal Component Analysis; SVM, Support Vector Machine; FAHS, Fully Automatic Heterogeneous Segmentation; BWT, Berkeley wavelet transformation; BRATS, Brain Tumor Image Segmentation Benchmark; DICOM - Digital Imaging and Communications in Medicine; CNN, Convolutional Neural Network.

Sharif *et al.* [5] constructed the modified deep learning architecture YOLOv2 from the existing deep learning architecture. This modified architecture was constructed using minimal cost of Convolutional layers and down sampling layers to maximize the classification rate of abnormal tumor pixel detection structure. The Homo-morphic Wavelet Filer (HWF) was used to suppress the level of noise contents from the brain samples. Further, the intrinsic features were computed from the wavelet filtered image and then non-Dominated sorted Genetic Algorithm (NDGA) was applied on the computed features to improving the sorting rate. Finally, the non-dominated features from NDGA were classified using YOLOv2 modified deep learning architecture. The main limitation of this work was that this work was tested on limited brain MRI image sample resources and hence there is no robust behavior of this proposed method.

Wong *et al.* used kernel linear segmentation algorithms on the source brain MRI image to locate the abnormal tumor pixels [6]. The authors developed segmentation network to identify the tumor pixels relating with abnormal category. The authors analyzed many segmentation algorithms on the source brain MRI images to validate the performance of the proposed work. The dilation of the segmentation algorithm detected the tumor boundary region of pixels in the classified pattern image and the results were verified by non-linear modeling methods. The authors obtained 87.1% of precision rate and 90.7% of Recall rate of the proposed method which used the proposed segmentation algorithm. The main limitation of this work was that this work was tested on limited brain MRI image sample resources and hence there is no robust behavior of this proposed method.

Jia *et al.* integrated SVM classification algorithm with the Fully Automatic Heterogeneous Segmentation algorithm (FAHS) for the detection and segmentation of abnormal tumor region of boundary pixels in brain MRI images [7]. This integrated algorithm reduced the cost of the execution time for the detection and location of tumor pixels. The authors validated the experimental results of the developed tumor detection algorithm on brain MRI images which were available in open access dataset models. The brain images in this dataset were split into number of sub band images and the proposed work was applied on each sub band images to cross check the experimental results of the proposed SVM based FAHS segmentation algorithm. The experimental results for the segmentation process of the proposed method were compared with other existing segmentation methods in terms of segmentation region of accuracy.

Table 7.1 shows the comparisons of the existing methods for brain tumor detection with their limitations.

7.3   Literature Survey Based on WMSN

Chiwariro *et al.* improved quality of service performance in WMSN using Multipath Routing Protocols (MRP) and Multi-channel Media Access Protocols (MMAP). This developed protocol-based networking algorithm was tested on transmitting and receiving the multimedia contents such as text, voice, and video over large number of sensor nodes [8]. The experimental results were conducted in high traffic environment mode. The algorithm complexity of this proposed method is high and not suitable for transmitting huge multimedia contents over the sensor nodes as the main limitation of this work.

Suseela *et al.* developed path selection methodology to select the individual optimized routing in network environment using Multi path routing algorithm [11]. The energy deficiency of each sensor node in WMSN was determined using Priority Based Multipath Routing Algorithm (PBMRA). The quality of service was improved by testing this proposed methodology on large sensor network environment in order to validate the effectiveness of the proposed method. The authors extensively compared the experimental results with other conventional path selection routing algorithms Ad-hoc On-demand Distance Vector (AODV), Dynamic Source Routing (DSR), and Destination Sequenced Distance Vector (DSDV). The data rate of the proposed path selection methodology was low and hence the priority of the dynamic nodes was not determined.

Mukherjee *et al.* used Distributed Artificial Intelligence (DAI) algorithm for improving the performance quality of the sensor networks [12]. The authors used various test bed methods to validate the effectiveness of the developed DAI algorithm. The source routing selection of this proposed method was extensively compared and analyzed using various routing protocols under different network environment constrains. The authors constructed dynamic channel modeling algorithm for allocate the power model for each sensor nodes in network environment. The authors compared the extensive simulation results with respect to different data rates.

Bavarva *et al.* used compressive sensing algorithm in WMSN which had the applications of MIMO in communication system [13]. The authors tested their developed sensing algorithm with respect to small and deep fade environments. The energy consumption of each sensor node and its data rate were analyzed using the proposed sensing algorithm and the experimental results were compared with conventional sensing algorithm in MIMO application environment. The authors also analyzed the security issues of the sensor nodes in WMSN environment under restricted region of simulation areas. The multimedia contents such as text, voice, and multimedia video were transmitted and received over the large number of sensor nodes in WMSN to analyze the impact of the developed compressing sensing algorithm.

Yadav *et al.* analyzed multimedia sensor networks with respect to various multimedia contents over large number of sensor nodes using path selection algorithm [14]. The path loss model of the MSN was analyzed to predict the energy loss of the sensor nodes. The authors obtain 96% of Packet Delivery Rate (PDR) and 187 mJ of energy consumption under limited constrained environments of networks. The authors compared the extensive simulation results with respect to different data rates. The multimedia contents such as text, voice, and multimedia video were transmitted and received over the large number of sensor nodes in WMSN to analyze the impact of the developed compressing sensing algorithm.

Table 7.2, the various wireless multimedia methods and their limitation with the conventional methods are compared with references [8, 11–14].

7.4   Literature Survey Based on Data Fusion

Zhang *et al.* constructed compressive sensing algorithm for fusion the multimedia data over the large sensor networks [15]. The independent data regions of the data samples were fused to improve the quality of the developed network model. The authors analyzed the performance of the developed data fusion model under different data modeling environments. The authors obtained 93.18% of accuracy which was tested on artificially developed benchmark datasets. The authors obtained 94.56% of accuracy which was tested on real time datasets.

Boulkaboul *et al.* developed data fusion method based on the principal of Dempster–Shafer (D–S) theory using an Adaptive Weighted Fusion Algorithm (AWFA) [16]. Basic Probability Assignment (BPA) was developed to construct the rules for fusing the multimedia data for different mode of applications on large scale network environments. The authors obtained 99.18% of accuracy which was tested on artificially developed benchmark datasets. The authors obtained 98.87% of accuracy which was tested on real time datasets.

Huang *et al.* developed and constructed medical tomography pixel-based replicas for fusing medical images for various healthcare applications [17]. The authors proposed various diverse data fusion approaches that could be applied to group medical imaging with Electronic Health Records (HER) to improve the medical imaging fusion rate. The authors presented

Table 7.2 Comparisons of the existing methods for analyzing the quality of service in WMSN with their limitations.

Author details	Year	Methodology	Limitations of the conventional method
Chiwariro et al. [8]	2020	MRP and MMAP	Algorithm complexity
Suseela et al. [11]	2020	Priority Based Multipath Routing Algorithm (PBMRA)	The data rate of the proposed path selection methodology was low and hence the priority of the dynamic nodes was not determined.
Mukherjee et al. [12]	2020	DAI algorithm	Low data rates
Bavarva et al. [13]	2018	compressive sensing algorithm	High Complexity
Yadav et al. [14]	2019	Path selection algorithm	Less PDR

contemporary knowledge, summarize significant results and deliver execution guidelines to assist as a direction for scholars interested in the implementation of multimodal fusion in medical tomography.

In Table 7.3 the authors Zhang [15], Boulkaboul [16] and Huang [17] have explained various data fusion methods and its limitations.

Table 7.3 Comparisons of the existing methods for data fusion with their limitations.

Author details	Year	Methodology	Limitations of the conventional method
Zhang et al. [15]	2019	Compressive sensing algorithm	High fused time
Boulkaboul et al. [16]	2020	Adaptive Weighted Fusion Algorithm (AWFA)	Low fusion rate
Huang et al. [17]	2020	Medical imaging pixel-based models	Complex algorithm

7.5   Conclusions

In this article, various conventional methodologies for data fusion, WMSN and brain tumor detection and segmentation algorithms are described. The limitations of each methodology are discussed with their experimental or simulation results under various environmental conditions.

References

1. Li, M., Kuang, L., Xu, S., Sha, Z., Brain tumor detection based on multimodal information fusion and convolutional neural network. *IEEE J.*, 7, 180134–180146, 2019.
2. Islam, Md.K., Ali, Md.S. *et al.*, Brain tumor detection in MR image using superpixel, principal component analysis and template based K-means clustering algorithm. *Mach. Learn. Appl.*, 5, 1–8, 2021.
3. Bahadure, N.B., Ray, A.K., Thethi, H.P., Image analysis for MRI based brain tumor detection and feature extraction using biologically inspired BWT and SVM. *Int. J. Biomed. Eng.*, 2017, Article ID 9749108, 1–10.
4. Jalali, V. and Kaur, D., A study of classification and feature extraction techniques for brain tumor detection. *Int. J. Multimed. Inf. Retr.*, 9, 271–290, 2020.
5. Sharif, M.I., Li, J.P., Amin, J. *et al.*, An improved framework for brain tumor analysis using MRI based on YOLOv2 and convolutional neural network. *Complex Intell. Syst. Springer*, 7, 2023–2036, 2021.
6. Wong, K.C., Syeda-Mahmood, T., Moradi, M., Building medical image classifiers with very limited data using segmentation networks. *Med. Image Anal.*, 49, 105–116, 2018.
7. Jia, Z. and Chen, D., Brain tumor identification and classification of MRI images using deep learning techniques. *IEEE Access*, 1, 1, 1–10, 2020.
8. Chiwariro, R. and N, T., Quality of service aware routing protocols in wireless multimedia sensor networks: Survey. *Int. J. Inf. Technol.*, 1, 200–210, 2020.
9. Khan, P., Kader, Md.F. *et al.*, Machine learning and deep learning approaches for brain disease diagnosis: Principles and recent advances. *IEEE*, 9, 37622–37655, 2021.
10. Wang, M., Yang, J., Chen, Y., Wang, H., The multimodal brain tumor image segmentation based on convolutional neural networks. *2017 2nd IEEE International Conference on Computational Intelligence and Applications (ICCIA)*, pp. 336–339, 2017.
11. Suseela, S., Eswari, R., Nickolas, S. *et al.*, QoS optimization through PBMR algorithm in multipath wireless multimedia sensor networks. *Peer Peer Netw. Appl.*, 13, 1248–1259, 2020.

12. Mukherjee, A., Goswami, P., Yang, L., DAI based wireless sensor network for multimedia applications. *Multimed. Tools Appl.*, 80, 16619–16633, 2020.

13. Bavarva, A., Jani, P.V., Ghetiya, K., Performance improvement of wireless multimedia sensor networks using MIMO and compressive sensing. *J. Commun. Inf. Netw.*, 3, 84–90, 2018.

14. Yadav, V. and Arora, G., Analysis of wireless multimedia sensor network. *2019 2nd International Conference on Power Energy, Environment and Intelligent Control (PEEIC)*, pp. 496–498, 2019.

15. Zhang, S., Chen, X., Yang, R., Li, P., Cai, Q., Research on data fusion method based on compressed sensing. *2019 IEEE International Conference on Artificial Intelligence and Computer Applications (ICAICA)*, pp. 90–94, 2019.

16. Boulkaboul, S. and Djenouri, D., DFIOT: Data fusion for Internet of Things. *J. Netw. Syst. Manage.*, 28, 1136–1160, 2020.

17. Huang, S.C., Pareek, A., Seyyedi, S. *et al.*, Fusion of medical imaging and electronic health records using deep learning: A systematic review and implementation guidelines. *NPJ Digit. Med.*, 3, 136, 2020.

18. Irmak, E., Multi-classification of brain tumor MRI images using deep convolutional neural network with fully optimized framework. *Iran. J. Sci. Technol. Trans. Electr. Eng.*, 45, 1015–1036, 2021.

19. Preethi, S. and Aishwarya, P., An efficient wavelet-based image fusion for brain tumor detection and segmentation over PET and MRI image. *Multimedia Tools Appl.*, Springer, 80, 14789–14806, 2021.

20. Chahal, P.K., Pandey, S., Goel, S., A survey on brain tumor detection techniques for MR images. Springer, *Multimedia Tools Appl.*, 79, 21771–21814, 2020.

21. Kapse, R.S., Salankar, S.S., Babar, M., Literature survey on detection of brain tumor from MRI images. *IOSR J. Electron. Commun. Eng.*, 10, 1, Ver. II, 80–86, Jan 2015.

22. Lima, S.A. and Islam, Md. R, A modified method for brain MRI segmentation using dempster-shafer theory. *2019 22nd International Conference of Computer and Information Technology*, IEEE, 2019.

23. Telrandhe, S.R., Pimpalkar, A., Kendhe, A., Detection of brain tumor from MRI images by using segmentation & SVM. *WCFTR'16*, IEEE, 2016.

24. Denzil Bosco, T., Lakshmi Narayanan, A., Veeramuthu, A., A new multimodal brain tumor image fusion for pre-processing of medical image database. *International Conference on Communication and Signal Processing*, IEEE, pp. 1724–1728, 2017.

25. Drevelegas, A. and Papanikolaou, N., Imaging modalities in brain tumors, in: *Imaging of Brain Tumors with Histological Correlations*, Springer-Verlag Berlin Heidelberg, Berlin, Germany, 2011.

Part II

DATA ANALYTICS APPLICATIONS

8

An Experimental Comparison on Machine Learning Ensemble Stacking-Based Air Quality Prediction System

P. Vasantha Kumari* and G. Sujatha

Department of Computer Science, Sri Meenakshi Govt. Arts College for Women (A)Madurai, Madurai Kamaraj University, Madurai, Tamil Nadu, India

Abstract

Air is most important factor for human life. Other than human life is wildlife and plants are depending on air for their survival. Air is polluted by the human behavior, industrialization, and urbanization. Prevention of this air pollution has become a necessary action in many cities. Air is polluted at intolerable levels by industries and heavy vehicular traffic in cities which affects human health conditions to a great extent. Forecasting and controlling the air pollution is the need of the hour to care for human beings from health hazards. The most important objective of this paper is to proposed new method to predict air pollution using data collected on monthly basis and give recommendations to prevent and control air pollution. Ambient air monitoring is the regular, continuing measurement of pollutant levels by measuring the amount and types of certain pollutants in the outside air. Investigative and protecting air quality in this earth has become one of the fundamental activities for every human in many industrial and urban areas at the present time. Based on the serious health concerns and the atmospheric pollution has become a main source of premature mortality among general public by causing millions of deaths for every year based on (WHO, 2014). Air Quality prediction used to alert the people about the air quality alarming conditions, and it's health effects and also support Environmentalists and Government to frame air quality standards and regulations based on issues of harmful and pathogenic air exposure and health-related issues for human welfare. Air Quality Index (AQI) is a measure of pollution level in the air. Predicting air pollution with AQI is one the major challenging area of Research nowadays. Machine Learning (ML) methods

Corresponding author: vasanthisundar2@gmail.com

K. Umamaheswari, B. Vinoth Kumar and S. K. Somasundaram (eds.) *Artificial Intelligence for Sustainable Applications*, (129–146) © 2023 Scrivener Publishing LLC

are used to predict the AQI. Machine Learning methods is a scientific approach to solve certain tasks and predict the value using techniques and Algorithms such as Supervised Learning (SL), Semi Supervised Learning (SSL), and Unsupervised Learning (USL). Machine Learning algorithms provide various methods to forecasting the air pollution levels. Ensemble method of Machine Learning algorithms is applied to predict the air quality and analyze these results to conclude with the comparison of other regression algorithms.

Keywords: Air quality index (AQI), machine learning (ML), Lasso regression (LR), support vector regression (SVR), random forest regression (RF), stacking, linear regression, gradient boosting regressor

8.1   Introduction

Air pollution is important thing for a number of pollution related diseases, including respiratory infections, heart disease, and stroke, lung cancer [1]. The human health effects of poor air quality are far reaching, but mainly affect the body's lungs and cardio vascular system. The increasing population, vehicles, and productions are dangerous of all the air at an alarming rate. In order to estimate the air impurity, contaminant constraints are considered in the lower altitudes of the troposphere, which are meticulous. Air excellence sensor devices extent the attentions of particles that have a sources of pollution and create the hazardous effects during or after the restore to health of air by human being. Particles like PM2.5, PM10 CO, NO2, NO etc. impact the quality of air. Automobiles releases release enormous amounts of nitrogen oxides, carbon oxides, hydrocarbons, and particulates when burning petrol and diesel. Prediction of these gas levels indicates the air quality to people.

8.1.1   Air Pollutants

Air pollution is resolute as the occurrence of pollutants in the atmosphere in huge amount for long periods. It can be solid particles liquid or gas. The air is polluted from various ways.

Primary Pollutants
Primary pollutants are one of the pollutants it emitted from the source directly to the air and sources can be either sandstorms or human-related, such as industry and motor vehicle emission. The common primary

pollutants are particulate matter (PM), nitrogen dioxide (NOx), sulphur dioxide (SO2), and carbon monoxide (CO) [2].

- Secondary pollutants
  This type of air pollutants are formed in the atmosphere, resulting from the chemical or physical reactions between primary pollutants. Photochemical oxidants and resulting particulate matter are the major examples of secondary pollutants.

Objectives of Air Quality Index (AQI)

- AQI used to comparing air quality environment at various locations and cities.
- It also helps to alert the people and identifying damaged standards and inadequate monitoring programs.
- AQI helps in analyzing the upgrading or degradation in air quality.
- AQI informs the public about ecological conditions. It is especially useful for old age people suffering from health issues caused by air pollution.

8.1.2 AQI (Air Quality Index)

AQI is used to determining Air Pollution Index which is the indicator of Pollution level of Air. The air pollution factors are used as parameters to calculate the AQI [15]. Based on this value the AQI is ranked by six types [4]. These ranks are listed in Table 8.1. Tasks such as playing a game or driving a car are examples where Reinforcement Learning is suitable. Unsupervised Learning is an approach that learns without any supervision and it used the data that is unlabeled or classified. Instead of responding to feedback as in Reinforcement Learning [3], unsupervised Learning identifies shared attributes and characteristics from Figure 8.2. Machine Learning Methods association problems, which try to describe parts of the data, and clustering problems, that seek to identify natural groupings. In supervised Learning, the algorithm attempts to learn from labeled data or classified data [5]. Such algorithms can be described as a data- driven approach, where historical data is used for predictions of the future. In the paper Air Quality is predicted with the help of three Machine Learning Algorithms and the results are compared against different parameters.

Table 8.1 AQI rank categories.

Rank	Category	Color	AQI value	Precautionary message
1	Good	Green	0-50	None
2	Satisfactory	Yellow	51-100	Unusually responsive people should consider reducing long-standing or heavy energy.
3	Moderately Polluted	Orange	101-150	Respiratory issues people and heart disease, the elderly and children should limit protracted exertion.
4	Poor	Red	151-200	People with respiratory issues or heart diseases the elderly and children should avoid long-standing exertion; Everyone else should limit prolonged exertion.
5	Very poor	Purple	201-300	Active children and adults, and people with respiratory disease, such as asthma, should avoid all outside exertion; Children to avoid outdoor exertion.
6	Serve	Maroon	301-500	Everyone should restrict any outdoor exertion; people with respiratory or heart disease, the old and Children should safe at home.

8.2 Related Work

The number of Machine Learning methods proposed for solving air pollution prediction problems in recent years. An outline of various air pollution forecasting algorithms is provided in [5]. Benzene can cause loss of white blood cells which leads to low immunity. It also causes anemia by reducing the production of red blood cells [6]. Klemm *et al.* have investigated the correlation between mortality and air pollution for two years period in Atlanta [7]. They found a significant increase in deaths due to respiratory problems and cancer with an increase of PM 2.5 levels. It is also observed that people above 65 years of age were getting affected by CO levels in the air. A stacking approach with SVR and k-NN as base models have got more accuracy in the prediction of super-resolution images and also achieved high consistency with human visual judgments [8]. A greedy stacking method for various biomedical disciplines with different data sets got more accuracy in prediction compared to linear, genetic algorithm stacking, and a brute force approach [10]. Wolpert and Macready have investigated some bootstrap algorithms and derived that the stacking method has shown improved performance [9]. Dragomir has performed the k-NN regression method to predict the quality of air in Ploiesti and obtained zero prediction error for 19 out of 29 instances. Shishegaran *et al.* have used four prediction models that are (1) Auto-Regressive Integrate Moving Average, (2) Principal Component Regression, (3) combination of 1 and 2, and (4) combination of model 1 with Gene Expression Programming to estimate daily AQI in Tehran, Iran [10]. Among these, the last model which is the non-linear ensemble regression model has shown the best results. In the present work, we have compared four regression models viz., linear regression, k-NN regression, decision tree regression, and stacking method in estimation of the air quality index (AQI) based on six air pollutants.

The paper explains and reviewed theory and applications of multiple predictive models as well as further compared advantages and disadvantages among models.

In [12] various different regression analysis techniques for accurate results are analyzed. It explains the relationship between a dependent and independent variable. This technique is used for forecasting or predicting, time series modeling, and finding the causal effect relationship of the variables of the model. Regression analysis is used to analyzing and modeling data. There are different kinds of regression techniques used to make predictions namely Lasso regression, Support vector regression, and Random Forest regression.

The system [11] has used to predict the next day pollution level using Lasso Regression and Multilayer Perceptron (ANN) Protocol. Based on basic parameters and analyzing pollution details and forecast future pollution for next day. Time Series Analysis is used for recognition of future data points and air pollution prediction.

In this paper [12] to predict the air pollution using Supervised Machine Learning approach considers four Machine Learning algorithms such as SVR. The absorption of air pollutants in ambient air is governed by the meteorological parameters such as atmospheric wind speed, wind direction, relative humidity, and temperature. These parameters are used to predict the Air Quality Index. The AQI is used to measure the quality of air.

The paper [13] is to take the publically available weather data from 2013 to 2020 and apply Machine Learning techniques to predict only the amount of PM2.5 concentration in the air given other environmental features. In this project the Machine Learning algorithms such as linear regression and so on are applied.

The air quality prediction was done either with Machine Learning techniques or big data techniques. In this paper [14] the air quality prediction is done by both techniques and the model accuracy is compared.

8.3   Proposed Architecture for Air Quality Prediction System

In this model used to predict the air quality using the machine learning approaches using air pollutant data without metrological data whereas the previous researches using the both metrological and air pollutant data to predict the air quality but in this model used only the air pollutant data. The desired data is downloaded from the Kaggle website. The proposed machine learning-based air quality prediction system is designed for purpose of comparing initial Machine learning algorithm. It is a layered architecture model (Figure 8.1). Based on the functionalities this architecture is divided in to five layers. The bottom most layer is data layer which is used to collect data from the Kaggle database. The next layer is data filtering layer that will clean data by removing the missing value and unknown value. The third layer is data processing layer used to split the data into testing and training data set. The next layer is prediction layer is used to forecast the AQI value using machine learning algorithm.

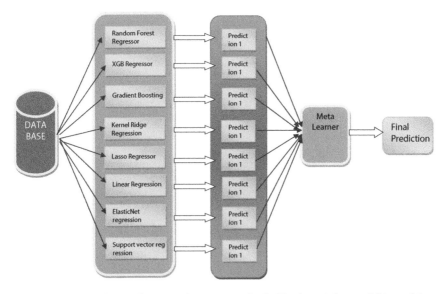

Figure 8.1 Air quality prediction architecture methods. This layer is heart of this model. The topmost layer is the output layer that takes the predicted AQI value.

Dataset Description

The dataset consists of around 29532 records and 13 attributes. The attributes are: 1. PM2.5, 2. NO, 3. PM10, 4. NOX, 5. NO2, 6. NH3, 7. O3, 8. SO3, 9. CO, 10. Benzene, 11. Toluene, 12. Xylene, 13. AQI value.

Data Extraction Layer

The Second layer model is data extraction layer. Data extraction is important step in Machine Learning model. The data set is having a large number of noisy data. The unknown data and missing data is removed by using the method pandas in python. Use Pandas packages to eliminate number of rows and columns with Null/NaN values. This function returns a new Data Frame and the source Data Frame remains unaffected data set. After removing the useless value the data set consists only of valued records. These records are used to build the model.

8.3.1   Data Splitting Layer

In this layer used to split the dataset into two as training dataset and testing dataset for applying proposed Machine Learning Algorithms. The first 12 parameters of the dataset are considered as input parameters X and the last parameter is taken as the output parameter Y. model takes the input as x

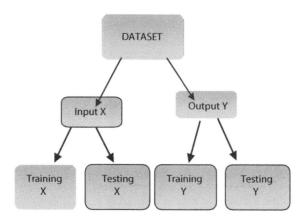

Figure 8.2 Dataset splitting.

and given the output to y. In Figure 8.2 the dataset is split by two part as training and testing.

8.3.2   Data Layer

This layer used to collect the data from the Kaggle [17] database. Kaggle is interactive online platform provides hundreds of databases and tutorials. The data is structured data type. This data is downloaded by .csv (comma separated value) format.

Prediction Layer
This architecture consists of two prediction layers, one is base learner another one is meta learner. These are used to predict the desired air pollution level. The output of base learner is getting and giving the input of meta learner. The Meta learner predicts the air quality. Machine Leaning methods are used to predict the output.

Lasso Regression
Lasso regression is regularization technique used for a more accurate prediction. The Lasso model uses shrinkage where data values are shrunk due to a central point as the mean. This particular type of regression for models showing variable selection/parameter elimination [12].

$$\sum_{i=1}^{n}(y_i - \sum_{j} x_{ij}\beta_j)^2 + \lambda \sum_{j=1}^{p} |\beta_j|$$

Support Vector Regression (SVR)
Support Vector Regression algorithm supports both linear and non-linear regressions of model. This model works on the principle of the Support Vector Machine (SVM) algorithm. SVR differs from SVM that it classifier used for predicting discrete categorical data labels while SVR is a regression that is used for predicting continuous ordered data variables.

Advantages of SVR

1. SVR is strong to the outliers.
2. Decision model can be updated easily.
3. Can use probability rules for multiple classifiers trained on the different types of data.
4. Measuring the confidence in classification by improve the prediction accuracy.
5. SVR performs less computation compared to other regression techniques in machine learning.
6. Easy implementation.

Random Forest Regression
Random Forest is a set of decision trees and it used to do regression and classification. Classification is used to find out the majority of selection. This algorithm can manage a variety of data such as binary data, categorical data, and continuous data and it is more accurate, robust. Random Forest is a multiple decision trees.

Kernel Regression
It is a non-parametric technique to estimate the conditional expectation of a random variable. The objective is to find a non-linear relation between a pair of random variables **X** and **Y**.

Elastic Net Regression
Elastic Net first emerged as a result of critique on Lasso, whose variable selection can be too dependent on data and thus unstable. The solution is to combine the penalties of Ridge regression and Lasso to get the best of both worlds.

Ensemble Methods

Ensemble is a machine learning technique that used to combines several base models of machine learning algorithm in order to produce one optimal predictive model.

- Bagging.
- Stacking.
- Boosting.

Bagging

Bagging is a technique for sinking prediction variance by producing supplementary data for training from a dataset by combining repetitions with combinations to create multi-sets of the original data. The algorithm for bagging is shown in Figure 8.3 and Structure of Bagging in Figure 8.4.

Stacking

Stacking regression is an ensemble learning technique that combines multiple base regression models through a metaregressor. The individual regression models are trained based on the complete training set; then the metaregressor is fitted based on the output meta-features of the individual regression models in the ensemble model [16]. Therefore, stacking regression is capable of improving the prediction accuracy by a linear combination of different predictors. In general, two fundamental principles should be followed when selecting base regressors. The first one is that the correlation between the individual regressors should be as small as possible so as to exploit the complementary characteristics between different base

1: Let T be the set of n training examples (x', y_i), $i \in 1, 2, \cdots, n$.

2: B is the number of base learners and L the base learning algorithm.

3: for$(i = 0; i < B; i++)\{$

4: Create a bootstrapped training set T_i of size n by sampling with replacement.

5: Learn a specific base learner $L_i(x, y)$ on T_i by using L.

6: $\}$

7: The final learning algorithm C is the ensemble of all base learners $\{L_i\}$ and a test example x^* is classified by using a simple majority voting method:

$$y' = \arg \max_y \sum_{L_i \in C} L_i(x',y)$$

Figure 8.3 Algorithm for bagging.

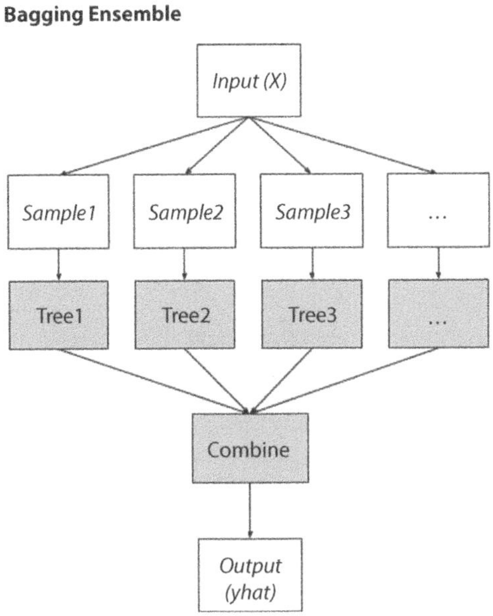

Bagging Ensemble

Figure 8.4 Structure for bagging.

regressors. The second is that the performance gap between different base regressors cannot be too large, otherwise the base regressor with poor performance will inevitably influence. The algorithm for stacking is shown in Figure 8.5, and the structure of stacking algorithm in Figure 8.6.

Algorithm 19.7 Stacking

Input: Training data $D = \{\mathbf{x}_i, y_i\}_{i=1}^m$ $(\mathbf{x}_i \in \mathbb{R}^n, y_i \in Y)$

Output: An ensemble classifier H

1: Step 1: Learn first-level classifiers
2: **for** $t \leftarrow 1$ to T **do**
3:      Learn a base classifier h_t based on D
4: **end for**
5: Step 2: Construct new data sets from D
6: **for** $i \leftarrow 1$ to m **do**
7:      Construct a new data set the contains $\{\mathbf{x}_i', y_i\}$, where $\mathbf{x}_i' = \{h_1(\mathbf{x}_i), h_2(\mathbf{x}_i),..., h_T(\mathbf{x}_i)\}$
8: **end for**
9: Step 3: Learn a second-level classifier
10: Learn a new classifier h' based on the newly constructed data set
11: **return** $H(\mathbf{x}) = h'(h_1(\mathbf{x}), h_2(\mathbf{x}),..., h_T(\mathbf{x}))$

http://rasbt.github.io/mlxtend/user_guide/classifier/StackingClassifier/

Figure 8.5 Algorithm for stacking.

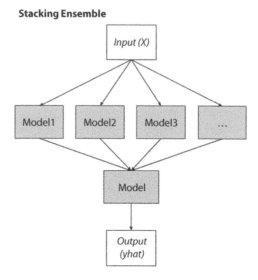

Figure 8.6 Structure for stacking.

Overview of Stacking

Stacking mainly differs from bagging and boosting on two points. First stacking often considers heterogeneous weak learners (different learning algorithms are combined) whereas bagging and boosting consider mainly homogeneous weak learners.

Boosting

Boosting is an iterative strategy for adjusting an observation's weight based on the previous classification. The algorithm of Boosting is shown in Figure 8.7 and the structure of boosting algorithm in Figure 8.8.

Output Layer

The top most layers of is output layer. In this layer take the predicted AQI value Y. Compared the predicted AQI and testing AQI based on this accuracy is generated.

8.4　Results and Discussion

Regression methods are used to predict the air quality and calculate the accuracy of the model. Based on these regression method outputs the meta learner is used to predict the air quality in better manner.

Boosting Algorithm

- Given example images $(x_1,y_1), ..., (x_n,y_n)$ where $y_i=0, 1$ for negative and positive examples respectively.

- Initialize weights $w_{1,i} = \frac{1}{2m}, \frac{1}{2l}$ for $y_i=0,1$ respectively. Where m is the number of positives examples and l the number of negatives examples.

- For t = 1,...,T (T weak classifiers)

1. Normalize the weights, $w_{t,i} = \frac{w_{t,i}}{\sum_{j=1}^{n} w_{t,j}}$

2. Select the best waek classifier with respect to the weighted error:

$$\varepsilon_t = min_{f,p,\theta} \quad \sum_i w_i |h(x_1, f, p, \theta) - y_i|$$

Define $h_t(x)=h(x,f_t,p_t,\theta_t)$ where $f_t,p_t y \theta_t$ are the minimizers of ε_t.

3. Update the weights: $w_{t+1,i} = w_{t,i}\beta_t^{1-e_i}$
   Where $e_i=0$ if example x_i is classfied correctly, $e_i = 1$ otherwise, and

$$\beta_t = \frac{\varepsilon_t}{1-\varepsilon_t}$$

- The final strong classifier is:

$$C(x) = \begin{cases} 1 \text{ if } \sum_{t=1}^{T} a_t h_t(x) \geq \frac{1}{2}\sum_{t=1}^{T} a_t \\ 0 \text{ otherwise} \end{cases}$$

Where $a_t = log \frac{1}{\beta_t}$ https://www.researchgate.net/figure/Boosting-Algorithm-11_fig1_309031690

Figure 8.7 Algorithm for boosting.

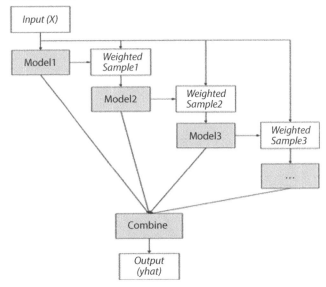

Figure 8.8 Structure for boosting.

Sample Data

The dataset contains air quality data and AQI (Air Quality Index) at hourly and daily level of various stations across multiple cities in India.

The same dataset is used for various algorithms to predict the air quality. The 12 input parameters of air pollution dataset values are shown Figure 8.9.

AQI is predicted from the testing dataset and the accuracy of the model is analyzed using various performance estimators like mean square error, root mean square error, absolute mean error, etc.

Root Mean Square Error (RMSE)

Root Mean Square Error (RMSE) is a normal deviation of prediction errors. RMSE measures, how to scope these residuals. The Result RMSE is graphically presented in Figure 8.10.

	Date	PM2.5	PM10	NO	NO2	NOx	NH3	CO	SO2	O3	Benzene	Toluene	Xylene	AQI	AQI_Bucket
0	1/1/2015	NaN	NaN	0.92	18.22	17.15	NaN	0.92	27.64	133.36	0.00	0.02	0.00	NaN	NaN
1	1/2/2015	NaN	NaN	0.97	15.69	16.46	NaN	0.97	24.55	34.06	3.68	5.50	3.77	NaN	NaN
2	1/3/2015	NaN	NaN	17.40	19.30	29.70	NaN	17.40	29.07	30.70	6.80	16.40	2.25	NaN	NaN
2	1/4/2015	NaN	NaN	1.70	18.48	17.97	NaN	1.70	18.59	36.08	4.43	10.14	1.00	NaN	NaN
4	1/5/2015	NaN	NaN	22.10	21.42	37.76	NaN	22.10	39.33	39.31	7.01	18.89	2.78	NaN	NaN
...	...	...	...	...	...	...	...	...	...	...	...	...	...	...	...
29526	6/27/2020	15.02	50.94	7.68	25.06	19.54	12.47	0.47	8.55	23.30	2.24	12.07	0.73	41.0	Good
29527	6/28/2020	24.38	74.09	3.42	26.06	16.53	11.99	0.52	12.72	30.14	0.74	2.21	0.38	70.0	Satisfactory
29528	6/29/2020	22.91	65.73	3.45	29.53	18.33	10.71	0.48	8.42	30.96	0.01	0.01	0.00	68.0	Satisfactory
29529	6/30/2020	16.64	49.97	4.05	29.26	18.80	10.03	0.52	9.84	28.30	0.00	0.00	0.00	54.0	Satisfactory
29530	7/1/2020	15.00	66.00	0.40	26.85	14.05	5.20	0.59	2.10	17.05	NaN	NaN	NaN	50.0	Good

29531 rows × 15 columns

Figure 8.9 Sample data.

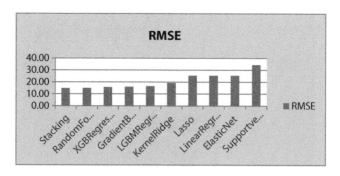

Figure 8.10 Comparison of RMSE value.

$$RMSE = \sqrt{\frac{1}{n}\sum_{j=1}^{n}(y_j - \hat{y}_j)^2}$$

Mean Square Error
The MSE is defined as Mean or Average of the square of the difference between actual and estimated values. The Result of MSE is graphically presented in Figure 8.11.

$$MSE = \frac{1}{n}\sum_{j=1}^{n}(y_j - \hat{y}_j)^2$$

MEAN ABSOLUTE ERROR: The mean absolute error (MAE) is very simple regression error metric to comprehend. To calculate the residual for every data point, taking only the absolute value of each, so that negative and positive residuals do not cancel out then take the average of all these residuals. The Result MAE is graphically presented in Figure 8.12.

$$MAE = \frac{1}{n}\sum_{i=0}^{n}|y_i - \hat{y}_i|$$

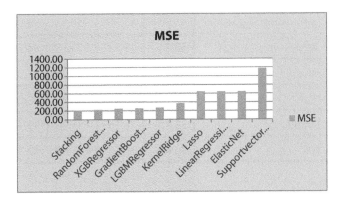

Figure 8.11 Comparison of MSE value.

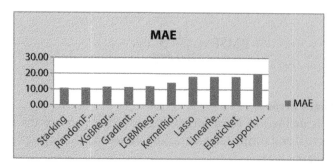

Figure 8.12 Comparison of MAE value.

Efficiency of the given model is analyzed using four performance estimators in Table 8.2. Based on these estimators the lowest error rate and highest accuracy rate of model it is best to predict the air quality as graphically presented in Figure 8.13. So the stacking method is used to reduce the error rate and improve the accuracy.

Table 8.2 Accuracy comparison of machine learning regression models with stacking.

Model	RMSE	MAE	MSE	Accuracy
Stacking	14.85	10.60	215.41	97.41
Random Forest Regression	14.96	10.80	223.76	97.31
XGB Regressor	15.78	11.50	248.96	97.01
Gradient Boosting Regressor	16.07	11.38	258.32	96.90
LGBM Regressor	16.53	11.93	273.15	96.72
Kernel Ridge	19.24	14.30	370.09	95.55
Lasso	25.42	18.15	646.26	92.23
Linear Regression	25.42	18.15	646.26	92.23
Elastic Net	25.42	18.15	646.27	92.23

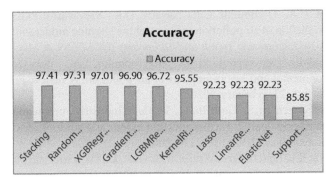

Figure 8.13 Prediction analysis of machine learning methods based on accuracy.

8.5   Conclusion

Air pollution is one of the dangerous problems in this world today and its prevention is stable scientific challenges of researcher. The AQI used to inform the quality of the air and its health effects it used for many people. The AQI is very important to sensitive people. Ensemble method of stacking in machine learning is used to reduce the error rate and improve the accuracy of the model. In future, attention of air pollutants is governed by the meteorological parameters such as atmospheric wind speed, wind direction, relative humidity, and temperature must be considered to reduce the error rate, and increase the accuracy of the model and the AQI is classified in to several categories based on this predicted value.

References

1. *7 Million premature deaths annually linked to air pollution*, Accessed: Apr. 27, 2019. Available: https://www.who.int/phe/eNews_63.pdf.
2. Sujatha, G., Vasantha Kumari, P., Vanathi, S., Machine learning approaches for air quality prediction – A review. *International Conference on Digital Transformation(AC- ICDT20)*.
3. Osisanwo, F.Y., Akinsola, J.E.T., Awodele, O., Hinmikaiye, J.O., Olakanmi, O., Akinjobi, J., Supervised machine learning algorithms: Classification and comparison. *International Journal of Computer Trends and Technology (IJCTT)*, 48, 3, 131, 133, 134, June 2017.
4. Sujatha, G. and Vasantha Kumari, P., Overview on air quality index (AQI). *J. Maharaja Sayajirao Univ. Baroda*.

5. Aditya, C.R., Deshmukh, C.R., Nayana, D.K., Vidyavastu, P.G., Detection and prediction of air pollution using machine learning models. *International Journal of Engineering Trends and Technology (IJETT)*, 59, 4, May 2018.
6. Manisalidis, Stavropoulou, E., Stavropoulos, A., Bezirtzoglou, E., Environmental and health impacts of air pollution: A review. *Front. Public Health*, 8, 1–13, February, 2020.
7. Jia, C., Batterman, S., Godwin, C., VOCs in industrial, urban and suburban neighborhoods-part 2: Factors affecting indoor and outdoor concentrations. *Atmos. Environ.*, 42, 9, 2101–2116, 2008.
8. Klemm, R.J., Lipfert, F.W., Wyzga, R.E., Gust, C., Daily mortality and air pollution in Atlanta: Two years of data from ARIES. *Inhal. Toxicol.*, 16, Suppl. 1, 131–141, 2004.
9. Zhang, K., Zhu, D., Li, J., Gao, X., Gao, F., Lu, J., Learning stacking regression for no-reference super-resolution image quality assessment. *Signal Process.*, 178, 2021.
10. Kurz, C.F., Maier, W., Rink, C., A greedy stacking algorithm for model ensembling and domain weighting. *BMC Res. Notes*, 13, 1, 1–6, 2020.
11. Aarthi, A., Gayathri, P., Gomathi, N.R., Kalaiselvi, S., Gomathi, V., Air quality prediction through regression model. *Int. J. Sci. Technol. Res.*, 9, 03, March 2020.
12. Sethi, J. and Mittal, M., An efficient correlation based adaptive LASSO regression method for air quality index prediction. *Earth Sci. Inf.*, 14, 1–10, 2021.
13. Zhu, S., Lian, X., Wei, L., Che, J., Shen, X., Yang, L., Qiu, X., Liu, X., Gao, W., Ren, X., Li, J., PM2.5 forecasting using SVR with PSOGSA algorithm based on CEEMD, GRNN and GCA considering meteorological factors. *Atmos. Environ.*, 183, 20–32, 1352–2310, 2018.
14. Nehete, R. and Patil, D.D., Air quality prediction using machine learning. *Int. J. Creat. Res. Thoughts (IJCRT)*, 9, 6, June 2021.
15. Sujatha, G., Vasantha Kumari, P., Vanathi, S., Air quality indexing system –A review. *AICTE Sponsored Two Days Online National Level E-Conference On Machine Learning as a Service for Industries MLSI 2020*, 4th–5th September 2020.
16. Air quality prediction using ensemble machine learning algorithm, *International Journal of Engineering Research & Technology (IJERT)*, Published by, www.ijert.org, ICACT – 2021 Conference Proceedings, 9, 8, 2021.
17. https://www.kaggle.com/rohanrao/noise-monitoring-data-in-india.

9

An Enhanced K-Means Algorithm for Large Data Clustering in Social Media Networks

R. Tamilselvan[1]*, A. Prabhu[2] and R. Rajagopal[3]

[1]*Chaitanya Bharathi Institute of Technology, Hyderabad, India*
[2]*CMR Technical Campus, Secunderabad, Hyderabad, India*
[3]*Alliance College of Engineering & Design Alliance University, Bengaluru, India*

Abstract

When given a large-scale set of data, data analysis becomes more difficult. Identifying societies or consumers' shared interests is particularly important for social network analysis. The enhanced information grouping for basic in interpersonal organization examination utilized in planning high dimensional information for successful information mining. The refined chart development in many existing works uses content of information as it were. The visual appraisal of information comprises of boisterous and scanty issue happen in refined diagram which makes the subsequent chart shaky and untrustworthy. Web-based media network information additionally contain connect data which gives comprises of (1) diagram development high-dimensional, quality worth information, for example, Facebook posts, tweets, remarks, and pictures, and (2) connected information that portrays the connections between web-based media clients just as who post the posts, and so on Existing works use the information interface for information bunching frequently inadequate, which means after effect of refined diagram are fragmented. The web-based media organization, the substance information regularly contains an enormous number of pointless highlights. The mind-boggling exercises of countless clients might create countless loud and inadequate of highlights. This paper proposes another k-means algorithm for huge information grouping utilizing refined chart in web-based media organization, utilizes an information bunching to track down the quantity of bunches in information. In this methodology we proposed algorithm for new k-means are

Corresponding author: nkltamil7@gmail.com

K. Umamaheswari, B. Vinoth Kumar and S. K. Somasundaram (eds.) *Artificial Intelligence for Sustainable Applications*, (147–162) © 2023 Scrivener Publishing LLC

shifts back and forth between two stages: In an element choice initial step, for observe the most agent subset of information grouping a transitional diagram instated with interface information. The second step for last coming about chart, which alluded to a refined diagram then, at that point, utilized informal organization information. A refined diagram bunching technique utilized on both the substance information and connection information. We efficiently plan and lead precise investigations to assess the proposed structure on datasets from true web-based media sites.

Keywords: Clustering, social network, distilled graph, high dimensional, social media data

9.1   Introduction

The task of categorizing a collection of articles into self-contained groups is known as clustering. Heaps of web-based media administrations are arising lately that permit individuals to convey and communicate them helpfully and effectively, e.g., Facebook and Twitter. Consistently, a great many photographs, recordings and messages are posted on long range informal communication sites like Facebook and Twitter, and we can likewise divide this substance between an enormous number of clients. In this manner, the informal organization examination turns out to be more troublesome when given huge scope information. In informal organization examination, a significant assignment is to find the fundamental networks or the clients' shared advantages [1]. In the greater part of the past investigations, the chart is frequently built utilizing all highlights on content information, and won't be refreshed or worked on after its development. Shockingly, in informal organization, the substance information regularly contains an enormous number of pointless elements. This is frequently accomplished by interpersonal organization information grouping on the substance information of the clients (e.g., post labels of the clients), in view of the way that clients in a similar local area regularly have comparative or associated content data [2]. The interpersonal organization information grouping, which breaks down informal communities as charts? In particular, the clients are acted as hubs, and the one-sided edges in charts utilized to measure the connections in clients. Subsequently, we can get the proclivity (similitude) data among hubs. By far most existing element determination algorithms work with "information containing uniform substances (or characteristic worth items) that are regularly thought to be free and indistinguishably disseminated." Notwithstanding, online media information differs as its important elements or cases are innately associated with one another [16]. Other than the substance data, interpersonal organization information likewise has interface data, (for example, the "follows" or companion associations). As referenced in [3, 4], connected clients in an informal organization are bound to have comparative subjects. In this way, it is naturally useful for local area revelation. Be that as it may, the connection information is regularly deficient or incorrect. We propose to utilize both the connection information and the substance information to build the diagram for interpersonal organization information grouping. In this technique, the diagram designed step by step. In every cycle, we distinguish the delegate highlights and bring up-to date the diagram in alternating way. In the first place, we update the chart by utilizing just the chose highlights. Then, at that point, given a built diagram, we further look for the most agent highlights subset with regard to the chart. The at last got chart, alluded to as refined diagram, is then utilized in ghastly grouping. We signify the proposed algorithm as k-means clustering. Extraordinarily, we perform highlight determination on posts (e.g., tweets, web journals, or pictures) with regards to web-based media with interface data among client and client or among client and posts [5].

Since ordinary element choice techniques can't exploit the extra data in connected information, we continue to concentrate on two key issues: (1) connection mining – extract unmistakable relations from connected information; (2) mathematical portrayal – addressing relations and coordinate them in a best in class highlight determination plan. Our algorithm is versatile for true huge scope interpersonal organizations. We approve the proposed algorithm by contrasting and other cutting-edge algorithms on certifiable information [6–8]. Our strategy exhibits serious or better exhibitions in the tests and shows remarkable proficiency, particularly when the quantity of the two connections as well as elements expanding.

The remaining part of the paper is structured as follows. Section 9.2 discusses about the related work. Section 9.3 explains about innovative K-means algorithm. Section 9.4 explains data partitioning. Section 9.5 explains about the experimental findings and outcomes. Section 9.6 conclusion is stated.

9.2   Related Work

This followed the part in survey probably the most related works in the informal community investigation, including highlight determination and ghastly examination techniques. Given a proper diagram, we propose an original algorithm to track down the most agent highlight subset. Rather than taking care of the issue with two-dimensional regularization, the proposed technique tends to move the issue to a curved enhancement issue with ensured execution and gives incredible comfort to control the quantity of chose highlights. In directed learning the objective idea is identified with class association, while in unaided learning the objective idea is typically identified with the inborn designs of the information. Basically, in the two cases, the objective idea is identified with partitioning cases into well divisible subsets as indicated by detachability. The test presently is the way to foster a brought together portrayal dependent on which various sorts of distinguishableness can be estimated.

In feature selection method has been broadly utilized in informal organization investigation. In administered highlight choice [9, 10], remove distinctive social relations to improve the component choice on interface information. In semi-regulated element choice, there is a co-grouping structure introduced to find the networks of clients in [11]. In solo component choice, there are techniques straightforwardly using content information for including determination [12], and strategies using join information to upgrade the element choice execution. For example, in it presents a social aspect structure learning strategy on connecting the information to support highlight determination. Otherworldly examination for K-means algorithms expects to find the nearby mathematical construction of information by means of diagram implanting. In the ghostly investigation, a comparability diagram is developed to catch the mathematical relationship among cases. In the diagram, cases inside similar groups are connected by closeness loads and edges. The edges connected between occurrences in various bunches are doled out low likeness loads. In particular, in the phantom investigation for interpersonal organization information bunching, various methodologies have been applied for building the comparability diagram. In a few words, for example, in [13], similitude chart is developed with just substance information. Nonetheless, the substance information might contain repetitive and boisterous elements [12], prompting the problematic and sullied closeness measures. Unearthly examination has likewise been installed with highlight choice algorithms. To save the information structure, a few methodologies proposed to gain proficiency with the diagram installing alongside highlight choice. The K-means algorithm performs element choice and subspace learning mutually. In [14], with the pre-determined similitude diagram, discriminative highlights can be chosen to safeguard the low dimensional space. The technique introduced in [11] uses the substance information by means of a straight relapse plan and embraces the connection information through a phantom grouping.

9.3   K-Means Algorithm

This paper proposes K-means algorithm, which is called huge information grouping. Past works and the model in ascertaining the likenesses utilizing just the substance data without any preparation, in which the diagram is normally developed utilizing all highlights. When the diagram is built, it won't be changed or improved. Sadly, practically speaking, the substance data frequently contains numerous loud, scanty, and repetitive elements. Utilizing every one of the elements might cause a critical predisposition of the genuine linkages of clients. To stay away from these issues, we need to find a refined chart that is developed utilizing just the genuine agent highlights. The normalized matrix is associated with G is defined as

$$L_1 = D_1 - A$$

Where D_1 is a diagonal matrix

$$D_1(i,i) = \sum_j A(i,j)$$

To keep away from the scale issue, we use the normalized graph Laplacian matrix:

$$L_1 = D_1^{-1/2} L_1 D_1^{-1/2}$$

The K-means algorithm is represented by the mean value of the objects and partitioning.

Algorithm 1 K-means

Inputs:
- K: Number of clusters
- D_1: data clustering.

Method used:
1. Select K objects from D_1 cluster.
2. Repeat the process
3. Assign every object to the group to the most common objects and based on the objects' mean value
4. Calculate the mean value
5. If no, then stop.

Output:
- A collection of K clusters

The K-means algorithm is used for cluster dispersion that is obtaining the value L. To divide the occurrences into c clusters, the spectral clustering algorithm was used. Let $X = (x_1 \ldots x_n)$ is a cluster predictor generator for the c classes $\{1, \ldots, C\}$ for n occurrences, where $X(i, j) = 1$. If x_i is assigned as the jth cluster; otherwise, 0. Because X is a discrete-valued matrix, NP optimization problem arises [18]. The predictor matrix by a measured cluster indicator matrix $F = X(XX^T)^{-1/2}$ enables its records to have any real-world values.

Algorithm 2 Weighted K-means Clustering for Social Media Networks

Inputs:
- $X \in R^{nxd}$: the content matrix
- $R \in R^{nnd}$: link matrix
- σ: and leverage parameters

Method:
1. Calculate the normalized matrix L according to (2).
2. Calculate the first c vectors of L.
3. Consider the vector representing to the j-th row of U
4. The cluster point $\{u\}_{i=1}^{n}$ clusters $\{1, \ldots, c\}$ through k-means algorithm.

Output:
- A set of K clusters

The weight of an incentive for an aspect in a group corresponds to the dispersion of the qualities from the center in the component of the group. Because the scatterings differ in different components of various K bunches, the weight esteems for various groups are distinct. The weight indicates a little scattering in one of group's elements. In this way, that aspect becomes most familiar in framing a group. This algorithm for subspace grouping seems to have an issue in taking care of scanty information. If the scattering of an aspect in a group turns out to be zero, then, at that point, the load for that aspect isn't calculable. The present circumstance happens much of the time in high-dimensional inadequate information. To make the loads calculable, a basic technique is to add a little consistent somewhere out there capacity to make all scatterings more prominent than zero [17, 18].

9.4   Data Partitioning

In this part, we present the exploratory outcomes on genuine information. This shows the examination after effects of the K-Means algorithm.

A genuine application for a retail organization in China. We utilized Enhanced K-means group high-dimensional inadequate deal information to rename providers dependent on their business practices. We further investigate the utilization of otherworldly clustering for the issue of visual information apportioning. The significant attributes of $I(\overline{D})$ in that can be taken advantage of for observing a decent applicant segment are the differentiation contrasts linking the dim squares across the fundamental askew and the pixels adjoining them. This algorithm expects, to create up-and-comer parcels by testing their wellness to the bunches proposed by the adjusted dim squares in $I(\overline{D})$.

Toward this end, a true capacity is characterized to certainly represent structures. An instinctively engaging estimate is the distinction of the mean difference uniting obvious groups (i.e., differences in nondark closes off-askew) and that inside evident bunches (i.e., differences in dim squares along the slanting) [21].

Let Y be a candidate create a partition in $\{C_i, 1 \leq i \leq c\}$ be the corresponding crisp c-partition to $U, |C_i| = n_i \forall_i$ and reduce the subscription of grouping anti-similarity membership among dark and no dark region in $I(\overline{D})$, F_b and variation within dark region in $I(\overline{D})$ are, respectively, represented by,

$$E_b = \sum_{i=1}^{c} (\sum_{s \in i, t \ni i} d_{st^*}) / \sum_{i=1}^{c} n_i (n - n_i), \qquad (9.2)$$

$$E_w = \sum_{i=1}^{c} (\sum_{s, t \in i, s \neq t} d_{st^*}) / \sum_{i=1}^{c} n_i (n - 1), \qquad (9.3)$$

We utilize a weighted k-means Algorithm [18] for this streamlining issue. As a specific type of transformative algorithm, a hereditary algorithms are carried out at a programmatic experience of theoretical portrayals (called a genome), up-and-comer arrangements (called people) to a advancement update develops toward improved arrangements. Development usually begins with a randomly selected population formed persons and happens over time [16, 17]. At each age, the health of each person in the population is examined, and numerous people were suddenly chosen from the existing populations and altered to shape some other populations, which is then utilized with mentioned focus. Typically, the algorithm ends when either a largest amount of ages has been reached, or a good wellness level has been achieved in the population, or there is no further advancement within different ages. This visual information parceling method is dependent on the grouping [18].

This analysis is utilized in the k-means algorithm (1) depends upon the eigende organization of a $N \times N$ matrix, which usually takes o(n³) time complexity, o(n²) space complexity. Plainly phantom disintegration was recalcitrant for enormous n, particularly on account of a dense matrix. This constraint makes the phantom Clusters technique unfeasible (or computationally infeasible) when dealing with huge informational indexes. Despite the fact that eigende piece should be possible (e.g., through disseminated equal algorithm), re-requesting such an enormous grid is likewise trying for the k-means algorithm, just as the powerlessness of showing such a huge picture because of the constraint of current screen goals. Extra procedures are required along such boundaries to measure the method to larger data widths whereas maintaining cluster performance. This broadens a sampling-based system in this paper [16–18].

9.5 Experimental Results

To assess our algorithms, we have done various investigations on falsely created informational collections, just as depiction of informational collections (summed up in Table 9.1). Except if in any case referenced, in the accompanying investigations, the distance matrix D is calculated with original attribute space.

9.5.1 Datasets

Nine Real-world informational collections with various data structure are utilized in our tests. The dispersed plots of these manufactured informational collections are in which each tone addresses an outwardly significant gathering. The initial six informational indexes are taken from [17], and the last 3 are produced by us. With the exception of S-7, which is a combination of 3 Gaussian shapes, any remaining informational collections include more unpredictable information structures, in which a conspicuous bunch centroid for each gathering isn't really accessible. As can be seen, a portion of these informational collections incorporate various scales between groups, or a few bunches concealed in a jumbled foundation just as data

Table 9.1 Description of data sets of various social media networks.

Name of the dataset	Type	Nodes	Edges	Description
Facebook	Undirected	4,038	87,234	Social media from Facebook (anonymized)
Gplus	Directed	106,614	13,673,553	Social circles from Google+
Twitter	Directed	83,306	1,768,249	Social circles from Twitter
gemFacebook	Undirected	124,833	1,390,293	Facebook dataset
feather-deezer	Undirected	26,281	92,552	Social network of Deezer users
Wikipedia	Directed, Signed	10,735	159,288	Wikipedia Requests from Admin

of the Real-world Datasets and consequences of assessing c (summed up in Table 9.2). Nine true informational indexes were likewise proposed to evaluate the algorithm; five of them come from the UCI Machine Learning Repository. -1, 4, 5, 8, and 9. To put it plainly, R-1 (bosom malignant growth) data set incorporates 683 examples, every one of which has nine credits and has a place with one of three classes. Repository-3 (face) informational collection was first utilized in [14], which is a subset of the informational index [21], including 1,756 pictures of three unique people. R-3 (hereditary) informational collection is a pairwise 194 × 194 lattice comprising of differences from just a bunch of 195 human quality items were grouped into four protein families. R-3 (iris) informational collection contains three actual classes, 55 examples every, in which each class alludes to sort a iris plant with 4 ascribes. R-5 (casting a ballot) informational index comprises of 435 US Representatives in the House individuals' decisions on 15 votes. R-6 (wine) informational index contains 177 wine occasions got from two distinct cultivars. R-7 (activity) informational collection [22] is a 100 × 100 grid comprising of pairwise dissimilarities got from 100 human activity cuts. R-8 (different elements) informational index comprises of paired examples per class. Picture highlights of 10 numerals are written by hand ('0'~'9'), 200. These digits are addressed as a 648-dimensional vector as far as six capabilities. R-9 (glass) informational collection incorporates 215 examples from 6 kinds of glass characterized as far as their oxide content [9] and [10].

9.5.2   Performance Analysis

By contrasting the group marks, the items given by the algorithms with the ground truth names, the visual system dividing algorithm exhibition is created (accessible for these 17 informational indexes). Precision metric has been generally utilized for bunching execution assessment [15, 16] and [18]. The delta function that approaches 1 if $z_1 = z_2$ and provided that and 0 in any case, and guide is the planning capacity that permutes grouping names to coordinate with comparable names. The K-means algorithm is

Table 9.2 Information of the real-world datasets and results of estimating.

Data	c_p	#attribute	n	c_{ov}^m	c_{sv}^m	c_{sv}^a
S-1	3	2	299	>=1	3	3
S-2	3	2	303	>=2	3	3
S-3	3	2	266	>=2	3	3
S-4	5	2	622	>=4	5	5
S-5	4	2	512	>=2	4	4
S-6	3	2	238	>=4	3	3
S-7	3	2	1000	3	3	3
S-8	2	2	2000	>=1	2	2
S-9	3	2	2000	>=2	3	3
R-1	2	9	683	>=3	2	2
R-2	3	12000	1755	3 or 4	3	3
R-3	3	-	195	>=3	3	3
R-4	3	4	160	>=2	2	2
R-5	2	17	425	>=2	2	2
R-6	3	12	179	>=3	3	3
R-7	10	-	100	>=9	10	10
R-8	10	6490	2000	>=7	9	9
R-9	6	9	215	>=4	6	6

typically utilized to acquire the lead planning [12, 13], an unearthly bunching for representation of our information parceling results on engineered and true informational indexes. The visual partitioning algorithm clustering accuracy is of the existing picture V_{ov} the clustering image V_{sv} is mentioned in Table 9.2.

9.5.3   Approximation on Real-World Datasets

This algorithm is tested in the present reality dataset. In the first place, we test the exhibition of refined chart adapting particularly to assess the exhibitions utilizing the quantity of nonzero things in the closeness grid. Moreover, to assess the ability to adapt the algorithms, this increases the number of interconnections and illustrates the research to notify the computation time, ACC and space complexity. This algorithm runs with ten emphases in spite of the stop condition, came to cycle 4. The test information was created with 1,000 occurrences, 2,000 highlights and 11% positive connections. For the comfort of perception. The inadequate portrayal of 2,000 × 2,000 closeness grid is web-based media organization. Each point in the figure is the likeness assessed between tests. This demonstrates that we are just given restricted connection data of information [20, 21]. After the fourth iteration of update M, the comparability network becomes more dense. From the point onward, loud connections were distinguished to emphasis 10. We have the accompanying perceptions:

- In general, the exhibitions of all algorithms arrive at the pinnacle while choosing at the maximum 1,200 highlights other than greatest 2,000 elements. This exhibits the significance of element choice while doing unearthly grouping.
- This algorithm outflanks all algorithms by and large on the grouping execution. In grouping by utilizing content and connection data, our algorithm and NetFS show much preferable bunching execution over others. This shows that the usage of connection data further develops the bunching execution on informal community information.
- This algorithm outflanks NetFS algorithm in by and large execution. The conceivable explanation is NetFS chooses highlight dependent in a low-dimensional space built by just connection data. Accordingly, it will be impacted by the boisterous connections. This algorithm repeatedly learns a refined chart with more operator include subset, that is more energetic and less delicate to data link.

The target of this examination was to assist a food retailer organization in China for classification to its providers as per providers' business practices. Provider classification alludes to the most common way of isolating providers of an association into various gatherings as per the qualities of the providers so that each gathering of providers can be overseen contrastingly inside the association. Provider classification is a significant stage in SRM for making better provider the board procedures to diminish the item obtaining hazard and costs and further develop business execution [18, 19]. Another k-means algorithm has subspace bunching for high-

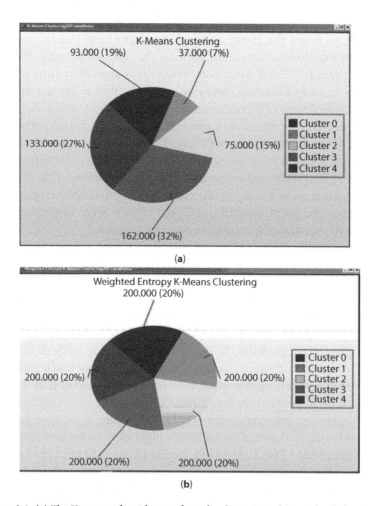

(a)

(b)

Figure 9.1 (a) The K-means algorithm perform for cluster 0 to cluster4 for different percentages of data sets, (b) The weighted entropy K-means algorithm performs for cluster0 to cluster4 for equal percentage of data sets.

dimensional meager information. In this, the time limit at the inside bunch scattering and boost the negative weight entropy in the grouping system. Since, the grouping system grants more aspects to make commitments to ID of each bunch, the issue of distinguishing bunches by barely any scanty aspects can be kept away from. In that capacity, the scarcity issue of high-dimensional information is handled. The preliminary results on both engineered and genuine informational collections demonstrated that the new proposed approach surpassed other k-means type algorithms as shown in Figure 9.1(a), for instance weighted entropy K-means grouping algorithm as we can see in Figure 9.1(b), for various bunches with equivalent rate.

The proposed approach can also be used to become acquainted with the illustrations in semi-regulated and administered learning environments. The weighted k-means algorithm is designed for unofficial organization's data enquiry, which is a typical unassisted selection situation up. Regardless, the suggested method is applicable to chart-based semi-managed teaching and guided training situations.

9.6 Conclusion

This chapter proposed an enhanced k-means for enormous information bunching on interpersonal organization media like Facebook, twitter, and so on, online media network information additionally contain interface data which gives comprises of (1) chart development high-dimensional, trait esteem information, for example, Facebook posts, tweets, remarks, and pictures, and (2) connected information that portrays the connections between web-based media clients just as who post the posts, and so forth In this algorithm, we all the while limit the inside bunch scattering and boost the negative weights entropy in the system grouping. Since, this bunching system grants most of the aspects to build commitments in distinguishing proof of all groups, the issue for recognizing groups scarcely any meager aspects can be stayed away from. All things considered; the sparsity issue of high-dimensional information is handled. The test results are true informational collections and have shown that the new proposed algorithm outflanked in another weighted k-means type algorithms deciding the quantity of bunches and dividing information in either social structure.

The proposed method can also be used to become acquainted with graphs in semi-directed learning and prescribed practice. Moreover, the scenario of personal and social organization data investigation is a typical unassisted picking up setting. The suggested strategy has been applied to chart-based semi supervised learning as well as controlled learning.

Another thought that we are at present pondering is that the vast majority of the grouping algorithms manage a steady k number of bunches, where truth be told this impedes the essential thought of why we are doing the bunching. Thus, anticipate coordinating this endeavors to taking care of a variable k rather than a consistent one, as this is exceptionally use in certifiable models where information is continually changing and k can't be fixed. We additionally plan to chip away at bunching algorithm kernelization; this implies that both the algorithm and information taken ought to be preprocessed utilizing explicit standards so they can improve the exhibition and the aftereffects of the grouping algorithm. The refined diagram and select the best agent include all the while for unearthly bunching via web-based media organization. We contrasted upgraded k-means algorithm and other cutting-edge baselines on true informational indexes.

Acknowledgments

The authors would like to express their gratitude to everyone at the Department of Information Technology in Chaitanya Bharathi Institute of Technology, Hyderabad, India and Dr. Rajanikanth Aluvalu, HOD, Information Technology, Chaitanya Bharathi Institute of Technology, Hyderabad, India for providing the valuable comments and suggestions of online data clustering using k-means algorithm for large data clustering for social media network, data partitioning and suggestions on experiments.

References

1. McPherson, M., Smith-Lovin, L., Cook, J.M., Brids of a feature homophily in social media networks. *Annu. Rev. Sociol.*, 27, 415–444, 2001.
2. Li, J., Hu, X., Wu, L., Liu, H., Robust unsupervised feature selection on networked data, in: *ICDM*, 2016.
3. Tang, J. and Liu, H., Unsupervised feature selection for linked social media data, in: *Proceedings of the 18th ACM SIGKDD International Conference on Knowledge Discovery and Data Mining*, ACM, pp. 904–912, 2012.
4. Li, J., Hu, X., Tang, J., Liu, H., Unsupervised streaming feature selection in social media, in: *Proceedings of the 24th ACM International on Conference on Information and Knowledge Management*, ACM, pp. 1041–1050, 2015.

5. Liu, W., Gong, D., Tan, M., Shi, J.Q., Learning distilled graph for large-scale social network data clustering. *IEEE Trans. Knowl. Data Eng.*, 32, 7, 1393–1404, 2020.

6. Wang, X., Tang, L., Gao, H., Liu, H., Discovering overlapping groups in social media, in: *Data Mining (ICDM), 2010 IEEE 10th International Conference on*, IEEE, pp. 569–578.

7. Wang, N., Liu, Z., Li, X., Graph-based semi-supervised feature selection for social media data, in: *Foundations of Intelligent Systems*, pp. 115–124, Springer, Berlin, Heidelberg, 2014.

8. Tang, J. and Liu, H., An unsupervised feature selection framework for social media data. *TKDE*, 26, 12, 2914–2927, 2014.

9. Ng, A.Y., Jordan, M.I., Weiss, Y. *et al.*, On spectral clustering: Analysis and an algorithm. *NIPS*, 2, 849–856, 2002.

10. Yang, Y., Shen, H.T., Nie, F., Ji, R., Zhou, X., Nonnegative spectral clustering with discriminative regularization, vol. 5, pp. 750–756, 2011.

11. Chiang, K.-Y., Hsieh, C.-J., Natarajan, N., Dhillon, I.S., Tewari, A., Prediction and clustering in signed networks: A local to global perspective. *J. Mach. Learn. Res.*, 15, 1177–1213, 2014.

12. Cai, D., He, X., Han, J., Document clustering using locality preserving indexing. *IEEE Trans. Knowl. Data Eng.*, 17, 12, 1624–1637, Dec. 2005.

13. Dhillon, Modha, D., Spangler, W., Visualizing class structure of multi-dimensional data. *Proc. 30th Symp. Interface: Computing Science and Statistics*, 1998.

14. Guattery, S. and Miller, G.L., Graph embeddings and laplacian eigenvalues. *SIAM J. Matrix Anal. Appl.*, 21, 3, 703–723, 2000.

15. Hu, X. and Xu, L., A comparative study of several cluster number selection criteria, in: *Intelligent Data Engineering and Automated Learning*, pp. 195–202, Springer, Berlin, Heidelberg, 2003.

16. Prabhu, A. and Usha, M., A secured best data centre selection in cloud computing using encryption technique. *Int. J. Bus. Intell. Data Min.*, 199–217, Inderscience Enterprises Ltd., 2019, https://doi.org/10.1504/IJBIDM.2019.096804.

17. Huband, J., Bezdek, J.C., Hathaway, R., Bigvat: Visual assessment of cluster tendency for large data sets. *Pattern Recognit.*, 38, 11, 1875–1886, 2005.

18. Jing, L., Ng, M.K., Huang, J.Z., An entropy weighting k-means algorithm for subspace clustering of high-dimensional sparse data. *IEEE Trans. Knowl. Data Eng.*, 19, 8, 1401–1414, Aug 2007.

19. Ling, R., A computer generated aid for cluster analysis. *Commun. ACM*, 16, 355–361, 1973.

20. Ng, A., Jordan, M., Weiss, Y., On spectral clustering: Analysis and an algorithm, in: *Advances in Neural Information Processing Systems*, MIT Press, Cambridge, MA, pp. 849–856, 2002.

21. Cai, D., Zhang, C., He, X., Unsupervised feature selection for multi-cluster data, in: *ACM SIGKDD*, pp. 333–342, 2010.
22. Tan, M., Tsang, I.W., Wang, L., Towards ultrahigh dimensional feature selection for big data. *J. Mach. Learn. Res.*, 15, 1, 1371–1429, 2014.

10

An Analysis on Detection and Visualization of Code Smells

Prabhu J.[1*], Thejineaswar Guhan[1], M. A. Rahul[1], Pritish Gupta[1] and Sandeep Kumar M.[2]

[1]*School of Information Technology and Engineering, Vellore Institute of Technology, Vellore, Tamil Nadu, India*
[2]*School of Computing Science & Engineering, Galgotias University, Uttar Pradesh, India*

Abstract

The term code smell indicates potential menacing practices in the source code of the software. It does not imply that the software will result in compilation errors or not produce the expected output. Still, the attributes such as performance, productivity, and software maintainability might have serious concerns, directly impacting the software code quality. The analysis is divided into 3 topics: Machine-Learning based code smell detection techniques, Code smell behavior on multiple computer languages, and the Comparison of the latest code smell detection tools. This paper provides an up-to-date review of the recent developments in code smell detection algorithms regarding Machine-Learning techniques. The study covers various aspects, from common findings of code smells in Machine-Learning based projects to detection of code smells in the API documentation. It is observed that the majority of the publications have focused on code smell characteristics over the Java environment. So, for our analysis, we choose to survey Scala, SQL, C#, Python, and JavaScript to understand the unexplored path better. Code Smell Detection tools follow various unique detection techniques and list the smell types identified for the developer to refactor. Subsequently, we conducted a comparative study on the few latest publications on detection tools compared and tabulated for their merits and demerits. This paper presents, which leads to improved software productivity comprehensive review of detection techniques and behavioral aspects of code smell which, when coupled with the detection tools.

Corresponding author: jprabhuit@gmail.com

K. Umamaheswari, B. Vinoth Kumar and S. K. Somasundaram (eds.) *Artificial Intelligence for Sustainable Applications*, (163–176) © 2023 Scrivener Publishing LLC

Keywords: Code smells, code smell detection tools, machine learning, deep learning, and smell detection

10.1 Introduction

The unhealthy exercises followed by developers due to strict deadlines posted by companies result in code smells to the software's source code. Though the logical component of the system may not be affected, code smell directly impacts the software code quality. So, the identification of code smells will avoid fatal problems during software maintenance. Throughout this paper, the focus will be on Machine-Learning based approaches for code smell detection, code smell characteristics in different languages, and the latest code smell detection tools. The advantage of using the Machine-Learning based technique would be to leverage the predictive power and autonomous nature of learning. In this study, Machine-Learning based approaches for the detection of code smells and refactoring-based practices are discussed. The characteristics of code smell vary from language to language. The properties of code smell on different languages, namely Scala, SQL, C#, Python, and JavaScript-based gaming applications, are inspected; the behavioral aspects of code smell in iOS and Android applications are inspected and evaluated. The usage of code smells detection techniques is made to reality with the availability of multiple tools, and analysis on various tools will be discussed. Along with that, the latest code smell detection tool publications listed below will be analyzed,

- Nanthaamornphong *et al.* [16] introduce Zsmell, a web application that detects code smells on Open Source Software's on GitHub based on software metrics.
- TAJS (Type Analyzer for JavaScript) [22] got restructured and furnished with contemporary techniques to generate $TAJS_{lint}$ [17], an automated code smell detection tool.
- Peruma *et al.* [18] present tsDetect, an open-source code smell detection tool. As a command-line tool, tsDetect can run as a standalone executable to analyze JUnit-based test files for the existence of test smells.
- CODECOD [19] is a crowdsourcing platform for performing manual detection in identifying code smells. The platform uses the partition-map-reduce method introduced by Kittur *et al.* [23] to carry out the Task decomposition process.

It proposes the Find, Verify, Vote method to be implied in the quality control phase.

- cASpER, an intelligence, is pledging for automated code smell detection and refactoring proposed by De Stefano *et al.* [20]. cASpER is an IntelliJ IDEA plugin that can detect code smells combining both structural and textual analysis. Moreover, it can refactor out the detected code smells.

10.2   Literature Survey

10.2.1   Machine Learning-Based Techniques

Bart van Oort *et al.* [1] discuss code smells in open source Machine Learning projects. Their analysis over finished projects on Kaggle and papers on code concludes that static code analysis is not prominent in machine learning based projects.

Labeled data is a necessity for training models. However, annotations differ from case to case. Luburić *et al.* [2] proposed a procedure to annotate code smells. They also develop a tool that helps them with the annotation procedure.

In their study, Guggulothu *et al.* [3] investigated the usage of multi-labelled classifiers to detect code smells. They experimented with various multi-label classification methods to make the most of the classifier to predict the presence of code smells.

Ensembling and Feature Selection are prominent techniques used in Machine Learning. Kaur *et al.* [4] experimented with four approaches to examine the performance. The first approach uses all the features of the dataset to train the model. The second approach involves using feature selection techniques and the selected features used to train and evaluate the model. The third approach utilizes ensemble aggregation techniques for feature selection. The fourth approach uses a voting classifier which also aids in feature selection. Based on the results produced, the second approach gave them the best results.

The study conducted by Agnihotri *et al.* [5] used object-oriented and software metrics to predict the presence of code smells on the JHOTDRAW dataset. Their inference lists seven software metrics, namely,

- LCOM to indicate lack of cohesion in a class
- MLOC to indicate the quality concerning the size of the code
- NOM as a measure of the size of code

- DIT as a measure of levels of inheritance
- WMC to measure the complexity of the code
- RFC and CBO were used as coupling metrics

Sharma *et al.* [6] discuss the usage of deep learning in code smells. They examine the usage of transfer learning for code smells in different languages. Also, they experiment with CNN (Convolutional Neural Network), RNN (Recurrent Neural Network), and autoencoders based architectures. This work encourages the usage of Deep Learning in the field.

Sidhu *et al.* [7] proposed a deep learning model to identify regions in UML (Unified Modeling Language) diagrams that could potentially lead to code smells. They collected 1000 UML images and trained their model to predict faults in refactored UML regions, preventing smells in the development phase.

Khan *et al.* [8] work on a methodology to detect smells in the API documentation. Smells in the documentation have led developers to lose productivity and create smells in their code. They find this inference by surveying 21 developers.

10.2.2   Code Smell Characteristics in Different Computer Languages

Bleser *et al.* [9] compare test smell in scala and java. Test smells cover faults in unit tests, and they conducted two studies, one of which is to examine the diffusion of code smells in projects. They found that the diffusion of test smells in scala projects is relatively smaller than in Java-based projects. Their second study aimed to check the ability of a developer to detect code smells. They took help from 14 developers and found that only five of them could explain the cause of a particular code smell they identified.

Muse *et al.* [10], in their paperwork on code smell induced by SQL in data-intensive systems. They mean the high volume of transactions between the data-intensive system's application logic on the server and the database. Firstly, they wanted to find the prevalence of SQL code smells in different projects. Their findings showed that Business domain projects had the most smells, and the most occurring smell was Implicit Columns. Next, do traditional code smells and SQL code smells co-exist. Results showed that they could co-exist, but their associativity was weak, which meant it is possible but not a compulsion for it to occur. Thirdly, can SQL code smells co-occur, and it is shown that there is no statistical association between them. Lastly, what's the duration of the existence of SQL smells; it is shown that most of the smells exist for a long period as they are not given frequent attention.

Sharma *et al.* [11] cover the characteristics of code smells in over 1988 C# Repositories and the correlation between design and implementation smells by using Designite to identify the bad smells. Manual verification on two repositories, namely RestSharp[2] and rtable[3], and their corresponding tool responses were validated, proving the tool efficient for large-scale mining study. Their computational results using Spearman's correlation coefficient report that the design smells and implementation smells are directly proportional to each other. Large-scale projects may not have a high smell density.

Gulabovska *et al.* [12] prove that symbolic execution techniques can outrun the existing AST-based tools. Static analysis for code smell detection performs a heuristic evaluation of the source code, which might be preferable for languages like C, C++, and Java. Researchers should focus on supporting dynamically typed languages by applying symbolic execution techniques.

The manual study of Agrahari *et al.* [13] on nine JavaScript games proved that almost eight out of nine games violated Data Locality, which refers to sorting data to enhance CPU caching. The fact that there is hardly a tool to identify the violation in gaming patterns provides the way for a new area of research. Researchers should train code smell detection tools for JavaScript programs to provide support for gaming sites by identifying the violation in gaming patterns exercised by developers while writing the source code for the gaming website, which might also provide significant growth in game development using JavaScript.

Rahkemaa *et al.* [14] compare code smells in mobile-based applications, mainly iOS and Android. The motive is to compare the code smells and deduce the number of similar smells, the density of code smells, and the frequency of code smells. The first problem they addressed was the similarity of code smells. Of the 19 code smells analyzed, 18 were the same for both applications. The density of code smells across all the projects was found to have a density of 41.7 smells/kilo-instructions in iOS and android to have 34.4 smells/kilo-instructions. However, the density varied across applications showed the difference of complexity in the structure of both the OS. Regarding the distribution of smells, they found that iOS applications have an even distribution of code smells in terms of project frequency.

10.3 Code Smells

Figure 10.1 demonstrates a mind map of all the concepts covered in the literature review.

This section covers an overview of the tools and techniques used in the literature covered. Scala is based on the Java Virtual Machine. It is a strong statically typed general-purpose programming language that leverages the power of both object-oriented programming and functional programming. Scala is now frequently used in Big-Data based systems. SQL or structured query language is used to design, program, and manage data stored in RDBMS or Relational database systems. In data-intensive systems, the volume of transactions is high. The word transaction means a unit of work performed against a database. C# is a statically typed multi-paradigm programming language that follows object-oriented and component-oriented programming disciplines. Gulabovska *et al.* [12] presented that magic number and duplicate abstraction are the respective smell types with high frequency in implementation and design smells. Python is a dynamically typed language, unlike Java, C, support and C++. PyLint is a widely popular tool that can perform in-time statistical analysis as a plugin when integrated with IDEs. Static analysis for code smell detection performs a

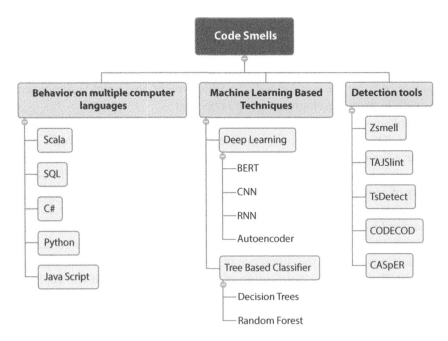

Figure 10.1 A mind map of all the concepts covered in the literature review.

heuristic evaluation of the source code, which might be preferable for languages like C, C++, and Java. JavaScript is still considered an unexplored language; the gaming support offered to the developers is immense. Since JavaScript-based gaming websites do not require a device native configuration, it stands out in the field of game development. Agrahari *et al.* [13] provided that the smell types "Excessive global variables" and "Lazy Object" had a high frequency inside the source code, also "Large Object" and "Dead code" were the smells with the least frequency in JavaScript based gaming projects.

Deep Learning is a subset of Machine learning and mainly uses neural networks to accomplish a task at hand. Various neural networks can be used to model different data types, namely tabular data, which can involve time-specific data, text, image, and audio. In the case of BERT, it is used to analyze text. BERT stands for Bidirectional Encoder Representations from Transformers and works based on transformers. Transformers can have an infinite span of attention when analyzing text data; therefore, they tend to perform very well on benchmark datasets. Convolutional neural networks (CNN) are prominently used in image-based tasks. This architecture works on the principle of convolution and captures feature maps of images used to predict the output. Images are 2-dimensional arrays, and CNN's accommodating images are known as 2-Dimensional CNN. At the same time, time-series data can be accommodated by 1-Dimensional CNN. RNN or Recurrent Neural networks are architectures used for sequential and time-series data. This type of architecture uses outputs of previous states to be used as current state input. This allows the information to propagate through time or states. As a result, RNN performs well; therefore the tools approximately up to 250-time steps. Auto encoders are neural networks that are typically used for representational learning. This includes the generation of new samples with noise or unlabeled data. Decision trees are models which use the structure of trees to make decisions. Simply, the model segments into multiple nodes wherein these nodes follow the structure of trees. So, while making predictions, the data flows through multiple nodes to get to a decision. The random forest, as the name suggests, combines multiple decision trees to make an ensemble prediction.

Before we enter into a brief discussion on code smell detection tools, it's important to look into various smells. Let's look into the commonly addressed twenty-two bad smells systematized by Fowler [21] in his book, "Refactoring: improving the design of existing code." The analysis conducted by Mathew *et al.* [15] categorizes the 22 smells under four categories: bloaters, object-oriented abusers, change preventers, dispensable, and couplers. Mathew *et al.* [15] help the developers to prioritize the smells in a fairly better aspect where object-oriented abusers break the Object-Oriented Programming principles, bloaters expand over time, resulting in increased software complexity, and change preventers prevent manipulations over dependent-code, couplers being code structures with high coupling and dispensable meaning irrelevant code. The tools vary like supported programming languages, especially Java; tools have many more tools than any programming language to analyze its source code efficiently. The tools also limit themselves to the types of code smells they can detect. According to Mathew *et al.* [15], there is a good count of tools that offer the detection of code smells "Duplicated code" and "Large Class." The tools do not differ much in their workflow. The tool's procedure to detect code smells involves hosting the tool as a stand-alone application or plug-in. The source code or the compiled byte code is fed to a model trained through befitting datasets that follow a distinctive technique depending on the tool. In parallel, the software metrics are also analyzed, and both of them combine to provide an output that unveils the code smells present in the software.

Tables 10.1 and 10.2 shows summary of latest machine learning detection techniques in code smells and comparison of latest code smells detection tool publications.

10.4 Comparative Analysis

Table 10.1 Summary of latest machine learning detection techniques in code smells.

Ref. no.	Objective	Merits	Demerits	Findings
[1]	Presence of code smells in Machine Learning Projects.	The difference between Machine Learning Development and conventional development is clearly defined.	None	Code Duplication is very common in all the projects analyzed. Static code analysis is not prominent in such projects as ML developers do not have SE backgrounds.
[2]	Annotation procedure for code smell-based modeling.	Annotations standards vary from dataset to dataset. This proposal pushes for common annotation practice.	The method of annotation is human-intensive. The process proposed is exhaustive for annotators.	Asking for an explanation for why a particular smell was annotated helps for a systematic annotation.

(Continued)

Table 10.1 Summary of latest machine learning detection techniques in code smells. (*Continued*)

Ref. no.	Objective	Merits	Demerits	Findings
[3]	Multi Labeled Classifier approach.	This approach enables capturing the collinearity between target classes which makes the prediction process a bit more explainable.	The current work only accounts for positive correlation; therefore, cases of negative correlation are yet to experiment.	Removing Disparity instances lead to an increase in the accuracy of the model.
[4]	Feature engineering methods for code smells.	Various experimentations on feature selection have been tried ranging from all features to Ensembling.	For the dataset used for training, only JAVA-based projects were used.	The modeling techniques used by them have all resulted in metric ranges of Accuracy: Greater than equal to 0.98 in the approaches Geometric Mean: Greater than equal to 0.92 in all approaches F-measure: Greater than equal to 0.91 in all approaches.
[5]	Code smell prediction using Object-Oriented Metrics.	Object-Oriented and software metrics used for analysis and modeling.	Only one project was used as a dataset, and only tree-based classifiers were used for modeling.	Dispersed Coupling smell is mainly dependent on MLOC and ocavg. Feature envy smell dependent on MLOC and LCOM. God class dependent on WMC, RFC, and CBO. Refused Parent smell dependent on NOM, WMC, and DIT.

(Continued)

Table 10.1 Summary of latest machine learning detection techniques in code smells. (*Continued*)

Ref. no.	Objective	Merits	Demerits	Findings
[6]	Code smell detection using Deep Learning.	Transfer learning is achieved from one language to another.	The language used for transfer learning should have a similar structure for the best results.	Performance between RNN and CNN are varying case by case. Auto encoders perform better than complex models using CNN and RNN.
[7]	Detection of faults in code refactoring to avoid code smells in later software cycles.	Encourages a standard for UML to make such tools to detect code smells in the software design phase.	A model trained will work only on class UML models.	They make a neural network-based model and successfully train it to achieve high accuracy.
[8]	Detecting smells in the API documentation.	The question of "How does this code smell occur?" has been answered in an unmatched manner.	The current work does not correlate between documentation smell and code smell.	The Best model, BERT, achieves F1-score in the range of 0.75-0.97.

Table 10.2 Comparison of latest code smells detection tool publications.

Ref. no.	Detection tool	Smell types supported	Merits	Demerits
[16]	Zsmell	Long Method, Large class, Lazy class, Long Parameter List, Cyclomatic Complexity, Multiple Returns, Message Chains.	The tool proved to be 100% effective. Also, the User Interface test provided satisfactory results.	The number of supported code smell types limits themselves to be seven.

(*Continued*)

Table 10.2 Comparison of latest code smells detection tool publications. (*Continued*)

Ref. no.	Detection tool	Smell types supported	Merits	Demerits
[17]	TAJS$_{lint}$	Argument Count Mismatch, Argument Type Mismatch, Array Length Assignment, Primitive Property Assignment, and Negative Array.	The tool accommodates 14 smell types, out of which 5 are proposed smell types, provide and 9 involve smells that are covered from industry tools and previous research works.	Some smell types have been hardly found in the tested Open Source Software's. Therefore, it is insufficient to accept the premise on efficiency and the number of smell types the code can detect.
[18]	tsDetect	Assertion Roulette, Conditional Test Logic, Construction Initialization, Default Test, Duplicate Assert, Eager Test, Empty Test, Exception Handling, General Fixture, Ignored Test, Lazy Test, Magic Number Test, Mystery Guest, Redundant Print, Redundant Assertion, Resource Optimism, Sensitive Equality, Sleepy Test, Unknown Test.	The Java-based tool achieves high detection accuracy with an average precision score of 96% and an average recall score of 97%. The tool has been designed in such a way to facilitate the addition of new smell types easily.	The tool should accommodate refactoring suggestions for the identified smell types.

(*Continued*)

Table 10.2 Comparison of latest code smells detection tool publications. (*Continued*)

Ref. no.	Detection tool	Smell types supported	Merits	Demerits
[19]	CODECOD	Since the tool implies manual detection, the set of supported smell types cannot be determined.	The empirical evaluation proved that the tool evidenced higher precision and recalls values with an average difference of precision of 0.07 and recall value of 0.19.	Though the tool provides better efficiency, it involves high expenses and workers with a high skillset and brief knowledge about code smell types.
[20]	cASpER	Feature Envy, Misplaced Class, Blob, and the Promiscuous Package.	Their report provides the smell type, degree of smelliness computed with both textual and structural algorithms, and the severity of the smell, which particularly helps developers to prioritize during the refactoring process.	For the product to hold up, it must add more code smell types into its tool.

10.5   Conclusion

The comparative analysis on code smell detection tools covers metrics such as efficiency and precision marked down along with the smell types and programming language supported by each tool. The majority of the detection tools focus on Java; the researchers should provide support for other programming languages. Furthermore, the tools must also focus on providing the developers with refactoring suggestions and highlighting the smell. We also covered an array of machine learning papers; so far, Machine Learning techniques have been used throughout out of requirements in code smell-based technology. However, Deep Learning's potential is still to be explored in the field, and this occurs as the size of the dataset being analyzed is quite small for a particular class to work on.

References

1. van Oort, B., Cruz, L., Aniche, M., van Deursen, A., The prevalence of code smells in machine learning projects, 2021, arXiv preprint arXiv:2103.04146.
2. Luburić, N., Prokić, S., Grujić, K.G., Slivka, J., Kovačević, A., Sladić, G., Vidaković, D., Towards a systematic approach to manual annotation of code smells, 2021.
3. Guggulothu, T. and Moiz, S.A., Code smell detection using a multi-label classification approach. *Software Qual. J.*, 28, 3, 1063–1086, 2020.
4. Kaur, I. and Kaur, A., A novel four-way approach designed with ensemble feature. Selection for code smell detection. *IEEE Access*, 9, 8695–8707, 2021.
5. Agnihotri, M. and Chug, A., Application of machine learning algorithms for code smell prediction using object-oriented software metrics. *J. Stat. Manage. Syst.*, 23, 7, 1159–1171, 2020.
6. Sharma, T., Efstathiou, V., Louridas, P., Spinellis, D., Code smell detection by deep direct-learning and transfer-learning. *J. Syst. Software*, 176, 110936, 2021.
7. Sidhu, B.K., Singh, K., Sharma, N., A machine learning approach to software model refactoring. *Int. J. Comput. Appl.*, 44, 2, 166–177, 2020.
8. Khan, J.Y., Khondaker, M., Islam, T., Uddin, G., Iqbal, A., Automatic detection of five API documentation smells: Practitioners' perspectives, 2021, arXiv preprint arXiv:2102.08486.
9. De Bleser, J., Di Nucci, D., De Roover, C., Assessing diffusion and perception of test smells in scala projects, in: *2019 IEEE/ACM 16th International Conference on Mining Software Repositories (MSR)*, 2019, May, IEEE, pp. 457–467.
10. Muse, B.A., Rahman, M.M., Nagy, C., Cleve, A., Khomh, F., Antoniol, G., On the prevalence, impact, and evolution of SQL code smells in data-intensive systems, in: *Proceedings of the 17th International Conference on Mining Software Repositories*, 2020, June, pp. 327–338.
11. Sharma, T., Fragkoulis, M., Spinellis, D., House of cards: Code smells in open-source c# repositories, in: *2017 ACM/IEEE International Symposium on Empirical Software Engineering and Measurement (ESEM)*, 2017, November, IEEE, pp. 424–429.
12. Gulabovska, H. and Porkoláb, Z., Evaluation of static analysis methods of python programs.
13. Agrahari, V. and Chimalakonda, S., An exploratory study of code smells in web games. arXiv preprint arXiv:2002.05760, 2020.
14. Rahkemaa, K. and Pfahla, D., Comparison of code smells in iOS and android applications, 2020.
15. Mathew, A.P. and Capela, F.A., An analysis on code smell detection tools. *Proceedings of the 17th SC@RUG, 2020*, p. 57, 2019.
16. Nanthaamornphong, A., Saeang, T., Tularak, P., Zsmell–code smell detection for open source software.

17. Almashfi, N. and Lu, L., Code smell detection tool for java script programs. *2020 5th International Conference on Computer and Communication Systems (ICCCS)*, IEEE, 2020.

18. Peruma, A., Almalki, K., Newman, C.D., Mkaouer, M.W., Ouni, A., Palomba, F., tsDetect: An open source test smells detection tool, in: *Proceedings of the 28th ACM Joint Meeting on European Software Engineering Conference and Symposium on the Foundations of Software Engineering*, 2020, November, pp. 1650–1654.

19. Paramita, A.J. and Candra, M.Z.C., CODECOD: Crowdsourcing platform for code smell detection, in: *2018 5th International Conference on Data and Software Engineering (ICoDSE)*, 2018, November, IEEE, pp. 1–6.

20. De Stefano, M., Gambardella, M.S., Pecorelli, F., Palomba, F., De Lucia, A., cASpER: A plug-in for automated code smell detection and refactoring, in: *Proceedings of the International Conference on Advanced Visual Interfaces*, 2020, September, pp. 1–3.

21. Becker, P., Fowler, M., Beck, K., Brant, J., Opdyke, W., Roberts, D., *Refactoring: Improving the design of existing code*, Addison-Wesley Professional, USA, 1999.

22. Jensen, S.H., Møller, A., Thiemann, P., Type analysis for JavaScript, in: *International Static Analysis Symposium*, 2009, August, Springer, Berlin, Heidelberg, pp. 238–255.

23. Kittur, A., Smus, B., Khamkar, S., Kraut, R.E., Crowdforge: Crowdsourcing complex work, in: *Proceedings of the 24th Annual ACM Symposium on User Interface Software and Technology*, 2011, October, pp. 43–52.

11

Leveraging Classification Through AutoML and Microservices

M. Keerthivasan[1*] and V. Krishnaveni[2]

Department of Computer Science and Engineering, PSG College of Technology, Coimbatore, Tamil Nadu, India

Abstract

Existing monolithic architecture used in ERPs (Enterprise Resource Planner) suffer from certain drawbacks such as increased complexity, increased startup time, reduced code readability and difficulty in debugging. This led to the emergence of micro-service architecture which approaches software development as an amalgamation of loosely coupled, independently deployable micro applications (Micro-Apps) of varied functionalities. These micro applications are privy to voluminous amount of data and incorporation of machine learning facility within them enables the users of the application to perform prediction of data circulated amidst the micro application. The aim of this work is to methodically obtain dataset and domain knowledge from consumers and make corresponding micro-apps composed for them by micro intelligence application platform capable of classification or regression while simultaneously making sure that the complexities of ML code such as model selection, hyper parameter tuning are abstracted from the client side using AutoML. The user interface is developed using angular JS and it is integrated to the backend AutoML code using rest APIs. Further the machine learning model arrived is serialized and stored along with the micro app details in a database. The runtime interface of the micro-application has a prediction service and is enabled to access the model that is deserialized and being run in a server. The functioning of proposed work is fully illustrated with the help of a three datasets namely Sonar, liver patients, and Insurance claim.

Keywords: Microservices, AutoML, classification, regression

Corresponding author: mkkvasan@gmail.com

K. Umamaheswari, B. Vinoth Kumar and S. K. Somasundaram (eds.) *Artificial Intelligence for Sustainable Applications*, (177–196) © 2023 Scrivener Publishing LLC

11.1 Introduction

IT organizations today enable business functions through Microservices to take the advantage of cost, granularity, and reuse. Microservices Architecture specifies a particular way of developing software, where applications are structured as a collection of autonomous services. With a staggering increase in the number of entrepreneurial firms each year and the elevated circulation of data among these firms and its customers, it is of paramount importance to implement a Service Oriented Architecture. Microservices architecture with its reduced code complexity, simplified deployment, straightforward internal workflows, and seamless maintenance is the obvious way forward. The main motivation of this project is to converge the fields of micro services and automated machine learning. This data serves as a basis to offer prediction services for Enterprise level micro applications. The objective of the work is to

- abstract the complexities of ML code
- adapt a domain agnostic approach
- provide Flexibility and Persistence

Abstract the complexities of ML code: Prior to the actual classification and regression process a dataset needs to be subjected to a variety of data and feature pre-processing. However, the Automated ML framework abstracts these complexities from the user.

Adapt a domain agnostic approach: The platform will be available to clients from different fields each with their own invoices, bills and other documents. Hence the entire setup from user interface to backend is independent of domain the client belongs to.

Provide Flexibility and Persistence: Since the prediction service is exposed as a micro-application it is independent from any other resource the client's enterprise may possess. Also storing the details of the ML model allows the clients to go back, update the details thus leading to the creation of new models [1–3, 5, 7].

This work is an amalgamation of a user interface, Backend database, and Machine learning code, all working together in unison to incorporate Machine learning capacity into a Micro-application. A user interface that collects information and a dataset needed for creating a machine learning model. This interface is created using HTML, CSS (Bootstrap) and Angular JS. A machine learning framework that accepts a dataset subjects it to a variety of algorithm and finds the most suitable machine learning

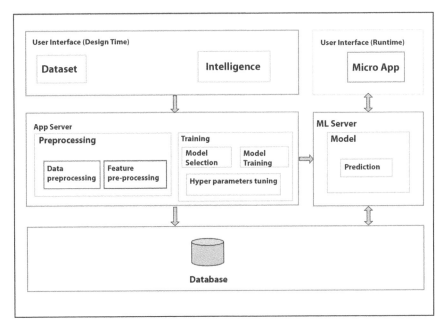

Figure 11.1 Block diagram of ML incorporated micro application.

algorithm which yields the highest possible accuracy. This Framework is formed using Auto sklearn, a backend that indexes and saves the information from the user interface to a database. The backend is accomplished using Core java, Apache Solr and HBase. The overall architectural flow of the work is shown in Figure 11.1.

11.2   Related Work

The existing work on Analysis of approaches and structures of automated machine learning framework reviews the current popular open source AutoML frameworks. The frameworks, namely, Auto-sklearn, TPOT, and Auto-Keras, aid in the further exploration of the work. The analysis and comparison of innovative structures, design-of-framework, and performance helps the practitioners to concretely decide on the choice of the framework for the work under consideration. Work titled automated machine learning in practice: state of the art and recent results, deals with the AutoML and its applications with benchmark results. A key take away for the researcher is the comprehensive overview of the current state of AutoML. Further Cutting-edge research is stimulated thorough analysis of independent benchmarks and out of the box available systems [4, 6, 8, 13, 15].

The work on automatic pipeline generation problem aims to address the broader perspective describing the optimal combination of preprocessors and classifiers, along with their respective parameters, discusses the possible strategies to automate the selection of Machine Learning algorithms and their parameters and analyses of the characteristics of the fitness landscape. Depending on the search, model quality target, and the data modeled, methods produce results that match the user expectations. Pipeline profiler is a graphical tool for the study of AutoML pipelines that allows comparison of the solution space.

The work entitled towards micro service architecture recovery, describes the elements required to build metamodel and specific-purpose abstraction of the micro services. Analysis of micro service-based research works will help the researcher to choose the right tool. A set of mapping rules which map between the software and the metamodel will help the developer to perform roundtrip engineering. "Architecting with Microservices: A Systematic Mapping Study," aims in identifying, classifying, and evaluating microservices in the research perspective. This enables researchers to understand how to architect with microservices, evaluation of the potential industrial use cases, and its implications [9, 10, 12, 14].

The work entitled "Contextual Understanding of Microservice Architecture: Current and Future Directions" aims in identifying, classifying, and evaluating microservices in the perspectives of industrial adoption. It compares based on deployment, user interface, Architectural scope, flexibility, integration mechanism, scalability, versioning and storage; further enables researchers to understand why to move from Service-Oriented Architecture (SOA) to Microservices; and provides a clear insight of the differences between these two architectures and their features. A comparative study on liver disease prediction using supervised machine learning algorithms aims in achieving effective diagnosis system for chorionic liver infection patients utilizing six distinctive supervised machine learning classifiers. There are six algorithms, namely, Random Forest, Logistic Regression, Decision Tree, SVM, K Nearest Neighbors, and Naïve Bayes. The performance of different classification techniques was evaluated based on accuracy, precision, recall, f1 score, and specificity. This gives an idea on how various classification algorithms work and the dataset details have been thoroughly discusses. Logistics Regression achieved the highest accuracy. The work on classification of liver patient dataset classifies data with and without disease. Even though the highest accuracy is reported using Random Tree algorithm, the execution time was higher than the other algorithms for this used in the investigation [11, 16–18].

11.3   Observations

In the past decade Machine learning research has gained a tremendous momentum. Practitioners applied machine learning to build patterns through models/algorithms. These models were used to make interpretations on new data. The steps were repetitive and encompass repeated trials in order to produce quality models. So practitioners faced tedious episodes of trials to obtain a quality models. AutoML attempts to simplify this by automating the intensive, time consuming, repetitive steps of training a machine learning model. AutoML allows data scientists to build efficient data models while sustaining quality. The Survey gives a clear knowledge on how the incorporation of machine learning feature into Micro-application can be performed. Further helps to focus how each function of an application can be designed and developed to exist as an independent service that can be modified without disturbing the rest of the application [17, 19, 20].

- Microservices architecture is a desirable option for modern Enterprise Applications
- Using Microservices it is possible to design and develop extendable solutions
- Agile delivery targeting fast, modular, decomposable services capable of continuous integration, deployment and delivery
- Very suitable for incorporation of AutoML into Micro-Applications

11.4   Conceptual Architecture

Layering refers to the organization of the system into functional components; each component interacts with its neighboring components by means of an interface and helps in achieving automation. This section discusses the proposed system realized as a layered architecture. The layers communicate with each other and are associated with its specific functionality. The merits of proposed system are maintainability, scalability, and transparency. The proposed system has four layers, and each layer has its own responsibility. The layers are namely External Interface Layer, Decision Engine, Processing Layer, and Physical storage Layer. The overall architecture is shown in Figure 11.2.

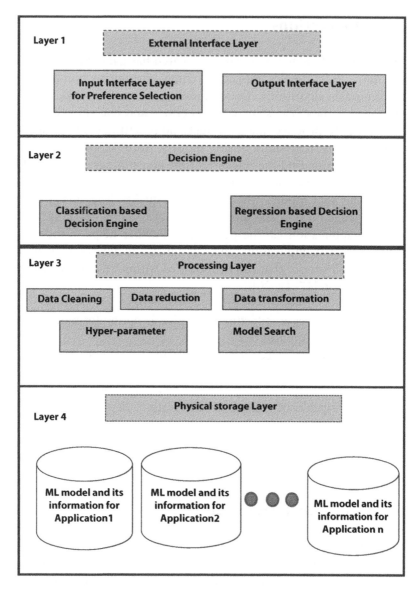

Figure 11.2 Conceptual architecture.

Layer 1: External Interface Layer

External Interface layer includes GUI Design for preference selector and Communicating to pre-processing level. Layer 1 Requirement and suitability of Angular JS are described as follows

(i) to expose the application as rich Internet Application, Angular JS is one of the best candidates for developing such rapid applications.

(ii) to provide developers an options to write client side applications using clean Model View Controller (MVC) architectural pattern and Angular JS supports the same.

(iii) Cross-browser compliance and the AngularJS automatically handles code suitable for each browser.

(iv) Data binding, Scope to refer to model, filter subset of items, create custom widgets, linking and dependency injection.

The elements of the interface layer are

1. AI model name: A text box that accepts name of the AI model created by the user

2. AI model description: A text area that allows user to describe about the AI model created so as to understandability of the created model

3. Training data Template: The term Template refers to the structure created by the user prior to AI model creation

4. Attribute to be predicted: A select box responsible for the selection of target field

5. Model Attributes: A multi select box responsible for the selection of input features

6. Training data Source: A select box that allows user to either use the data within platform or externally upload data

7. File Upload: A file upload box is responsible for the submission of external dataset. It is enabled only if the user selects upload external data in the previous select box

In this work the MVVM pattern of angular JS was the key factor in making sure that once selected target field cannot be selected as input feature. MVVM refers to Model View ViewModel Design pattern. The MVVM is derived from Model View Controller (MVC) Design structure. The aim of MVC model is to separate content from presentation and data preprocessing from content. The Model in MVC is the data itself. View represents the data while controller acts as mediator between model and view. However, in MVVM the controller gets replaced by the ViewModel. The ViewModel is a script which updates any change made in the model get reflected in the view and vice versa. This is known as 2-way binding. This phenomenon of 2-way Binding, grants different elements in the UI the ability to share data.

Layer 2: Decision Engine

Regression and Classification algorithms are Supervised Learning algorithms. The proposed system choses between classification or regression based on the following criteria as shown in Table 11.1.

Nature of Classification Algorithm: In Classification, the target field must be a discrete. The classification algorithm maps the input features (x) to the discrete target field (y). Classification tries to find the decision boundary, which can divide the dataset into different classes.

Nature of Regression algorithms: In Regression, the target field must be continuous. The regression algorithm maps the input features (x) to the continuous target field (y). Regression tries to find the best fit line, thus predicting the output more accurately. Regression algorithms is used to solve problems such as Weather Prediction, House price prediction, etc.

Layer 3: Processing Layer

Automated machine learning works on the basis of different techniques such as Bayesian optimization, evolutionary methods, random search, grid search and the like. For the proposed system the technique used should be

Table 11.1 Characteristics of classification and regression problems.

Based on the listed characteristics of problems an algorithm has been developed to check whether the given dataset has to undergo classification or regression		
Property	**Classification**	**Regression**
Output type	Discrete	Continuous
What are you trying to find	Decision boundary	Best fit line
Evaluation	Accuracy	Sum of squared error

Step 1: Count the total number of Values in a field. Assign the value to Variable *TOTAL*

Step 2: Count number of unique values in the field. Assign the value to Variable *UNIQUE*

Step 3: IF (*UNIQUE*> (*TOTAL*/2)

       Call for Regression

  ELSE

       Call for Classification

robust and also monitor a list of previously generated probabilistic models. As Bayesian optimization satisfies both the afore-mentioned requirements, Auto sk-learn which employs this Bayesian optimization technique was selected as the final tool to be used. This tool searches for the best model and also tunes the hyper-parameter to obtain the most suitable Machine Learning model. Bayesian Optimization uses the following steps to perform model selection and hyper-parameter tuning. Algorithmic representation of above mentioned Bayes optimization Procedure.

Procedure Bayes Optimization (i, f, C)

//Initialize M, D where M refers to probabilistic model and D refers to configurations//
for j ← 1 .....i do
      cj is to Select next configuration
      yj ← f (cj)
      Update D, D U(cj; yj)
      Update the statistical model (M)
end for
end procedure

Step 1: Objective functions Surrogate probability model is constructed.
Step 2: Those parameters that performs best on the surrogate probability model is computed.
Step 3: The computed hyperparameter is applied to the true objective function.
Step 4: The new surrogate model is updated.
Step 5: Step 2–4 is repeated until the declared maximum iterations is reached.

Prior to model selection and hyper-parameter tuning, autosk-learn was used to perform the following data pre-processing functionalities.

Bayesian Optimization in a Gaussian Process

A function $f X \to \mathbb{R}$ is to be optimised over some set X (here the set X is the set of hyperparameters and f is expensive to compute.

Bayesian Optimization : f is modeled as a probability distribution, computed at parameter values $x1, x2, x3 \ldots xD$. $f(x1), f(x2) f(x3) \ldots f(xD)$ are known as the observed variables present in the model

$$P(f(x)|f(x1), f(x2), \dots, f(xD))$$ (11.1)

The selected probabilistic model should be cheaper to computer than f(x). f(x) for values of x is yet to be observed can be estimated from conditional distribution. This conditional distribution is used to choose the next value of x that is computes f(x) as a process of optimization is being continued. Key benefit of Bayesian optimization is that it uses all information from previous computations of f(x). Two major decisions for Bayesian optimization

1. The prior: The probability distribution over functions that are to be used. This encodes the assumptions made about function f. The standard way to do this is with a Gaussian process prior.
2. The Acquisition function: The selection of next point to sample given a conditional distribution over the values of f(x).

Gaussian process as a prior for Bayesian optimization: To use a Gaussian process for Bayesian optimization the domain of the Gaussian process X I selected to be the space of hyper parameters, and defines some kernel that is believed to match the similarity of two hyper parameter assignments. Typically the kernel is based on intuition about the problem.

Expected improvement EI acquisition function refers to minimization of the expected improvement in the value of newly formed Ybest.

$$P(f(x_*) < y_{best} = P\left(\frac{f(x_*) - \mu(x_*)}{\sigma(x_*)} < \frac{y_{best} - \mu(x_*)}{\sigma(x_*)} \right) = \Phi\left(\frac{y_{best} - \mu(x_*)}{\sigma(x_*)} \right)$$ (11.2)

Probability of improvement PI acquisition function refers to maximization of probability that will observe an improvement from the next point searched

$$E[min(f(x_*) < y_{best}, 0)] = E\left[min\left(\frac{f(x_*) - \mu(x_*)}{\sigma(x_*)} < \frac{y_{best} - \mu(x_*)}{\sigma(x_*)}, 0 \right) \right] . \sigma(x_*)$$ (11.3)

$$E_u[min(u-c,0)] = \int_{-\infty}^{c} (u-c).\phi(u)\,du = [-\phi(u)-c.\Phi(u)]_{-\infty}^{c} \quad (11.4)$$

$$[-\phi(u)-c.\Phi(u)]_{-\infty}^{c} = -\phi(c)-c.\Phi(c) \qquad (11.5)$$

then the acquisition function is

$$\alpha_{EI}(y_{best},\mu,\sigma) = -\left(\phi\left(\frac{y_{best}-\mu}{\sigma}\right) + \frac{y_{best}-\mu}{\sigma}.\Phi\left(\frac{y_{best}-\mu}{\sigma}\right)\right).\sigma \quad (11.6)$$

Data and Feature Preprocessing

1. Data Cleaning: Data cleaning refers to the method of f removing, data within a dataset. To handle irrelevant and missing parts and noisy data the following actions are taken.

> If (missing data)
> **Action 1:** Ignore the record totally
> // suitable for large dataset where the absence of minimal number of records may affect the accuracy.

> **Action 2:** Fill the Missing values
> // Fill the missing values, mean, median or mode
> P.S Suitable for smaller datasets where the absence of single record may record the accuracy

> If (Noisy Data):
> Noisy data refers to meaningless and cannot be interpreted by machines.
> Reasons: faulty data collection, data entry errors

> Action: Binning Method
> Sort data and smooth it.
> Divide into segments of equal size
> Handle each segment separately.
> Replace all data in a segment by its mean or boundary values

2. Data Transformation: This step is performed to transform the data into Machine Learning friendly form. This Involves following ways:

> **Normalization( )**
> // Scale the data values in a specified range (-1.0 to 1.0 or 0.0 to 1.0)
> **Attribute Selection()**
> // Construct new attributes from the given set of attributes
> **Discretization( )**
> // Replace the raw values of numeric attribute by interval levels
> **Concept Hierarchy Generation**
> // attributes are converted from level to higher level in hierarchy.

3. Data Reduction: It reduces data storage overheads by efficiently reducing the redundant data. Data Cube Aggregation, Numerosity Reduction, and Principal Component analysis are certain techniques to perform data reduction.

Layer 4: Physical Storage Layer

The aim of this layer is to add persistence to the project work. After filling the details in the layer 1 External User interface, the user is directed to the runtime interface where the prediction service can be used. However, without the physical storage layer a model once created cannot be altered.

Table 11.2 Classification and regression algorithms supported by auto-sklearn.

Classification algorithms		Regression algorithms
1. AdaBoost (AB)	9. Linear SVM	1. Stochastic gradient descent regression
2. Bernoulli naive Bayes	10. Kernel SVM	2. Lasso Regression (Least absolute selection and shrinkage operator)
3. Decision tree (DT)	11. Multinomial naive Bayes	3. Elastic Net Regression
4. Extremely randomized trees	12. Passive aggressive	4. Ridge Regression
5. Gaussian naive Bayes	13. Quadratic Discriminant Analysis	5. Ensemble Regression
6. Gradient boosting (GB)	14. Random forest (RF)	6. Support Vector Regression (Radial Basis function)
7. kNN	15. Linear Class (SGD)	7. Support Vector Regression (Kernal = Linear)
8. Linear Discriminant Analysis		

Hence the physical storage layer's function is to store the ML model details, specific meta data and the serialized form of Machine learning model created in a database for easy storage and retrieval. Indexing is a technique used on data that is to be stored in database prior to its introduction into the database. This leads to organized storage and a simplified retrieval.

SOLR is an open-source parallel SQL supporting search platform that performs NRT (Near Real Time) search. NRT makes the data that is being indexed readily available for search because Solr does not block updates

Table 11.3 Layers and corresponding responsibilities.

Layer	Software components	Responsibilities
External Interface Layer	Input Interface Layer for Preference Selection	GUI Design for preference selector and Communicating to pre-processing level
	Output Interface Layer	
Decision Engine	Classification Based Decision Engine	Algorithm to Find if given dataset is suitable for classification or regression
	Regression Based Decision Engine	
Processing Layer –	Data Cleaning	Data cleaning through handling i. Missing Data, ii. Noisy Data, iii. Normalization, iv. Attribute Selection, v. Discretization, vi. Concept Hierarchy generation, vii. Data reduction using aggregation, attribute subset selection, and viii. dimensionality reduction
	Data Reduction	
	Data Transformation	
	Model Search	
	Hyper Parameter Tuning	
Physical storage Layer	Databases and Data sets	Indexing and Storing the database and ML model details
Languages and Frameworks and editors used: Angular JS, HTML, CSS, Java, Bootstrap4, Auto Sk-learn, Pandas, VS Code, Google colab, Eclipse, HBase, SOLR		

while commit is being performed. This is due to the availability of "soft commit" which is less expensive variant of commit statement that makes data available for search when it is in progress. Secondly Solr runs on top of Lucene, a java search library which performs inverted indexing. An inverted index maps terms to the documents where they are present Hbase is used for storage and Solr is used for indexing. Table 11.1 depicts the characteristics of Classification and Regression Problems, Table 11.2 comprehends Classification and Regression algorithms supported by auto-sk learn, and Table 11.3 describes the layers and corresponding responsibilities

11.5   Analysis of Results

The working of project is explained through three example test cases

1. Case 1: Sonar Dataset – Classification
2. Case 2: Indian Liver Patient Data set – Classification
3. Case 3: Automobile Insurance claim dataset – Regression

Case 1: Sonar Dataset – Classification

This dataset was used by Gorman and Sejnowski to study the study of classification of sonar signals and predict whether the sonar signal is reflected off a mine or rock. Here the sonar signals are obtained by bouncing them of a metal cylindrical rock. In the dataset each pattern is a combination of 60 numbers confined within the range 0.0 to 1.0. When the energy of a particular frequency band is integrated over a period of time the numbers afore mentioned is arrived. The 61st column consists of either the letter 'R' or 'M' indicating if that particular signal was reflected of a rock ('R') or a mine ('M'). The dataset contains 208 such observations of sonar signals

a. Set of Sampling Apertures
b. Sampling aperture super imposed over short term Fourier transform
c. Spectral envelope (Calculated by integration over each sampling aperture

Case 1: ML Model Evaluation details

Best model for the Sonar dataset as predicted by the proposed ML framework is shown in Figure 11.3. The results obtained by using the best model is described with the help of a confusion matrix as shown in Figure 11.4.

```
auto-sklearn results:
  Dataset name: 895eb0abbd8857d94c2a66baf6d71c28
  Metric: accuracy
  Best validation score: 0.914286
  Number of target algorithm runs: 47
  Number of successful target algorithm runs: 38
  Number of crashed target algorithm runs: 1
  Number of target algorithms that exceeded the time limit: 8
  Number of target algorithms that exceeded the memory limit: 0
```

Figure 11.3 Best model for Case 1 – Sonar dataset.

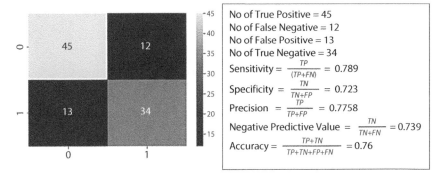

Figure 11.4 Model performance metrics for Case 1 – Sonar dataset.

Case 2: Indian Liver Patient Data set – Classification

This data set contains 441 male patient records and 142 female patient records. The patient details stored contains the following information: Age of the patient, Gender of the patient, Total Bilirubin – Direct Bilirubin, Alkaline Phosphatase, Alamine Aminotransferase, Aspartate Aminotransferase, Total Proteins, Albumin, Albumin and Globulin Ratio, Diagnosis. The dataset contains 416 liver disease patients and 167 non liver disease patients.

Case 2: ML Model Evaluation details

Best model for the Sonar dataset as predicted by the proposed ML framework is shown in Figure 11.5. The results obtained by using the best model is described with the help of a confusion matrix as shown in Figure 11.6.

```
auto-sklearn results:
  Dataset name: 25a39c844142a2f66cb8320c2f16d60f
  Metric: accuracy
  Best validation score: 0.751938
  Number of target algorithm runs: 53
  Number of successful target algorithm runs: 51
  Number of crashed target algorithm runs: 0
  Number of target algorithms that exceeded the time limit: 2
  Number of target algorithms that exceeded the memory limit: 0
```

Figure 11.5 Best model for Case 2 – Liver Patients dataset.

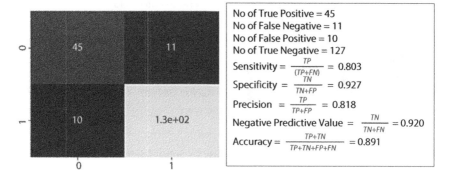

Figure 11.6 Model performance metrics for Case 2 – Liver Patients dataset.

Case 3: Automobile Insurance claim dataset – Regression

It is a regression problem that involves predicting the total payment for all claims in Swedish currency (kronor), given the total number of claim. There are 63 such records in the dataset. The variable names are Number of claims, Total payment for all claims in thousands of Swedish Kronor.

Case 3: ML Model Evaluation details

Best model for the Sonar dataset as predicted by the proposed ML framework is shown in Figure 11.7.

```
auto-sklearn results:
  Dataset name: ff51291d93f33237099d48c48ee0f9ad
  Metric: r2
  Best validation score: 0.844561
  Number of target algorithm runs: 58
  Number of successful target algorithm runs: 48
  Number of crashed target algorithm runs: 9
  Number of target algorithms that exceeded the time limit: 1
  Number of target algorithms that exceeded the memory limit: 0

MAE: 24.797
```

Figure 11.7 Best model for Case 3: Automobile Insurance claim dataset – Regression.

11.6   Results and Discussion

Though there are research works undertaken in the area of microservices and machine learning separately, this work understands the afore-mentioned researches and aims to expose Machine learning as micro service. The machine learning entity like other microservices is loosely coupled. Hence it has better testability, swappable components, scalability, and Isolation. The project tries to redefine ERPs as plugin architecture with various components getting added and removed according to client's requirements without any hindrance. From the client's point of view the end to end experience from the selection of the data set to running of prediction service will be seamless due to selection of most appropriate tools for every layer in the conceptual architecture.

The main motive of this work is "composing a micro application from an existing dataset and use the data present in it to create a prediction service" and was successfully completed. The usage of automated machine learning made sure that the first objective of "abstracting the complexities of ML code from client" was achieved. The three cases of datasets showcased for classification regression were taken from biomedical, Communication, Finance fields respectively indicating the domain agnostic nature of project i.e. second objective of Creating a domain agnostic system' is achieved. There were 48 and 53 target algorithms run for Case 1 and Case 2 to achieve an accuracy of 76% and 89%, respectively; 58 target algorithms run for Case 3 achieving a mean absolute error of 24.797. Despite the efficient selection of individual tools and platform the system suffers from acute integration issues. Accuracy as obtained in the machine learning algorithm can be further improved if implemented with the deep learning heuristics techniques. However, the increased time taken during neural network technique implementation will not go hand in hand with Collabrr platforms' aim to compose and deliver micro-application almost instantly.

With a rapid evolution in the field of security, there is possibility to incorporate authentication into the prediction service. Based on the authenticated ID, the personnel of an enterprise can be classified into different levels, while some can create and alter an ML model, some can use only the prediction service, and the rest can only view the results of prediction service.

References

1. Apache cTAKES™, natural language processing system for extraction of information from electronic medical record clinical free text, 2021, http://ctakes.apache.org/index.html.
2. Černý, T., Donahoo, M., Trnka, M., Contextual understanding of microservice architecture: Current and future directions. *ACM SIGAPP Applied Computing Review*, vol. 17, pp. 29–45, 2018, 10.1145/3183628.3183631.
3. Lynch, C.M., Abdollahi, B., Fuqua, J.D., de Carlo, A.R., Bartholomai, J.A., Balgemann, R.N., van Berkel, V.H., Frieboes, H.B., Prediction of lung cancer patient survival via supervised machine learning classification techniques. *Int. J. Med. Inform.*, 108, 1-8, 1386–5056, 2017, https://doi.org/10.1016/j.ijmedinf.2017.09.013.
4. Freire, J. *et al.*, PipelineProfiler: A visual analytics tool for the exploration of AutoML pipelines. *IEEE Trans. Vis. Comput. Graph.*, 27, 2, 390–400, Feb. 2021, doi: 10.1109/TVCG.2020.3030361.
5. Tuggener, L., Amirian, M., Rombach, K., Lörwald, S., Varlet, A., Westermann, C., Stadelmann, T., Automated machine learning in practice: State of the art and recent results. *2019 6th Swiss Conference on Data Science (SDS)*, Bern, Switzerland, pp. 31–36, 2019, doi: 10.1109/SDS.2019.00-11.
6. Kamdar, J.H., Jeba Praba, J., Georrge, J.J., Artificial intelligence in medical diagnosis: Methods, algorithms and applications, in: *Machine Learning with Healthcare Perspective. Learning and Analytics in Intelligent Systems*, vol. 13, V. Jain and J. Chatterjee (Eds.), pp. 27–37, Springer, Cham, 2020, https://doi.org/10.1007/978-3-030-40850-3_2.
7. Kadhm, M.S., Ghindawi, I.W., Mhawi, D.E., An accurate diabetes prediction system based on K-means clustering and proposed classification approach. *Int. J. Appl. Eng. Res.*, 13, 6, 0973–4562, 2018, https://www.researchgate.net/publication/323945877_An_Accurate_Diabetes_Prediction_System_Based_on_K-means_Clustering_and_Proposed_Classification_Approach.
8. Alshuqayran, N., Ali, N., Evans, R., Towards micro service architecture recovery: An empirical study. *2018 IEEE International Conference on Software Architecture (ICSA)*, Seattle, WA, USA, pp. 47–4709, 2018, doi: 10.1109/ICSA.2018.00014.

9. Di Francesco, P., Lago, P., Malavolta, I., Architecting with microservices: A systematic mapping study. *J. Syst. Software*, 150, 77–97, 2019, https://doi.org/10.1016/j.jss.2019.01.001.

10. Ge, P., Analysis on approaches and structures of automated machine learning frameworks. *2020 International Conference on Communications, Information System and Computer Engineering (CISCE)*, Kuala Lumpur, Malaysia, pp. 474–477, 2020, doi:10.1109/CISCE50729.2020.00106.

11. Rahman, A.K.M., Shamrat, F.M., Tasnim, Z., Roy, J., Hossain, S., A comparative study on liver disease prediction using supervised machine learning algorithms. 8, 419–422, 2019.

12. Shah, P., Kendall, F., Khozin, S., Artificial intelligence and machine learning in clinical development: A translational perspective. *NPJ Digit. Med.*, 2, 69, 1–5, 2019, https://doi.org/10.1038/s41746-019-0148-3.

13. Maliha, S.K., Ema, R.R., Ghosh, S.K., Ahmed, H., Mollick, M.R.J., Islam, T., Cancer disease prediction using naive bayes, k-nearest neighbor and J48 algorithm. *2019 10th International Conference on Computing, Communication and Networking Technologies (ICCCNT)*, pp. 1–7, 2019, https://doi.org/10.1109/ICCCNT45670.2019.8944686.

14. Singaravelu, M., Rajapraksh, S., Krishnan, S., Karthik, K., Classification of liver patient dataset using machine learning algorithms. *Int. J. Eng. Technol. (UAE)*, 7, 323–326, 2018, 10.14419/ijet.v7i3.34.19217.

15. Uddin, S., Khan, A., Hossain, M., Comparing different supervised machine learning algorithms for disease prediction. *BMC Med. Inform. Decis. Mak.*, 19, 281, 1–16, 2019, https://doi.org/10.1186/s12911-019-1004-8.

16. Garciarena, U., Santana, R., Mendiburu, A., Analysis of the complexity of the automatic pipeline generation problem. *2018 IEEE Congress on Evolutionary Computation (CEC)*, Rio de Janeiro, Brazil, pp. 1–8, 2018, doi: 10.1109/CEC.2018.8477662.

17. https://www.cs.cornell.edu/courses/cs4787/2019sp/notes/lecture16.pdf.

18. https://www.kaggle.com/edhenrivi/introduction-classification-sonar-dataset.

19. https://machinelearningmastery.com/standard-machine-learning-datasets/.

20. https://automl.github.io/auto-sklearn/master/.

Part III

E-LEARNING APPLICATIONS

12

Virtual Teaching Activity Monitor

Sakthivel S.* and Akash Ram R.K.

Department of Electronics and Communications Engineering, Amrita Vishwa, Vidyapeetham, Chennai, India

Abstract

In the current COVID-19 scenario, every aspect of daily life is reliant on the virtual world, and a virtual classroom is no exception. During this pandemic, we have learned that adjusting to a new normal is the best way to survive. As a result, online classes became the sole way to get an education. Adapting teaching tactics to the students' attention status can make eLearning platforms more personalized. Students' attention states are divided into three categories: attentive, drowsiness, and yawning. The analysis of student involvement helps to nurture those emotions and behavioral patterns that are helpful to gaining knowledge, therefore boosting the instructional process effectively. To keep an eLearning classroom running well, you'll need the correct monitoring software. The suggested attention estimation technique aims to bridge the gap between an online classroom and a traditional offline classroom. So, I felt these add-ons are required: Network Speed, Attention Detector, Head Movements, Efficient Attendance system, and Text classification. By implementing these add-ons, we can achieve student-centered teaching.

Keywords: eLearning, attention states, head pose estimation, attendance's system, Eye Aspect Ratio (EAR), facial feature detection

12.1   Introduction

A teacher can instantly detect a student's emotional state and change lectures accordingly, maximizing their attention and engagement. To give a high-quality eLearning system the software should be very user friendly and also needs to monitor the students so they should be dynamic in their

---

Corresponding author: sakthijaya10022@gmail.com

K. Umamaheswari, B. Vinoth Kumar and S. K. Somasundaram (eds.) *Artificial Intelligence for Sustainable Applications*, (199–218) © 2023 Scrivener Publishing LLC

approach. To deliver a tailored learning process, today's eLearning attempts to be firmly student-centered/student-based. Nowadays the lessons taught by the instructors are not effectively conveyed to the student's online mode of education. Although online and remote modes of education are not the same, they can easily be turned into ineffective platforms for learning if the teachers do not provide high-quality and interesting instruction. Many teachers were caught off guard by the COVID-19 outbreak, and they were obliged to teach typical offline courses on an online platform. In addition, in order to provide the most effective learning experience possible, this condition necessitates the provision of content with high-quality course materials. Providing course information to students, conducting lectures, and providing study resources as a reference are some of the top priorities that can be problematic in this mode of eLearning platforms. In this perspective, using a student-centered teaching method makes perfect sense for the online mode of education. In order to achieve the goals of this paper, students should be engaged in classes in addition to having access to all of these priorities. This is a crucial component that encourages a thorough comprehension of the concepts, making it a key aspect of the learning process.

Instructors should adapt and employ some online technologies to meet all of these goals. Only then can students be guaranteed a high-quality and engaging experience; here is where the student-centered idea comes into play. According to the feedback of many educators online, this form of teaching can be divided into three main interactive ways that focus on different parts of engaging and learning. The three forms of relationship are important for an active eLearning experience those are student content engagement, student's interaction with themselves, and student instructor engagement. Student–content interaction focuses on an active learning experience with content that incorporates student-involved activities, so students will do something useful and in connection with the course content supplied in addition to reading. This would allow them to reflect on their grasp of the material through tasks such as drafting a summary of the chapters taught, jotting down significant points and takeaways, and formulating their questions from the syllabus to stimulate the students' thinking process. All of these tasks can be given as a follow-up assignment, along with polls and flipping the web conference lecture to allow students to prepare and present their own subjects.

Then there's the student-student interaction, which makes students feel like they're part of a community even though they're all attending classes separately. This is possible through activities such as role-playing, debate, peer-group projects such as writing assignments, presentations, study groups, and so on. When this type of interactive academic environment between the students is created, it will kick start the students' higher-order thinking skills, which are impossible to develop through studying the subject. Student-instructor contact is the next and final type of primary interaction required in digital classrooms. It is also one of the most important of the three. Since all other interactions are really supplements to the main meal, designed to increase student engagement, improve thinking abilities, and promote productivity, this interaction serves as the foundation for the entire teaching system.

More than just questions and answers must be exchanged between the instructor and the pupils. Regular, substantive, and instructor-led interactions are expected from the teachers. Participation in class material conversations with students, as well as putting effort into each assignment, such as creating a video to explain the task and sharing it alongside the assignment, are examples of this, as well as meetings to address various class-related issues, acquainting students with them by demonstrating active social involvement, and providing feedback on classes and assignments. The proposed model's extensions and tools help with the majority of these interactions. Many of the requirements of digital classrooms and the methodologies described above can be automated, and some time-consuming processes can be handled so that educators can devote more time to student-centered instruction.

The attention monitor tool presented in this paper as shown in Figure 12.1 uses a process of eye tracking to do face detection effectively. This mainly measures the eye movement compared to the head position to know where the student is looking at. Even emotion can be detected with eye-tracking hardware and a statistical program. This mainly lets us know about the level of excitement shown with the help of the frames taken while the classes via webcam. There are many parameters like pupil size, blink rate, and gaze. Especially the pupil size can let us know whether the

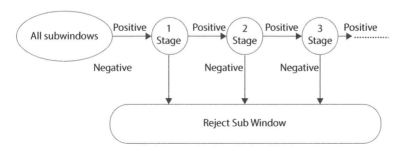

Figure 12.1 Schematic depiction of the detection cascade.

emotional reaction is positive or negative to the class serving as real-time feedback to instructors. This method helps us include a feature that lets us know and flash the direction the student is looking on the monitor so that they could get back on track with the class immediately.

Internet-based applications attempt to meet contemporary educational needs by bridging the gap [1] between traditional teaching methods and future developments in technology-enhanced learning. Various developed e-learning systems fall short of this goal by lacking features such as customized media settings, monitoring learners' input, and relevant remarks of the students [2]. The current evaluation monitors the student's focus and warns them when necessary. It also detects the head movements (rotational and translational) of a user's head, as well as the directionality of his eye look, are two significant issues for assessing the attention of the student when beside a computer monitor. This need is reflected in the development of cutting-edge technologies that can measure a student's focus during eLearning classes. Biometric sensors can provide valuable insight into a student's mental health [3], but they can also cause physical discomfort for the student, as well as hardware costs and logistical issues. As a result, non-invasive systems such as log analysis [4] and inexpensive devices already installed on PCs [5], such as a webcam [6], are recommended.

A good face detection system should be able to recognize a person's face in a photograph or video frame. It shouldn't matter what posture the face is in for this purpose, nor what age, gender, or ethnicity the persons/people to be classified are. In addition to this, Changes in illumination or other environmental constraints should not affect a good face detection model [7]. For detecting faces we can use the face library which is available in OpenCV, which includes Face detection model that has been pre-trained as well as the ability to train your own classifiers. Frontal face, facial landmark, and full person detection are all supported by Haar-like and local binary pattern data which are pre-trained classifiers. Several thousand images of faces and images where faces are not there should be collected if you need a self-trained classifier are utilized. A good training set takes into account faces of various ages, genders, ethnicities, facial hair, lighting, and hairstyles. Because of the complexity of the training approach, only pre-trained classifiers like Haar cascade and the local binary pattern are used for frontal faces detection.

Cascaded classifiers are used to implement the Haar cascade and the local binary pattern classifier in order to swiftly eliminate images which doesn't have faces while maintaining high accuracy for positive outcomes (FACES) (see Figure 12.2). Before recognizing faces, several

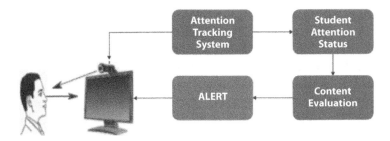

Figure 12.2 Alert system block diagram.

pre-processing measures such as resizing the image to a lower resolution are taken to accommodate for changes in illumination, face orientation, background, and hairstyle. This, it is assumed, permits the classifiers to be used not only to confined environments, but also to any [8]. The Haar cascade classifier is considered as a viable face detection algorithm. Even though OpenCV's LBP classifier is efficient in terms of time, but it's less precise and so it cannot consistently recognize faces in an artificially lit office space. The Haar cascade classifier seems to be a little slower than Local binary patterns classifier, but it can still categorize images into faces and non-faces consistently in an unconstrained environment. The equivalent Haar cascade eye detectors are used to identify the left and right eye in a picture.

Present log-in based attendances system is also not that much trustworthy so we have used facial recognition attendances system [9] this was to ensure that not only student is inside the eLearning platform but also paying attention to the class. So, it is vital to have an efficient attendance marking system. Most of the time the faculty members get a common excuses like network issue from students for not answering when they were called so to avoid this, we will update the network speed in a shared excel sheet. Online classes end up causing students to get more documents relating to their subjects, so we have created a text classification system based on the Nave-Bayes Algorithm to classify them according to their subjects.

12.2 Related Works

There are various researches in this literature that deal with detecting a student's facial emotion. Only a few of them concentrate on detecting the students' attention. In [10] the author proposed that the user's comfort and emotional state are inextricably linked. The author devised a system for the perception of posture [11] through the analysis the amount of pressure the body exerts on the chair. For this, they employed a chair with pressure sensors. The technology employs computer vision techniques to map in real time the pressure distribution obtained from sensors on the seat. [12] proposed a neuro-fuzzy method for inferring a student's focus status in front of a monitor utilizing a web camera. In [6] the author proposed detecting the position and movement of particular spots surrounding the eyes, as well as the position of the iris, to measure the level of attention and interest of a user reading content on a computer. The system examines user behavior and generates a model which segregates the status into an six learner state levels which are frustrated, not focusing on the content, looking tired, distracted by the surroundings, focusing on the content, on all ears).

This paper [13] focuses on improving the students' presence and attention in online classes since many of the students try to skip the classes whenever possible. To create a more responsible and monitored online mode of education a method is proposed that involves a calculated outcome of roll numbers which changes every session. Here there was a sample of 20 students taken and every session had five different roll numbers who should be answering in order to get the attendance. In the case of having several classes on the same day, this system will cover every roll number at least once a day. After the implementation of this concept, the attendance and the response from the students' side has been highly increased when compared to the before week, this system was implemented to the week after its implementation. This may be because many students would have been aware of this and stayed attentive in classes which were the main objective of this paper. This also shows the gradual increase in the attentiveness in classes in graphs where the average response of the students per day is measured on a scale of one to five, where the five credits are given to a student if there are 5 classes in a day and as per the questioning system if they respond every time.

This smart online monitoring system is developed based on a shuffling algorithm to shuffle students' roll numbers for the questions to be asked by the teacher. Here the shuffling is done with the implementation of the Fisher-yates shuffle algorithm, this is used so there won't be any repetition of roll numbers in the same session. The simulation of the Fisher-Yates algorithm is done through hash mapping as this allows the model to pick M number of elements from the whole set ranging from 0 to N where $0<M<N$. This paper suggests having this feature of theirs be added to online platforms like Microsoft, Google, and Zoom as add-ons to get

this effective tool for monitoring everywhere thereby increasing the standard of online classes.

Unlike the previous paper, the proposed solution by the paper [26] for effective attendance and attention monitoring in the online mode of learning uses signal processing applications, particularly image processing. The main intention of this paper is to design a virtual teaching activity monitor which can efficiently follow students' activities and report actual non-attentive conduct by not marking students' attendance. Because internet teaching has so many limits and drawbacks, it must be successfully countered by some effective technique. The method described in the paper for this purpose follows a unique procedure in which the students are unaware of the instances and frames taken and used for effectively marking attendance.

This data is directly obtained from the students' webcams, after which it is processed locally and then further processed by the client, i.e., the instructor, to filter out the necessary observations, and then the computed data is delivered to the teachers for their use. Before capturing the images for marking attendance, it checks the internet connectivity to ensure that it is working well, thus if the students' internet is not working properly, the pictures will not be taken since it is a real explanation.

The LBPH algorithm is then used to match the faces while processing the data taken in the face recognition process to monitor the students. The crucial data will be sent to the teacher and then uploaded to a database. Following that, each student's attention history and status will be displayed in their respective account, which can be viewed by students for reference so that they may see what their respective attendance percentage is and pay more attention to courses if necessary. This technique is incredibly compact for today's times, as well as totally automated, thus there will be no manual errors in this model.

This research [14] focuses on a daily online attendance monitoring system that has a simple process and produces accurate data. As opposed to offline classrooms, where teachers are fully permitted to check and supervise student presence, the online classroom setting is frequently left unmonitored. This system was created to address this issue, and the results are well-organized and easily available to the administrator or teacher, as absentees are represented in the attendance report by a blank seat. Once students have logged into the class, cameras check their presence. If the student is in front of the camera facing the screen and the seat is occupied, the attendance will be supplied; if a vacant seat is identified, the student will be marked absent. Because it will be updated on a regular basis, any modifications will be stored for inclusion in the final report, as well as letting the teachers know when the student was absent.

The entire report generating process is automated, resulting in a faster workflow than human attendance monitoring and registration, which is less reliable and efficient than the model suggested in the study. Because all of these data are processed, saved, and delivered to teachers, it's difficult to overlook any information on a student's attendance. Using image processing, the major goal of this work was to create a simple, rapid, and automatic attendance report that was easy to read. This strategy also resulted in a significant rise in average student attendance since pupils were more responsible because they were monitored during class hours. This paper also includes a rating of students' attendance on a scale of one to five, as well as a classification to provide final comments on the attendance marked. Because everything is automated, it also eliminates the possibility of human error. From the perspective of image processing applications, this model focuses primarily on facial recognition, which is employed in the context of an attendance monitoring system.

12.3 Methodology

12.3.1 Head Movement

We can obtain the 3D coordinate information of each frame image using a typical facial statistical measurement model, and then the rotation and translation matrices, which represent the mapping relationship between 2D and 3D models. To determine a student's 3D posture in a photograph, the coordinates are required:

1. 2D coordinates: As illustrated in Figure 12.3, a few points in the image's 2D x and y coordinates are required. In the instance of a face, we can choose the corners of both the eyes, the nose tip, the mouth's left and right corner, and so on. The face landmark detector in Dlib gives us a lot of options to pick from. The nose tip, chin, left eye's left corner, right eye's right corner, mouth's left corner, and mouth's right corner will all be used in this paper.

2. Locations of identical coordinates in 3D: The 3D coordinates of the 2D feature points are required. These are called as World Coordinates (also known as Model Coordinates in OpenCV docs).

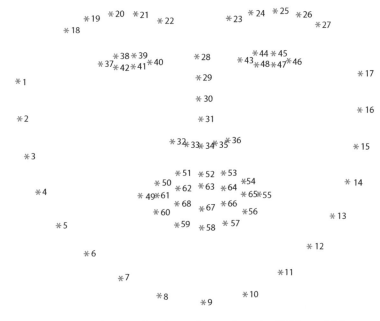

Figure 12.3 Sixty-eight facial landmark coordinates from the iBUG 300-W dataset.

a) The mouth's left corner coordinates are: [-150, -150, -125]
b) The mouth's right corner coordinates are: [150, -150, -125]
c) Chin coordinates are given by [0, -330, -65]
d) The right eye's right corner coordinates are: [225, 170, -135]
e) The left eye's left corner coordinates are [-225f, 170f, -135]
f) Nose tip is given by [0, 0, 0]

In OpenCV, to estimate pose, there are two ways one is solvePnP and the other is solvePnPRansac functions. Here we have used solvePnP function, the solvePnP function in OpenCV is mostly used for pose estimation. We can utilize the coordinates of a person's key features to follow their activity by observing their gestures if we have the coordinates of their key features. It is commonly used to prevent malpractice via video monitoring a person using artificial intelligence, particularly in online tests. Other applications of solvePnP in position estimation include motion tracking, augmented reality, and robot training. We can then find the angle of deviation of these points and then we will be able to determine at which direction the student is looking at we have three possibilities in our model i.e., Forward, Looking Left, and Looking Right.

12.3.2   Drowsiness and Yawn Detection

Many methods have been developed for detecting drowsiness in a video sequence. Different methods such as correlation between opened and closed eye patterns are matched [15] a heuristic image intensity projected perpendicularly or flatly oriented over the eye [16] active shape models [17] fitting of a mathematical model to find the eye lids [18] and Sparse tracking is used to estimate motion in the ocular area from optical flow. [19] or adaptive thresholding with frame-to-frame brightness discretization, have been used to interpret the status of the eye lids whether it's in an open state or closed state from a picture. The earlier methods had the primary flaw of implicitly imposing too strict setup requirements, such as a relation to camera-to-face posture (motion of the forehead), quality of an image, illumination, the principles of mobility, and so on. In spite of their actual real time environment's performance, unprocessed picture intensity heuristic techniques are usually extremely sensitive. Here we are using facial landmark detection as shown in Figure 12.3 to find important face characteristics like the eyes, brows, nose, ears, and lips. Here we have used Haar cascade classifier to detect the face. The Haar cascade classifier is a simple face identification approach that can be used as a foundation for more complicated algorithms. Many diverse things, such as faces, cars, or even humans, can be learned using a large dataset. Haar classifier characteristics (Two Haar characteristics are shown in Figure 12.4) are used to classify images that are generated with integral photographs, really quickly. As a result, local knowledge can be taken into account.

There seem to be 180,000 different Haar-like features in images with a resolution of 24x24 pixels. The feature set included around 180,000 of them, which were reduced to 6000 using machine learning techniques, which will be explained in greater depth here. Because they will be too random to find anything, the majority of these features will be irrelevant to the face features. So, they needed a Feature Selection technique to pick a subset of characteristics from a large set that would not only select the features that performed better than the others, but also exclude the ones that were irrelevant. They employed the AdaBoost Boosting Technique, in which each of the 180,000 features was individually applied to the images to create Weak Learners. Some of them had low error rates because they were better at distinguishing Positive from Negative images than the rest, while others were not. These weak learners are programmed to misclassify

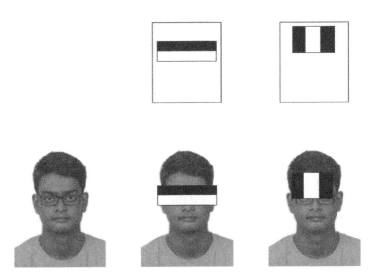

Figure 12.4 The first two Haar-like features.

a small number of images. They are capable of outperforming a random estimate. Their final collection of features was reduced to a total of 6000 by using this strategy.

The next level is the Attentional Cascade [20] in two stages. In this instance, not every function needs to be activated on every window. We might conclude that the facial attributes are missing if a feature fails on a certain window. As a result, we can navigate to the following windows, which may contain face traits. Various characteristics are applied to the images in stages. The features in the earlier stages are simpler than those in the latter stages, which are complex enough to recognize the smallest details on the face. Only once the first stage's features have been discovered in the image will the second stage processing begin. The procedure repeats itself as per Equation 12.1, with the window being passed on to the next step if it passes the first, and being discarded if it fails the second.

$$Hf(x) = 1, \text{ if } p_j f_j(x) < Pj\theta j$$
$$0, \text{ else}$$

(12.1)

There are 38 stages in total, with approximately 6000 features. In the first five levels, there are 1, 10, 25, 25, and 50 features, with the number increasing in succeeding stages. The early stages with fewer and simpler features removed the majority of the windows without any facial features, lowering the false negative ratio, whereas the later stages with more complex and numerous features can focus on lowering the error detection rate, lowering the false positive ratio, and achieving a low false positive ratio.

The EAR (Eye Aspect Ratio) must be computed from landmarks in an image, which is utilized to assess the eye-opening state. Right and left eye is depicted with six x and y coordinates (Q1, Q2, Q3, Q4, Q5 and Q6 as shown in Figure 12.5), starting at the eye's left corner, as though watching the camera, and proceeding circular motion rotating in the right direction around the rest of the region. There is a correlation between the breadth and altitude of these coordinates. We may then come up with a formula that expresses the correlation termed the EAR (Eye Aspect Ratio) based on work done by [21].

$$\text{Eye Aspect Ratio} = \frac{\|Q2 - Q6\| + \|Q3 - Q5\|}{2\|Q1 - Q4\|} \tag{12.2}$$

The distance between perpendicular eye points is computed in the dividend, while the divisor calculates the distance between flat eye coordinates. Once we have determined EAR (Eye Aspect Ratio), we can use it to identify whether or not the student is DROWSY – When the eyes are awake, the EAR (Eye Aspect Ratio) will be relatively constant, but will rapidly approach 0 during drowsiness, then increase when the eye opens. The dividend computes the distance between perpendicular eye landmarks, while the divisor computes the distance between flatly oriented eye landmarks.

So, when the EAR tends to zero, we will alert the student the same process has been implemented for yawn detection here we have extracted the mouth's points of interest (49–68 facial-points in Figure 12.3).

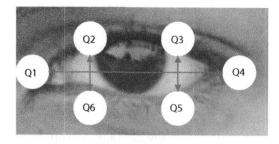

Figure 12.5 The six facial landmarks associated with the opening of an eye.

12.3.3   Attendance System

To implement the facial recognition-based attendances system [9] first we must train our model with the student's images dataset shown in Figure 12.6, training a Deep Convolutional Neural Network [22] is the most reliable approach to measure a face. A Deep Neural Network reliably returns a collection of 128 points on a face when a picture is fed through it. These measures serve as the face's unique identity. These measurements are referred to as embeddings. We need to train the model to obtain 128 measures for every face in our dataset. 128 measurements of each face are referred to as an embedding by machine learning experts. In machine learning, the concept of reducing complex raw input, such as a photograph, to a list of machines generated digits comes up quite often. Run the students' face photographs through the pre-trained model to acquire the 128 measurements for each face. The values for our test image are shown in Figure 12.7. The matching is done by utilizing a basic machine learning classification technique like the linear SVM classifier to discover the individual who has the nearest parameters to our test image in our database of known people. If the person matches any of the test images, the Support Vector Machine returns the student's ID number/Roll Number, after getting the roll Number we will update the attendances in the excel sheet.

12.3.4   Network Speed

This feature helps to monitor the student's internet connectivity [23]. It is a feature written in Python for monitoring real-time internet usage and speeds for both download and upload. We will also upload the time at which the student has taken the speed test. So, the student can update the network speed periodically.

Figure 12.6 Dataset used for building our model.

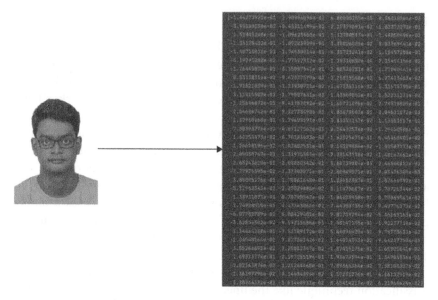

Figure 12.7 One hundred twenty-eight feature values have been extracted from student image.

12.3.5   Text Classification

Text classification has long been regarded as a critical way for managing and processing a large number of digital documents that are widely distributed and growing. Especially in the online classes we used to get large number of documents for references or study purpose mostly these things are sent on daily basis but if the student didn't classify it on regular basis, he/she is going to have a hard time before exams. So as to classify them we have used Naive Bayes classifiers [24, 25]. Naive Bayes classifiers have been widely used for text categorization and content analysis machine learning problems. The Bayes' Theorem Equation 12.3 forms the base from which we have derived the Naïve Bayes algorithm. It's a group of algorithms that all work on the same principle: each pair of features being classified is independent of the others. The dataset consists of two elements which are a description matrix and a resultant vector:

- The Description/feature matrix (R) contains the values of dependent features for each of the dataset's vectors (row). w is the number of features, so R = (r1,r2,r2, rw).

- The Resultant/targeted vector (S) for each row of the feature matrix, holds the value of the class/group variable.

$$P(Y|Z) = \frac{P(Z|Y)P(Y)}{P(Z)} \tag{12.3}$$

We state our problem as follows: we define information matrix as R and the resultant vectors as s:

$$P(s|R) = \frac{P(R|s)P(s)}{PR)} \tag{12.4}$$

where s denotes a variable's class and R denotes a dependent feature vector of dimension w, namely the $R = (R_1, R_2, R_3...R_w)$, and w is the number of variables/features in the sample.

Consider that all of R's qualities are mutually independent, and that they are conditional on the category s and applying the "nave" conditional independence assumptions we get Equation 12.5.

$$P(s|r_1, r_2,...r_w) = \frac{P(s)\prod_{i=1}^{w} P(xi|y)}{P(r1)P(r2)......P(rw)} \tag{12.5}$$

Lastly, we must simply identify the output with the highest probability for all potential values of the class variable s in order to determine the probability of a given sample for all possible values of the class variable s:

$$s = \arg\max yP(s)\prod_{(i=1)}^{n} P(ri|s) \tag{12.6}$$

12.4   Results and Discussion

As you can see in Figure 12.8, the attention states are found in the first image the student is looking forward and his eyes are wide-open but in the second one the student's eyes are slight closed and his head is tilted left so we display the Drowsiness alert and at last image the student is yawning so we throw a yawn alert. Below (see Figure 12.9) is the network speed

Figure 12.8 Attention states.

	A	B
1		
2	Rollnumber	In Time
3	19D010	22:40:36
4	19D004	22:44:47
5	19D062	22:45:12
6	19D005	22:45:14
7	19D066	22:45:15
8	19D015	22:45:19
9	19D039	22:45:38
10	19D023	22:45:44
11	19D029	22:45:54
12	19D025	22:45:59
13	19D019	22:46:10
14	19D012	22:46:10

Figure 12.9 Attendances using facial recognition (Excel sheet and real-time example).

of a student that has been uploaded in the excel sheet. We can see that it has been uploaded with the date and time so that Professors/Teachers can verify. For the attendances system the camera will recognize a person's face in real time, compute face encoding for the identified face, and compare the encodings to the encodings computed during the model's training and if it's matched then will update the attendances in excel (see Figure 12.10) sheet. Here (see Figure 12.11) I have used newspaper articles as a dataset (11,314 documents, 1,385,334 words in total) to classify and got an accuracy score of about 87% which is a decent one we can increase it by increasing the features but by doing this we are over-fitting our model and the time taken will also be more.

	A	B	C
1			
2	Date and Time	Download	Upload
3	24-09-2021 23:29:37	28.55	19.65

Figure 12.10 Network speed.

	precision	recall	f1-score	support
0	0.88	0.90	0.89	114
1	0.63	0.83	0.71	152
2	0.96	0.65	0.78	139
3	0.61	0.82	0.70	152
4	0.76	0.89	0.82	138
5	0.85	0.82	0.84	153
6	0.83	0.69	0.75	147
7	0.81	0.90	0.85	137
8	0.94	0.91	0.93	131
9	0.91	0.94	0.93	135
10	0.98	0.95	0.97	136
11	0.93	0.97	0.95	145
12	0.92	0.69	0.79	157
13	0.98	0.94	0.96	151
14	0.96	0.88	0.92	155
15	0.84	0.94	0.88	159
16	0.89	0.91	0.90	140
17	0.96	0.92	0.94	149
18	0.84	0.85	0.84	138
19	0.81	0.60	0.69	101
accuracy			0.85	2829
macro avg	0.87	0.85	0.85	2829

Figure 12.11 Text classification results.

12.5 Conclusions

Teachers and Professors can use this computerized technology to gain a better understanding of their students and design their course content that is more suitable for online education. As the pandemic is going to over now these could be implemented in the offline classes too, so the teacher or the professor can deliver the content even more effectively and also statistic data collection of student's attentions can give insights about student's interest and the professors can guide the student accordingly. eLearning platforms like NPTEL can use this to alert the student when required. In future OCR (Optical Character Recognition) could be used to convert the exam sheets into digital docs which can be provided to text classification for correction. So, by putting the principles outlined above into practice, we were able to develop a Virtual Teaching Activity Monitor.

References

1. Athi Narayanan, S., Prasanth, M., Mohan, P., Kaimal, M.R., Bijlani, K., Attention analysis in e-learning environment using a simple web camera. *IEEE International Conference on Technology Enhanced Education*, 2012.
2. Ashwin, T.S. and Guddeti, R.M.R., Unobtrusive behavioral analysis of students in classroom environment using non-verbal cues. *IEEE Access*, 7, 150693–150709, 2019.
3. Conati, C., Chabal, R., Maclaren, H., A study on using biometric sensors for monitoring user emotions in educational games, in: *Proc. of Workshop on Modelling User Affect and Actions: Why, When and How. UM'03 9th International Conference, UM 2003*, Johnstown, PA, 2003, June.
4. Cocea, M. and Weibelzahl, S., Can log files analysis estimate learners' level of motivation?, in: *Proceedings of the Workshop Week Lernen - Wissensentdeckung - Adaptivität (LWA2006)*, University of Hildesheim, Hildesheim, pp. 32–35, 2006.
5. Zhu, M., Martinez, A.M., Tan, H.Z., Template-based recognition of static sitting postures, in: *Computer Vision and Pattern Recognition Workshop, CVPRW '03*, 2003.
6. Asteriadis, S., Tzouveli, P., Karpouzis, K., Kollias, S., Estimation of behavioural user state based on eye gaze and head pose–application in an e-learning environment. *Multimedia Tools Appl.*, 41, 3, 469–493, 2009.
7. Li, S.Z. and Jain, A.K., *Handbook of face recognition*, Springer-Verlag London Limited, London, UK, 2011.
8. Bergh, T.F., Hafizovic, I.U., Holm, S., Multi-speaker voice activity detection using a camera-assisted microphone array. *The 23rd International Conference on Systems, Signals and Image Processing: Bratislava, Slovakia*, 2016.
9. Bah, S.M. and Ming, F., An improved face recognition algorithm and its application in attendance management system. *Array*, Elsevier Inc., 5, 100014, 2020, https://doi.org/10.1016/j.array.2019.100014.
10. Fenety, P.A., Putnam, C., Walker, J.M., In-chair movement: Validity, reliability and implications for measuring sitting discomfort. *Appl. Ergon.*, 31, 4, 383–393, 2000.
11. Tarzia, S.P., Dick, R.P., Dinda, P.A., Memik, G., Sonar based measurement of user presence and attention, in: *Ubicomp '09: Proceedings of the 11th International Conference on Ubiquitous Computing*, pp. 89–92, 2009.
12. Asteriadis, S., Karpouzis, K., Kollias, S., A neuro-fuzzy approach to user attention recognition, in: *ICANN '08: Proceedings of the 18th International*

Conference on Artificial Neural Networks, Part I, pp. 927–936, 2008, https://doi.org/10.1007/978-3-540-87536-9_95.

13. Sharma, M., SOCMS: Smart online class monitoring system. *J. Stat. Manage. Syst.*, 24, 251–261, 2020.

14. Bernard, A., Santos, G., Balba, N.P., Rebong., C.B., Attendance monitoring system for selected schools in the philippines with an inclusion of optimization query algorithm. *14th World Conference on Applied Science, Engineering and Technology*, 2018.

15. Chau, M. and Betke, M., Real time eye tracking and blink detection with USB cameras. Technical report, Boston University Computer Science Department, 2005.

16. Dinh, H., Jovanov, E., Adhami, R., Eye blink detection using intensity vertical projection, in: *International Multi-Conference on Engineering and Technological Innovation, IMETI*, 2012.

17. Sukno, F.M., Pavani, S.K., Butakoff, C., Frangi, A.F., Automatic assessment of eye blinking patterns through statistical shape models. *7th International Conference on Computer Vision Systems*, pp. 33–42, 2009.

18. Yang, F., Yu, X., Huang, J., Yang, P., Metaxas, D., Robust eyelid tracking for fatigue detection, in: *19th IEEE International Conference on Image Processing*, pp. 1829–1823, 2012.

19. Drutarovsky, T. and Fogelton, A., Eye blink detection using variance of motion vectors, in: *Computer Vision - European Conference on Computer Vision*, pp. 436–448, 2014.

20. Viola, P. and Jones, M., Rapid object detection using a boosted cascade of simple features, in: *Proceedings of the 2001 IEEE Computer Society Conference on Computer Vision and Pattern Recognition*, CVPR, 2001.

21. Soukupová, T. and Cech, J., Real-time eye blink detection using facial landmarks, enter for machine perception, in: *21st Computer Vision Winter Workshop, Rimske Toplice, Slovenia*, 2016.

22. Sawhney, S., Kacker, K., Jain, S., Singh, S.N., Garg, R., Real-time smart attendance system using face recognition techniques. *IEEE 9th International Conference on Cloud Computing, Data Science & Engineering (Confluence)*, 2019.

23. Bauer, S. and Clark, D., *Understanding broadband speed measurements*, Massachusetts Institute of Technology, Cambridge, 2010.

24. Li-guo, D., Peng, D., Ai-ping, L., A new naive bayes text classification algorithm. *TELKOMNIKA Indones. J. Electr. Eng.*, 12, 2, 2014, http://dx.doi.org/10.11591/telkomnika.v12i2.4180.

25. Bauer, S., Clark, D.D., Lehr, W., Understanding broadband speed measurements. *TPRC Conference*, August 15, 2010.

26. Saha, D., Mukherjee, I., Roy, J., Sarkar, B., Bhattacharjee, R., Attendance and attention monitoring - a perspective in digital pedagogy. *J. Phys.: Conf. Ser.*; Bristol, 1797, 1, Feb 2021, https://dx.doi.org/10.1088/1742-6596/1797/1/012067.

AI-Based Development of Student E-Learning Framework

S. Jeyanthi[1]*, C. Sathya[2], N. Uma Maheswari[2], R. Venkatesh[3]
and V. Ganapathy Subramanian[4]

[1]*Department of Computer Engineering, Government Polytechnic College,
Kaniyalampatti, Karur, Tamil Nadu, India
[2]Department of Computer Science and Engineering, PSNA College of Engineering
and Technology, Dindigul, Tamil Nadu, India
[3]Department of Information Technology, PSNA College of Engineering and
Technology, Dindigul, India
[4]FreddieMac, Reston, Virginia, USA

Abstract

Artificial intelligence associating with the machine learning through processing of natural language is one of the necessities for demand of emerging industries. AI framework is called exchange frameworks, expressed discourse frameworks, or chatbots. The proposed framework aims in approaching a typical way to develop a chatbot for student education sectors using machine learning. The proposed system is intended with different conversational models to aid in the field of educational system for learning. Nowadays most of the curriculums are conducted via virtual platforms. Students look with certain problems during the practical sessions, such as, how to use the software, how to install the software, etc. The proposed chatbot is a full-on-full educational oriented chatbot giving various experiences for the users and it provides exact answer for the question which is related to the particular practice. In the today's world demanding of the number of e-learners are numerous, our framework may be made used to get on the spontaneous replies instead of manual response to respond. Learners need not depend upon someone else to guide them while facing software related technical issues. Instead, he/she can make use of the chatbot to solve the problems on his/her own. The proposed framework provides the student with a specific solution to his/her issue, rather than getting multiple solutions in the internet. The system is modeled

*Corresponding author: sjeyanthi@psnacet.edu.in

K. Umamaheswari, B. Vinoth Kumar and S. K. Somasundaram (eds.) Artificial Intelligence for Sustainable Applications, (219–230) © 2023 Scrivener Publishing LLC

to address the queries which the users feed in through text. The developed frame-work is useful for the students and parents to get their queries sort out instead being held in a wait list.

Keywords: Artificial intelligence, chatbot, conversational models, e-learner, machine learning, natural language processing

13.1   Introduction

With emerging trends of artificial intelligence chatbots are support-ing humans in many fields. A chatbot is a software tool which devel-ops interaction between user and computer using natural language. Conversation between chatbot and user will be short, anywhere and anytime service can be granted. Wide availability of platforms helps in easy development of chatbots in a convenient manner. Chatbots task can be classified into request and response in the form of queries. Based on the query request chatbot understand and interprets the semantics of query. Relevant matched response is retrieved from the database and given to the user. In recent days; e-learning is popular among students, researchers, and teachers. Chatbots connects new manner for humans and with computers in an interaction and intelligent method. Natural Language Processing is the core behind the rise of chatbots. Chatbots are more efficient than human and there is a chance for reaching large audience. Chatbots acts as virtual assistants who make a feel like one-to one teaching with its interactive capability of responding to messages or dialogues. AI based development of student chatbot systems is proposed to obtain the beneficial and applicable information from one or more knowledge bases.

13.2   Objective

Nowadays maximum of the classes are conducted via online platforms. Learners may come across certain problems during the practical sessions such as software installation, software usage, and syntax of the various commands, etc. In order to reduce the dependency upon someone else for the learner to guide them while facing software related technical issues, chatbot can be used to solve the problems by self. The study aims to pro-vide the learner with a specific solution for an issue, rather than getting multiple solutions in the internet. The purpose of the proposed system is to design and develop a learner chatbot using NLP and ML which helps user, communicates to provide service.

13.3   Literature Survey

Rajkumar *et al.* [1] involved distinguishing the personality types of the user's framework consist of introvert, extrovert, and style of learning. Naïve Bayes, N48, and Canopy algorithms are implemented and the results are compared with the past works.

Honda *et al.* [2] proposed symbolic process with question interaction system in connection of advanced deep learning methods and the achieved results compared with conventional methods. Ait-Mlouk *et al.* [3] built the interactive system with relevant of SPAROL queries and made it essential for data retrieval, data acquisition, intent classification, query understanding and continuous learning.

Srivastava *et al.* [4] diagnosis bot is developed that draws in patients in the discussion on clinical questions, issues which are used to find in view of their analyzed appearance and profile. A recall of 65% and a precision of 71% are obtained for individual user experiences.

Lal *et al.* [5] proposed framework based on HCI which can interact with the patients question and support the improvement of the nature of medical care administrations given to a person is constructed. The advancement of the techniques in the current industry like data analytics, MLP and ML are used for possible attainment of capable arrangement. Helpful for patients to know about their health conditions, discharge summaries, and furthermore details.

Rahman *et al.* [6] built a health assistance chatbot named "Disha" is developed with the help of machine learning algorithms. Disha can be made used for Bangla speaking patients so that their queries can be met in their own language improved accuracy was achieved by implementing six different machine learning algorithms.

Kumar *et al.* [7] built a system using the non-linear approach of ML for the input and the output obtained is generated as a statistical model. Kumari *et al.* [8] method is made any number of times until correctness is achieved. Ready to send messages, pictures, sounds, connections, and messages progressively as reactions to inquiries from clients. Polignano *et al.* [9] shows that that chatbot that is made used for educational institutions as the replacement for enquiry desk is intensively developed. Makhamova *et al.* [10] modelled to address the queries which the users feed in through text. Shingte *et al.* [11], Ansari *et al.* [12] scheme is useful for the learners to get their queries sort out instead being held in a wait list. In the previous research, they proposed for the enquiry kind of chatbot which answer related to learners.

13.4   Proposed Student E-Learning Framework

In the current scenario states that due to the demand of increasing the number of e-learners in the learning environment proposed framework can be used to get immediate response. The proposed interactive education oriented chatbot for e-Learning framework shown in Figure 13.1. This chatbot will help the student to answer all expected queries with the possible answers. Our proposed educational chatbot utilized approach of machine learning algorithms.

Queries can be raised directly in the internet by the student instead of working on manual. But, it gives numerous answers for such questions and the student might get confused to choose the best one. When the exact purpose of query is narrowed down then the solution is simple. Our proposed model, work with the set of all possible formation of questions and answers that can be based on input query raised by the learners and model is trained with machine learning for providing relevant response.

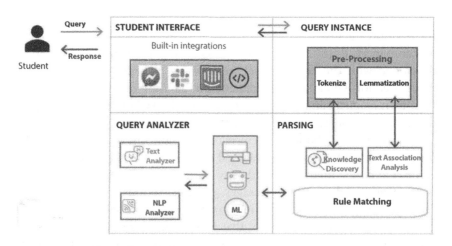

Figure 13.1 Student e-learning framework.

13.5   System Architecture

Detailed view of the proposed student e-learning system is used to relate the working principles of chatbot and its constraints and relationship among the components in the process of chatbot integrations. The detailed view of chatbot using ML and NLP depicts in Figure 13.2.

In Figure 13.2 illustrates the overall view of the deployment of the entire system. It also shows the behavior of the system in an abstracted way. The overview of the proposed system, initially the input collection of data in JSON format is pre-processed with word tokenization. Lemmatization finds the root-word in the query and helps in predicting the answer i.e. classes pickle and continue with that words converted to numbers which is called as Bag of words contain vector representation. Word pickle is defined as set of list that consists of pickles are well-defined words conversion.

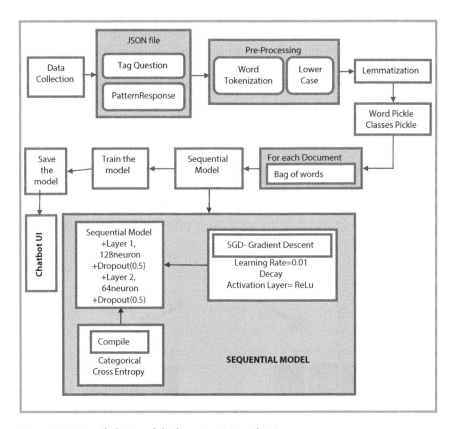

Figure 13.2 Detailed view of chatbot using ML andNLP.

In proceeding with the process of tokenization, classes pickle is used to predict the response list for its relevant word. Sequential model is the actual neural network which comprises of two layers with dropout of 0.5 and activation layer as ReLU. The well trained dataset is promoted for sequential model building that contains the computations of neural network and deploys the model of the system.

13.6   Working Module Description

The chatbot understands the objective of sender, find out the type of essential response message (a follow-up question, direct response, etc.), and use exact syntactic and lexical rules while framing the response. Few prototypes may use further meta information from data, such as speaker id, gender, emotion. Sometimes, sentiment analysis is used to allow the chatbot to 'understand' the mood of the user by analyzing verbal and sentence structuring clues. In Figure 13.3 portrays processing of query in detailed and well defined method with the support of AI model includes query generation, request ranking and ended with query processing.

Our proposed AI Model system looks for the relevant tags and checks if something relevant is found. Now arises two possibilities: In the first case, the model finds something relevant to the query entered, and provides the corresponding solution to the query being asked. Meanwhile, in the second scenario, the model fails to identify any kind of relevance to the query being asked with the existing tags in the JSON file. In such a case, the bot prompts for even more elaborated query to the user. Finally, on providing the relevant solution to the student, it is now left to the student to decide whether the solution is provided with the method to

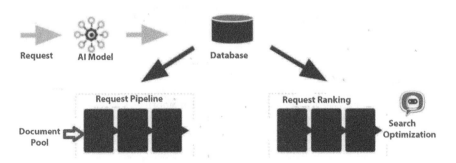

Figure 13.3 AI model of query process.

resolve the issue that the learner faces. If the student is satisfied with the answer being given by the chatbot, then the student ends the query conversation with the chatbot. If not, then the user again tries to enter even more elaborated query and the process continues until the learner is provided with the solution to the issue being faced. The dataset is stored in JSON format, which is used for training of the model. Training is done for 200 epochs. Also, final accuracy of 96 percent is achieved after completing the training of the dataset.

13.6.1   Data Preprocessing

To build the trustworthy model, suitable data is to be used. Data preprocessing is the fundamental need in order to have attained the data. The phases of pre-processing involves tokenization, removing stop words, stemming, lemmatization, parts of speech tagging, named entity recognition and chunking shown in Figure 13.4.

Pre-processing process will get better the excellence of the data used in the response retrieval and its keywords are tabulated in Table 13.1.

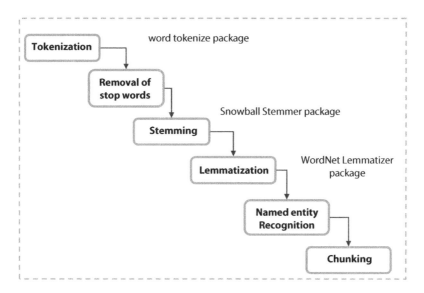

Figure 13.4 Steps involved in data preprocessing.

Table 13.1 List of keywords in pre-processing.

Keywords	Definition
Tokenization	*To make each word from set of lines*
Removing stop words	*To discards stop words before processing*
Stemming	*Stemming outputs the word by chopping off suffixes or prefixes used with a word*
Lemmatization	*Identification of the root word*
Named entity recognition	*Named entity recognition used for labeling real-world objects into pre-defined categories*
Chunking	*Process of adding the syntactical structure and meaning to the sentences*

13.6.2   Driving Test Cases

Our proposed testing for chatbot can be categorized into in the various testing like conversational design testing, entities testing, fulfillment testing, user acceptance testing, and automation testing tools which are in the phases of chatbot like understanding, answering, and navigation. Some of the chatbot tools like botium box, selenium, gupshupproxy bot, and test fairy will use the chatbot for testing and share the reports and other needed remarks with the stakeholders. The performance of the chatbot can be evaluated and verified by the various automated testing tools with the comparison of input query and relevant response matches. To build chatbots in successful manner, different testing phases like pre-launch and post-launch tests were conducted. The information regarding testing types to be made on the system is shown in Table 13.2.

13.6.3   System Analysis

System analysis is the procedure of reviewing a method so as to find out its goals, purposes and in turn develop systems and methods that will achieve them in an efficient way. Analysis and synthesis, as scientific methods, always go hand in hand; they complement one another. Every synthesis is built up on the results of a preceding analysis, and every analysis requires

Table 13.2 Experimental results of various test cases.

S. no.	Output detail	Preconditions	Accept/ Reject	Outcome
1	Query Acceptance	No Preconditions required	Accept	Accept successfully
2	Response to the query	Query has to be accepted	Accept	Responded successfully
3	Produce accurate response	Query has to be accepted	Accept	Accurate response observed
4	Check for brief description of the query	Pass ambiguous query as input	Accept	Ambiguous queries identified successfully
5	Prompt for detailed description of query	Pass ambiguous query as input	Pass	Prompted successfully

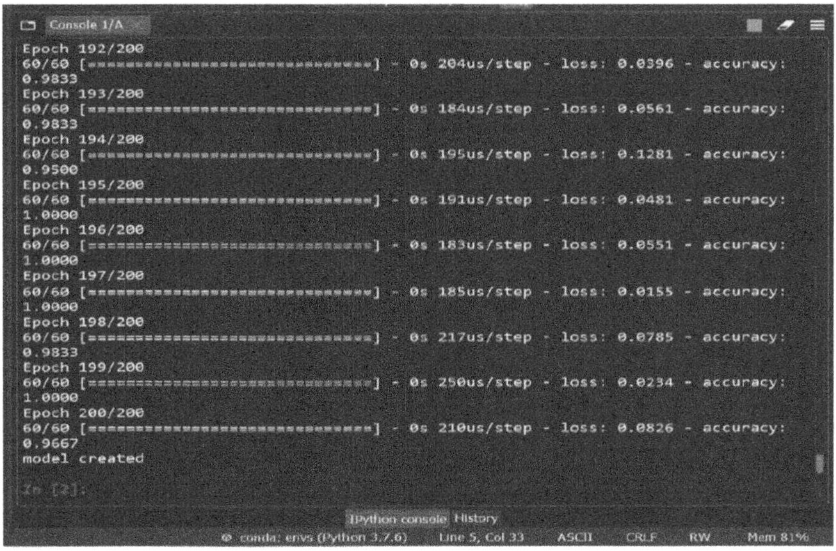

Figure 13.5 Dataset training.

a subsequent synthesis in order to verify and correct its results. The model for dataset training shown in Figure 13.5.

13.7   Conclusion

Traditionally there exists no chatbot to address the difficulties faced by the students while at the beginning stage of using a new platform. In the present day system, if a student encounters a technical issue while working with software, queries will be raised to someone or refer internet. The first option depends on the availability of the corresponding person, whereas the second alternative provides multiple solutions that often lead to a state of confusion in the minds of the students in deciding which solution to go with. Especially, in this time of pandemic as everything has turned out to happen virtually, there develops an increasing demand for such proposed chatbots that could evidently help in easy troubleshooting of the technical issues that the students experience.

13.8   Future Enhancements

In the proposed AI based development of student e-learning framework is an interactive model supported for virtual learner's community. Some future enhancements for the proposed systems can be improved by look and feel of the UI, deploying the chatbot to make it serve as a stand-alone application, including voice recognition so that making more convenient for the user and extending the usage of chatbot to support even more software manuals

References

1. Rajkumar, R. and Ganapathy, V., Bio-inspiring learning style chatbot inventory using brain computing interface to increase the efficiency of e-learning. *IEEE Access*, 8, 67377–67395, 2020.
2. Honda, H. and Hagiwara, M., Question answering systems with deep learning-based symbolic processing. *IEEE Access*, 7, 152368–152378, 2019.
3. Ait-Mlouk, and Jiang, L., KBot: A knowledge graph based chatbot for natural language understanding over linked data. *IEEE Access*, 8, 149220–149230, 2020.

4. Srivastava, P. and Singh, N., Automatized medical chatbot (medibot). *2020 International Conference on Power Electronics & IoT Applications in Renewable Energy and its Control (PARC)*, pp. 351–354, 2020.

5. Lal, H. and Lal, P., NLP chatbot for discharge summaries. *2019 2nd International Conference on Intelligent Communication and Computational Techniques (ICCT)*, pp. 250–257, 2019.

6. Rahman, M.M., Amin, R., Khan Liton, M.N., Hossain, N., Disha: An implementation of machine learning based bangla healthcare chatbot. *2019 22nd International Conference on Computer and Information Technology (ICCIT)*, pp. 1–6, 2019.

7. Kumar, P., Sharma, M., Rawat, S., Choudhury, T., Designing and developing a chatbot using machine learning. *2018 International Conference on System Modeling & Advancement in Research Trends (SMART)*, pp. 87–91, 2018.

8. Kumari, S., Naikwadi, Z., Akole, A., Darshankar, P., Enhancing college chat bot assistant with the help of richer human computer interaction and speech recognition. *2020 International Conference on Electronics and Sustainable Communication Systems (ICESC)*, pp. 427–433, 2020.

9. Polignano, M., Narducci, F., Iovine, A., Musto, C., De Gemmis, M., Semeraro, G., HealthAssistantBot: A personal health assistant for the Italian language. *IEEE Access*, 8, 107479–107497, 2020.

10. Makhkamova, O., Lee, K., Do, K., Kim, D., Deep learning-based multi-chatbot broker for Q&A improvement of video tutoring assistant. *2020 IEEE International Conference on Big Data and Smart Computing (BigComp)*, pp. 221–224, 2020.

11. Shingte, K., Chaudhari, A., Patil, A., Chaudhari, A., Desai, S., Chatbot Development for Educational Institute, June 6, 2021, http://dx.doi.org/10.2139/ssrn.3861241.

12. Ansari, M., Shaikh, S., Parbulkar, M.S., Khan, T., Singh, A., Intelligent Chatbot. *International Journal of Engineering Research and Technology, (IJERT)* NREST, 09, 04, 2021.

Part IV
NETWORKS APPLICATION

14

A Comparison of Selective Machine Learning Algorithms for Anomaly Detection in Wireless Sensor Networks

Arul Jothi S.* and Venkatesan R.

Department of Computer Science and Engineering, PSG College of Technology, Coimbatore, India

Abstract

Wireless Sensor Networks endure from a wide range of faults and anomalies which hinder their smooth working. Anomaly Detection (AD) in wireless sensor networks is a crucial research area, to make sensor nodes to be more protected and consistent. Due to energy constraints and less computation capability of sensor networks AD should focus on the essential boundaries of sensor networks. AD techniques can be categorized as statistical approaches, clustering, and machine learning. Wireless sensor networks observe active environments that vary rapidly overtime. These lively actions are besides the source from peripheral issue or instigated by the developers. In this paper, machine learning techniques that are suitable for anomaly detection and their challenges have been discussed based on the performance metrics factors. Accuracy, precision, and recall contribute to major performance analysis for the implemented model which has been discussed with weather dataset. The research issues of various anomaly detection techniques have been presented with a brief discussion on certain adaptive algorithms.

Keywords: Wireless sensor networks, anomaly detection, machine learning, performance metrics

Corresponding author: saj.cse@psgtech.ac.in

K. Umamaheswari, B. Vinoth Kumar and S. K. Somasundaram (eds.) *Artificial Intelligence for Sustainable Applications*, (233–248) © 2023 Scrivener Publishing LLC

14.1 Introduction

Sensor networks make use of a device that detects or measures a physical property and can record, indicate, or respond to it. Wireless device networks assist observations and create supremacy over physical environments from inaccessible locations with higher correctness. They are suitable for use in fields like natural observation, armed forces, and obtaining sensing information. Due to the economical temperament and ad-hoc scheme of sensor nodes, they have diverse power and device limitations.

Sensor nodes are compactly covered in wireless device networks which allow substantial environments to turn out dreadfully within the reach and broadcast such knowledge. These features are supported by a group of sensor nodes. The nodes can be united or compressed together to transmit compact data. The localized traffic is extended with global information in an individual cluster. This assemblage of sensor nodes in an exceedingly tight set up in large scale is recognized as cluster. The process of combing data into a compressed behavior in a single cluster is called data fusion or data aggregation.

The constraints in sensor resources in terms of storage, execution, and communication and battery usage make WSNs susceptible to a variety of malevolent assaults. Integrity must be achieved from the data obtained in WSNs. Timely analysis of data collected from sensors has a higher significance.

An anomaly or outlier in a compilation of data is characterized as an examination that emerges to be conflicting with the remainder of the data set [1]. Transgression in the network is branded by evaluating the sensor data readings or traffic-correlated features in the network.

Implementation of anomaly detection in data aggregation for increasingdata accuracy in wireless sensor networks is a key challenge. This can aid in reducing inaccurate data transmission with less process overhead and less energy consumption which depends on the development of proficient distributed algorithms.

14.1.1 Data Aggregation in WSNs

Data aggregation desires a scheme for joining the sensed data into high-quality information [2]. Data aggregation is bounded as the method of gathering the data from several sensors to eliminate the terminated transmission and estimate the quantified response about the sensed environment by providing fused data to the base station [3].

The aggregated data is progressed to the base station over the intermediate nodes. Usual case is calculating the mean or considering the highest calculated readings from the entire sensors [7]. The primary procedure of data aggregation is pretty direct: data from all the sensor nodes in the network travels wirelessly from the sources to a receiver along a tree. The intermediary nodes in the tree perform some form of accretion task on the data which have been collected from few or all of their offspring nodes. This aggregated value, with supplementary organizational values is then dispatched [8].

Data aggregation is used to avoid data redundancy, diminish data broadcast, and enhances data accuracy in WSNs [9].

14.1.2   Anomalies

Anomaly or outlier detection denotes identifying patterns in a specified dataset that do not match to recognized standard behavior. These arrangements thus sensed are called anomalies, and frequently interpret to critical and actionable information in numerous application areas [10]. Anomalies are also stated as outliers, surprise, aberrant, deviation, peculiarity, etc. Figure 14.1 illustrates anomaly detection setup for the proposed work.

Anomalies in data occur due to various causes that are harmful activities like credit card fraud, cyber-intrusion, terrorist activity, or breakdown of a system [11]. All of these have a common characteristic that they are interesting to the analyst.

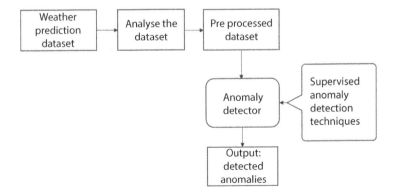

Figure 14.1 Anomaly detection system setup.

14.2 Anomaly Detection in WSN

Authorizing sensor data feature is crucial for the precise conclusion. Prevention based techniques are not consistent as they cannot defend sensor nodes from data variation. Hence, anomaly detection models are proposed to discover any unbalanced activities in sensor data streams [4].

Patterns that deviate from normal behavior are said to be anomalies or a set of observations that is incorrect while analyzing remaining datasets in the database [5].

14.2.1 Need for Anomaly Detection in WSNs

The core intend of anomaly detection is to reach an elevated anomaly detection rate with least power consumption. The intent is to deliver elevated data accuracy and high utilization of resources in parallel, at some stage in the design of an anomaly discovery process [5]. Some of the complexities are regarded through the formulation of proposed anomaly detection techniques and they are as follows [6].

Communication Cost: The charge of data broadcast is more than the charge of data processing. Accordingly, power utilization is concerned by the quantity of communication overhead that is endured by the dissemination process.

Active Data Flow: Generally, no previous knowledge exists to construct the standard dissemination of reading data (normal reference model). Despite this information is obtainable at a precise time, it is insufficient for the later due to the active flow that alters the environment of the dissemination.

Network Expandability: Various WSNs utilization develops overtime to such a degree few nodes may be appended to the set-up. Because of network size increase the huge collection of data formed leads to a weakness in real-time detection.

High Dimensional Data Stream: The upsurge of data magnitude earns an elevated computational charge which exhausts power and storage of sensors.

Computational Cost: WSNs are contrived using cheap sensors that need to be resource controlled in terms of memory and processing. The procedure of anomaly detection in WSN involves the use of the computational and storage resources for handling data in real-time.

14.3   Summary of Anomaly Detections Techniques Using Machine Learning Algorithms

Table 14.1 shows the machine learning algorithms classification based on the following, desirable properties of anomaly detection techniques.

14.3.1   Data Dimension Reduction

The quantity of data broadcasted in the WSN is to be reduced due to resource restriction. Intricacy in terms of transmission and processing should be minimized. In WSN's, data flow can be univariate or multivariate [12]. Univariate flows are represented by collection of readings from an exceptional kind of sensor.

Multivariate flows are represented by collection of readings acquired from various sensing entity with same characteristic sensor node [13].

Table 14.1 Summary of anomaly detection techniques that adopts machine learning approaches.

Approach	Class	Data dimension	Adaptability with change	Correlation exploitation
[15, 16]	Neural Networks	Multivariate	Adaptive	Spatial & Temporal
[17]		Univariate	Adaptive	Spatial & Temporal
[18–20]	Support Vector Machines	Multivariate	Adaptive	Spatial & Temporal
[21, 22]	Bayesian Statistics	Multivariate	Non-Adaptive	Spatial & Temporal
[23, 24]	Principal Component Analysis	Multivariate	Non-Adaptive	Temporal

14.3.2   Adaptability with Dynamic Data Changes

Generation and transmission of data in WNS can direct to a bottleneck in the study necessary to expand familiarity [14]. Consequently, it is enviable to computerize the working of frequently flowing data, to identify factors that are of actual notice to construct and refurbish the data performance pattern.

14.3.3   Correlation Exploitation

The characteristics of the correlation in the WSN are:

1. Spatial correlation: WSN applications entail perceptually intense sensor employment to realize acceptable treatment.
2. Temporal Correlation: Several WSN applications including event occurrence may necessitate sensor nodes from time to time to carry out inspection and broadcast the sense incident features.

14.4   Experimental Results and Challenges of Machine Learning Approaches

The experimental result shows the comparative analysis of various machine learning algorithms for unsupervised weather datasets.

14.4.1   Data Exploration

Weather dataset is mostly used for data analysis, to predict weather conditions in real-time which should be accurate. A lot of works has been done on detecting and removing outliers and missing data for weather prediction analysis.

The dataset is weather data from kaggle repository of size 168 kb has 11 dimensionality features, which is complex to consider for outlier detection. Dimensionality reduction is used to make easy exploration and visualization of data. PCA is an analytical method utilizing a linear variation to translate an event examined with dependent variables into a collection of discriminate variables called principal components. The attributes selected for outlier detection are based on the following box plot,

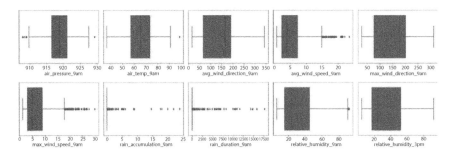

Figure 14.2 Boxplot view to analyze the distribution of data attributes.

From the box plot in Figure 14.2 the attributes rain_acculumation_9am and rain_duration_3pm cannot be considered for outlier detection since their distribution are uneven.

14.4.1.1   Pre-Processing and Dimensionality Reduction

The dataset extracted may contain missing data and outlier. So the collected data are pre-processed to remove missing data present in it. The dataset taken has 15 dimensionality features, which is complex to consider for outlier detection. In order to reduce the dimension, Principal Component Analysis (PCA) is used. Dimensionality reduction is used to make easy exploration and visualization of data. "PCA is a mathematical

	x	y
0	0.480918	-0.201376
1	0.316910	-0.127188
2	0.144667	-0.341601
3	-0.274952	-0.371676
4	-0.056744	-0.184913
5	-0.431227	-0.249246
6	0.005630	0.368016
7	-0.487462	0.124675
8	-0.099948	0.073113
9	0.224317	0.019887
10	0.411825	-0.572891
11	0.051063	0.656965
12	-0.324820	0.133744
13	-0.244184	0.413930
14	0.186591	-0.570819
15	0.359427	0.427402
16	0.663193	-0.018477
17	-0.296801	-0.120182
18	0.015616	-0.399693
19	0.389453	-0.176678
20	0.091840	0.321066
21	-0.063791	0.556531

Figure 14.3 Dimensionality reduction using PCA with two principal components.

statistical procedure that uses an orthogonal transformation to convert a set of observations of possibly correlated variables into a set of values of linearly uncorrelated variables called principal components. It is a technique used to emphasize variation of feature to bring out strong patterns in a dataset and not emphasize on characteristics of dataset". The trial and error method is used to choose the number of dimensions that need to be reduced to taken into considerations. Figure 14.3 shows reduction of dimensions implemented using PCA for visualization and accuracy purpose.

14.4.1.2   Clustering

Clustering algorithm forms different clusters based on certain criteria and condition given by programmer for the given dataset. The dataset taken is unsupervised which can be grouped and labeled using clustering algorithm shown in Figure 14.4. "DBSCAN is a density-based clustering application with noise: given a set of points in some space, it groups the points that are closely packed together, marking and identifies as outlier's points that lie alone in low-density regions in space. DBSCAN is robust to outlier and some noisy data". This method is proposed since the prior knowledge of the number of cluster is not needed. It is also suitable even if there is noise data. Here two values (i.e.) min point (the number of points should be there in order to consider it as a cluster) and epsilon (distance measure-Euclidian distance) are used to identify clusters. The fixed min point value is considered as 13 and epsilon value as 0.25 using trial and error method.

"K-Means clustering is a method of vector quantization, originally from signal processing, that is popular for cluster analysis in data mining.

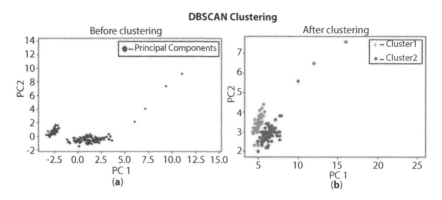

Figure 14.4 Scatter plots of (a) data with dimensionality reduction (b) PC after DBSCAN clustering.

K-means clustering aims to partition N observations into k clusters where each observation belongs to the cluster with the nearest mean, serving as a prototype of the cluster". K-Means clustering is also used to compare and analyze suitability of DBSCAN clustering. In DBSCAN algorithm, the number of cluster formed for given data can be covered. The supervised clustering algorithm (K-Means cluster algorithm) is considered to confirm whether clusters shaped from the DBSCAN is similar to the cluster shaped from K-Means algorithm. After clustering, data is attributed with cluster types and this is used for further outlier detection purpose investigated using various machine learning algorithm.

14.4.2   Outlier Detection

The outlier detection model is implemented using various machine learning techniques (Multilayer Neural Network, Support Vector Machine, and Bayesian Network). The parameters considered for outlier detection are training set (60%), test set data (40%), activation function.

14.4.2.1   Neural Network

The Multilayer neural network is built as shown in Figure 14.5 with input layers, 50 hidden layers and output layers. Three activation functions:

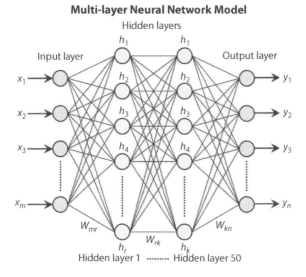

Figure 14.5 Design of multi-layer neural network model for outlier detection.

sigmoid function, Rectified Linear Unit (ReLU) function, and Tanh function are implemented and compared to extract best model that classifies the data based on threshold for normal and abnormal behavior. The model is trained and weights are adjusted using back propagation (gradient descent method). Once the model is perfectly trained, test data is fed and classify the output as normal data or outliers.

14.4.2.2   Support Vector Machine (SVM)

The chore of Support Vector Machine for given weather dataset is to classify and detect the outlier. But if we do not have class labels or outputs of our feature set then it is considered as an unsupervised learning algorithm. Then we can use clustering and label it, classify it using SVM [23]. SVM is a supervised machine learning algorithm that classifies data based on a region analyzed based on the input data [24]. SVM classifier SVM classifier treated as one of the dominant classification algorithms. There are 2 kinds of SVM classifiers:

- Linear SVM Classifier – In linear classification model, the data points plotted are expected to be separated by some distance. It predicts a straight hyper plane dividing into classes. The focus is to maximize the distance between the data and the hyper plane.
- Non-Linear SVM Classifier – In real world problem the model can never be linear, so straight linear hyper plane cannot be used. Hence Non-Linear Classifiers are used by

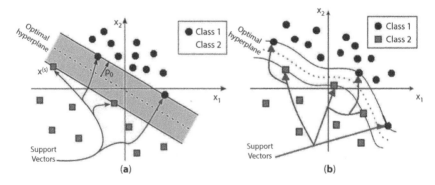

Figure 14.6 (a) SVM Linear Classifier. (b) SVM Non-Linear Classifier with optimal hyperplane.

applying the kernel trick to maximum-margin hyper plane. The data points are plotted in a higher dimensional space.

Figure 14.6 depicts a visualization of SVM classifier, mutually with linearly distinguishable and non-linearly distinguishable classes.

14.4.2.3   Bayesian Network

Bayesian network is a presumption explicit representation that corresponds to collection of attributes and their restricted criterion by a way of digraph with no cycles [18]. They seems to be perfect for enchanting an happening that arise and predicts the probability so as all of numerous potential recognized origins was the causative aspect.

Generally as in [25], a Bayesian network on a set of variables $X = x_1, x_2...,x_n$ has

(1) a possible relationship between variables in X determined as a network structure S and

(2) a variable in X each associated to a set P of local probability distributions associated with each.

For each variable $X_i : X_i \perp nondescendants\ X_i \mid Pa^S\ X_i$

Where the symbols,

- Pa denotes, parents of variable
- X_i in network structure S and
- symbol $\perp$ denotes conditional independence.

Let S be network structure with parameters P, then the conditional dependency distribution for X is given by Equation 14.1.

$$P(X) = \prod_{i=1}^{n} P(x_i \mid Pa_i) \tag{14.1}$$

Equation 14.1 illustrates the joint probability distribution for assessing quality of weather sensor data. A set of data variables $X = [x_A, x_B...x_G]$ is described on the source and consequence analysis allied with the network. Figure 14.7 represents the Conditional Probability Distribution (CPD) with each node conditionally dependent on other. The nodes that point towards a particular node are known as its parents.

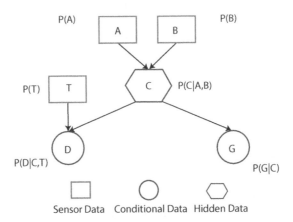

Figure 14.7 A Bayesian network in which each node is associated with a variable conditionally towards other variables. The node A and node B are the sensed weather data readings associated with node C conditionally to provide inference. The conditional data quality relates to hidden data for node D and node G. The conditional probability distribution of the network will be skilled from interpretation of weather sensor data readings.

14.5 Performance Evaluation

From the experimental results of the various machine learning techniques for detecting outliers, the performance of the model is calculated and represented in Table 14.2 in terms of accuracy, recall, and precision. The confusion matrix has been defined for the model with

Accuracy = referred to as an overall classification rate, shows the ratio of number of correct classifications against the number of instances.
Precision = Precision, expressed as TP/(TP + FP), shows the relation of right detections to gross detections.
Recall = Recall, expressed as TP/(TP + FN), shows the ratio of existing anomalies in the data that are detected.

Figure 14.8 shows the performance metrics of individual machine learning algorithms. From the results it is evident that neural network-based model ensures high accuracy with minimum time for detecting anomaly for the given dataset. Enhancing the neural network models makes it adapt to high dimensional data and apply detection techniques on various applications.

Table 14.2 Summary of adaptive machine learning algorithms performance metrics.

Machine learning techniques	Activation function	Accuracy	Precision	Recall
Neural Network	Sigmoid	0.93	0.89	0.90
	RELU	0.94	0.90	0.93
	Tanh	0.93	0.88	0.91
Support Vector Machine		0.80	0.80	0.80
Bayesian Network		0.92	0.68	0.53

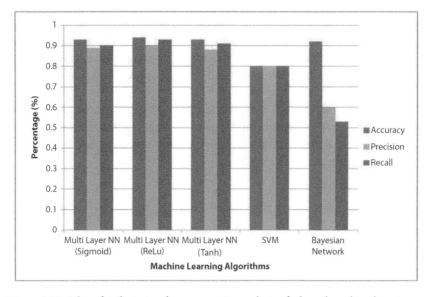

Figure 14.8 A bar plot depicting the comparative analysis of adapted machine learning algorithms.

Based on the analysis the following issues and challenges of machine learning algorithms are identified.

- Elevated computing constraint is the key concern of PCA-based data aggregation results. Apart from increasing throughput, these solutions sophisticatedly deal with the soaring dimensionality of aggregated data by maintaining merely significant information.

- Bayesian Network is capable of providing high accuracy but the precision and recall were not achieved as per the expectation. This may lead to identifying false positives in the dataset as outlier.

14.6 Conclusion

Anomaly detection is a vital glitch that has been explored within various research areas and real time application fields. Numerous anomaly detection methods seem to be precisely available for convinced application areas, while others are further broader. The proposed adaptive machine learning algorithms in this paper attempts to offer a wide-ranging outline of the study on machine learning techniques for anomaly detection on weather data in wireless sensor networks. Existing techniques were grouped into diverse groups' contingent to the fundamental approach implemented by respective techniques.

From the experimental analysis, it is evident that an ideal anomaly detection system should produce higher accuracy with minimal energy consumption. It is practicable to employ an anomaly detection method for improving data accuracy in WSNs.

References

1. Ayadi, H., Zouinkhi, A., Boussaid, B., NaceurAbdelkrim, M., A machine learning methods: Outlier detection in wireless sensor networks. *IEEE International Conference on Sciences & Techniques for Automatic Control and Computer Engineering*, 2016.
2. Singh, S.P. and Sharma, S.C., A survey on research issues in wireless sensor networks. *Trans. Wirel. Sens. Netw.*, 2, 1, 1–18, March 2015.
3. Rawat, P., Singh, K.D., Chaouchi, H., Bonnin, J.M., Wireless sensor networks: A survey on recent developments & potential synergies. *J. Supercomput.*, 68, 1–48, 2014.
4. Roy, S., Conti, M., Setia, S., Jajodia, S., Secure data aggregation in wireless sensor networks. *IEEE Inf. Forensics Secur.*, 7, 3, 1040–1052, 2012.
5. Wang, D., Xu, R., Hu, X., Su, W., Energy-efficient distributed compressed sensing data aggregation for cluster-based underwater acoustic sensor networks. *Int. J. Distrib. Sens. Netw.*, 2016, 1–14, 2016.

6. Haque, S.A., Rahman, M., Aziz, S.M., Sensor anomaly detection in wireless sensor networks for healthcare. *Sensors*, 15, 4, 8764–8786, 2015.

7. Mitchell, R. and Chen, I.-R., A survey of intrusion detection in wireless network applications. *Comput. Commun.*, 2, 42, 1–23, 2014.

8. Xie, M., Han, S., Tian, B., Parvin, S., Anomaly detection in wireless sensor networks: A survey. *J. Network Comput. Appl.*, 34, 4, 1302–1325, 2011.

9. O'Reilly, C., Gluhak, A., Imran, M.A., Rajasegarar, S., Anomaly detection in wireless sensor networks in a non-stationary environment. *IEEE Commun. Surv.*, 16, 3, 1413–1432, 2014.

10. Dau, H.A., Ciesielski, V., Song, A., *Anomaly detection using replicator neural networks trained on examples of one class*, Springer International Publishing Switzerland, Simulated Evolution and Learning. SEAL, Lecture Notes in Computer Science, vol. 8886, pp. 311–322, Springer, Cham, 2014.

11. Xu, S., Hu, C., Wang, L., Zhang, G., Support vector machine based on k-nearest neighbor algorithm for outlier detection in wireless sensor networks. *IEEE International Conference on Wireless Communications, Networking & Mobile Computing*, 2013.

12. Bilge, L., Sen, S., Balzaroti, D., Kirda, E., Krugel, C., Exposure: A passive DNS analysis service to detect and report malicious domains. *ACM Trans. Inf. Syst. Secur.*, 16, 4, 1–28, 20142014.

13. Nanduri, A. and Sherry, L., Anomaly detection in aircraft data using recurrent neural networks. *Integrated Communications Navigation & Surveillance*, IEEE, 2016.

14. Manikandan, R.P.S., Kalpana, A.M., Naveena Priya, M., Outlier analysis and detection using K-medoids with support vector machine. *IEEE Computer Communication & Informatics*, 2016.

15. Erfani, S.M., Rajasegaran, S., Karunasekera, S., Leckie, C., High-dimensional &large scale anomaly detection using a linear one-class support vector machine with deep learning. ELSEVIER, *J. Pattern Recognit.*, 58, 121–134, 2016.

16. Amer, M., Goldstein, M., Abdennadher, S., Enhancing one-class support vector machine for unsupervised anomaly detection, in: *Proceedings of the ACM SIGKDD Workshop on Outlier Detection and Description (ODD '13). Association for Computing Machinery*, pp. 8–15, New York, NY, USA,

17. Yuan, H., Zhao, X., Yu, L., A distributed bayesian algorithm for data fault detection in wireless sensor networks. *IEEE International Conference on Information Networking*, 2015.

18. Bhajantri Lokesh, B. and Nalini, N., Bayesian network-based fault tolerance in distributed sensor networks. *J. Telecommun. Inf. Technol.*, 4, 44–52, 2014.

19. Rassam, M.A., Zainal, A., Maarof, M.A., One-class principal component classifier for anomaly detection in wireless sensor networks. *IEEE International Conference on Computational Aspects of Social Networks*, 2012.

20. AahmadiLivani, Abadi, M., Alikhani, M., Outlier detection in wireless sensor networks using distributed principal component analysis. *J. AI Data Min.*, 1, 1–11, 2013.

21. Gharbel, O., Ayedi, W., Snowsi, H., Abid, M., Fast & efficient outlier detection method in wireless sensor networks. *IEEE Sens. J.*, 15, 6, 3403–3411, 2015.

22. O'Reilly, C., Gluhak, A., Imra, M.A., Distributed anomaly detection using minimum volume elliptical principal component analysis. *IEEE Trans. Knowl. Data Eng.*, 28, 9, 2320–2333, 2016.

23. Ghorbel, O., Abid, M., Snowsi, H., A novel outlier detection model based on one class principal component classifier in wireless sensor networks. *IEEE International Conference on Advanced Information Networking & Applications*, 2015.

24. Camacho, J., Villegas, A.P., Teodoro, P.G., Fernandez, G.M., Principal component analysis based multivariate statistical network monitoring for anomaly detection. *J. Comput. Soc.*, Elsevier, 59, 118–137, 2016.

25. Koller, D. and Friedman, N., *Probabilistic graphical models: Principles and techniques*, The MIT Press, Cambridge, USA, 2009.

15

Unique and Random Key Generation Using Deep Convolutional Neural Network and Genetic Algorithm for Secure Data Communication Over Wireless Network

S. Venkatesan[1]*, M. Ramakrishnan[1] and M. Archana[2]

[1]Department of Computer Applications, Madurai Kamaraj University, Madurai, Tamil Nadu, India
[2]P.A. College of Engineering and Technology, Pollachi, Tamil Nadu, India

Abstract

Wireless network plays a dynamic role in the high-speed communication of data across the globe. Achieving highly secure data communication and protecting the confidential data from illegal access are the key concerns in the wireless network. Encryption and decryption ensure better data security by using public key cryptography. However, the public key could be easily hacked by unauthorized user. This makes the network vulnerable to the attacks. To ensure improved data security, there is a need to create encryption key and decryption key that are unique in nature, diverse and random. In the proposed work, the cryptographic keys are generated by using Elliptic Curve Diffie-Hellman (ECDH) with Deep Convolutional Neural Network (DCNN) and Genetic Algorithm (GA). High data confidentiality and data integrity are achieved by preventing unauthorized manipulations and denial of the message. The GA generates a population having maximum fitness value, which acts as the transitional cipher text applied as input to the DCNN to encrypt the original message. The DCNN uses its security key in the form of weights, by using the backpropagation algorithm. The ECDH algorithm generates unique, encrypted messages by using the DCNN keys that cannot be accessed deprived of authorization. The keys possess the randomness essential for both security and key strength. Hence, the proposed work improves data security by

---

*Corresponding author: venkatesan708@gmail.com

K. Umamaheswari, B. Vinoth Kumar and S. K. Somasundaram (eds.) *Artificial Intelligence for Sustainable Applications*, (249–264) © 2023 Scrivener Publishing LLC

evaluating the performance of DCNNs and GAs on the user data over the elliptic curves with high accuracy.

Keywords: Deep convolutional neural network (DCNN), elliptic curve diffie-hellman (ECDH), genetic algorithm, wireless network

15.1 Introduction

There will be a decrease in the data credibility if the data is not protected appropriately from the security attacks. Also, the copyright/patent and data privacy are also easy to be infringed. Currently, Artificial Intelligence (AI) technology is being used widely in the educational and industrial applications. Machine Learning (ML) is one of the significant AI technologies, which is successfully used in the field of natural language processing, pattern recognition, computer vision, image processing, etc. At present, the existing security ML approaches face a lot of challenges. Secure data processing and preserving the data privacy are the significant challenges in wireless network.

In wireless networks, the security is more perilous than the wired networks, when the data communicated over the wireless network is disseminated to the neighborhood. Owing to the open transmission nature of the wireless network, the data communication interactions are prone to the adversary attacks. In order to safeguard the wireless communication signals from the malicious attacks, various security measures must be provided adequately to the user. In the prevailing wireless communication systems, security issues are handled by using various encryption techniques. At the transmitter side, the input message is encrypted with a cipher key, before the transmission of signal.

The receiver can decrypt the message by using the same cipher key. Though encryption is a process of protecting the message in the upper layers, it does not prevent detection of the signal by the malicious adversaries present in the intermediate layers. Also, encryption increases the network overhead and power consumption to enable the authentication, which may not be viable in some applications [1]. Data security in the wireless network needs to adjust itself to the new communications paradigm by becoming extra adaptive and flexible [2].

Multilayer Neural Networks (NNs) are computational-based learning network used to transmit the input data across a series of linear operators and simple non-linearities. The properties of the shallow communication networks, with a single hidden layer, are taken as disintegrations in the groups of the ridge functions [3]. But, these approaches do not extend to the networks having multiple layers. DCNN introduced by Le Cun [4], are applied with the linear convolutions trailed by the non-linearities, over more than five layers. This complex programmable machine, well-defined by billions of the filter weights, takes us to a different arithmetic world. Many researchers pointed out that the DCNN are computing gradually with the increase in the depth [5–7].

The main purpose of the Cryptography algorithm such as Riverst-Shamir-Adleman (RSA) algorithm, Advanced Encryption Standard (AES) and Data Encryption Standard (DES) is to prevent the unauthenticated access to the confidential information by applying complex arithmetic and logic to make information jumbled, and also to retrieve the original data. Various cryptography algorithms have been developed. Conventional cryptography ciphers use exhaustive serial operations by applying complex mathematical formulas and massive prime numbers, while making the encryption and decryption process to consume more computational resources and become vulnerable. On the other hand, recently ML and AI technologies have achieved significant improvements in the field of cryptography [8].

ECDH key is applied to secure data in the wireless network [9]. Due to the intensive nature of the ECDH key, it required long execution time and complex computations [10]. To mitigate this, DCNN is applied to decrease the encryption and decryption time. The GA generates a population with maximum fitness value, which acts as the intermediate cipher text for the encryption process. This cipher is applied as input to the DCNN for encrypting the original message. In DCNN, own key is used in the form of its weights, by using the backpropagation algorithm. The ECDH algorithm generates unique, encrypted messages by using the DCNN keys that cannot be illegally accessed. The keys own the property of randomness needed for better security and key strength. Hence, the proposed approach improves the data security by evaluating the performance of DCNNs and GAs on the user data over the elliptic curves with the maximum accuracy.

The manuscript is organized as follows: Section 15.2 describes the existing cryptographic approaches. Section 15.3 explains the proposed work including ECDH algorithm, Genetic algorithm, and DCNN. Section 15.4 presents the performance evaluation results of the proposed ECDH-DCNN algorithm. The work is concluded in Section 15.5.

15.2   Literature Survey

Jogdand and Bisalapur [11] and Kinnzel and Kanter [12] proposed a neutral network based key exchange mechanism depending on the synchronization of two parity machines for the sender and receiver. The outputs of the parity machines were compared to perform the training process. Key randomness was achieved and security was improved. In [12], two multilayer NNs are trained on their shared output bits. A secret key was generated over a public communication channel, by training the parity bits on the output bits of the respective partner. The key generation by the mutual learning of the tree parity machines was made secure.

Klein *et al.* [13] applied a novel phenomenon combining the neural network and chaos synchronization for creating a secure cryptographic secret-key by using a public channel, for ensuring better safety against the attackers. Klimov *et al.* [14] analyzed the security of the key exchange protocol depending on the mutually learning NNs. Convergence of two parties to a common key was explained and unlikeness of the attacker using a similar NN converging to the same key was also analyzed. Volna *et al.* [15] applied NNs that are trained and tested for the encryption and decryption of the original plain text. The input message was converted into American Standard Code for Information Interchange (ASCII) code and the order of bit for each code was obtained. Division of the code into six-bit blocks is performed; the divided blocks are used as input for the encryption process.

Neural cryptography is a public key exchange algorithm that works based on the NN synchronization principle. By using the NN algorithm, two NNs update their own weight through the process of exchanging the output obtained from each other. Weights of two NNs will become same, once the network synchronization is completed. The weights of the NN can be used for the secret key. But, all the existing works are based on the real NN model. Few works study the neural cryptography according to the complex-valued NN model. Dong and Huang [16] proposed neural cryptography based on the Complex-Valued Tree Parity Machine (CVTPM) Network. The proposed model ensured better security due to the complex value of the input, output, and weights of the CVTPM network.

Shi *et al.* [17] introduced Continuous Variable-Quantum NN (CV-QNN) for efficient extended cryptography to encrypt and decrypt data. The proposed scheme guaranteed high information security and quickens the encryption process in a simultaneous way. Encryption and decryption of the classical and quantum data was performed efficiently.

15.3   Proposed Work

Ensuring secure data communication over the insecure networks and protecting the secret and sensitive data from the unauthenticated access over the public networks is a main concern in the cloud servers. In this proposed work, asymmetric cryptography using ECDH with DCNN and GA is applied for the encryption and decryption processes, to generate both public and private keys. Data confidentiality, sender, and recipient authentication, data integrity for the prevention of manipulations, and prevention of the denial of the message by either sender or recipient are achieved. In this work, ECDH keys are used along with the Genetic Algorithm.

The GA performs replication of the randomness property, where a population of entities adapts to its environments through a natural selection process and system behavior. The GA creates a population with a high fitness value, which serves as the intermediate cipher text for encryption process. DCNN uses the intermediate cipher text to encrypt the original message. Backpropagation algorithm is used in DCNN, in which the key is used in the form of its weights and biases. ECDH, GA and DCNN keys are used for generating unique encrypted messages that are accessed by the authorized personnel. Hence, the data security is enhanced by evaluating the performance of DCNNs and GAs on the user data over the elliptic curves with the maximum accuracy [18].

15.4   Genetic Algorithm (GA)

GA is an iterative procedure involving the population size of the individuals encoded based on the fitness function. Based on the principle of the existence of the fittest chromosome, more adaptive chromosomes are maintained and less adaptive chromosomes are rejected while generating a new population. This process is repeated continuously until the termination conditions are fulfilled [19]. Figure 15.1 presents the flowchart of the GA.

15.4.1   Selection

It selects the chromosomes that are permitted to reproduce. The highly fittest chromosomes produce more descendants than the least fit ones. Consider the two offspring 'f1' and 'f2' carefully chosen from two parents.

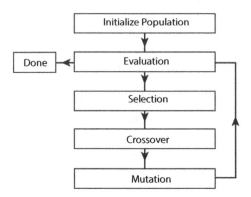

Figure 15.1 Flowchart of genetic algorithm.

15.4.2   Crossover

It combines the parent chromosomes and mimics the biological recombination between two single chromosomes to produce a new offspring. The progressive value of the crossover probability C_p and average crossover probability are computed as

$$C_p = F_{sum_s} - F_{sum_p} \qquad (15.1)$$

$$\bar{C}_p = \frac{1}{N_c} \sum C_p \qquad (15.2)$$

Where F_{sum_s} and F_{sum_p} denotes the fitness sum of the two offspring and parent individuals, respectively.

15.4.3   Mutation

It randomly changes the bit values at the randomly selected locations in the chromosome. Mutation is performed if the successive iteration values are same. Resulting offspring is considered after the mutation operation is done. The growth value of the mutation probability M_p is defined as

$$M_p = F_{new} - F_{old} \qquad (15.3)$$

Where F_{new} is the fitness of the new offspring and fold the fitness of the original individual. The average mutation probability value is calculated using the following equation

$$\bar{M}_p = \frac{1}{N_m} \sum M_p \qquad (15.4)$$

15.4.4 ECDH Algorithm

ECDH algorithm is an unidentified key agreement procedure that lets two parties A and B, to create a shared key over an insecure communication channel. In this channel, each party will have a pair of elliptic curve public-private key.

The idea of Elliptic Curve Cryptography (ECC) is proposed depending on the elliptic curve theory, for planning the public key cryptographic framework. General type of elliptic curve 'E' over a main finite field F_p is:

$$Y^2 = X^3 + AX + B \qquad (15.5)$$

The points on 'E' over the main finite field along with an extra point 'Ó' is called as the point at infinity or the zero point. It is denoted as:

$$A = \{(X, Y): X, Y F_p, E(X, Y) = 0\}(1) \qquad (15.6)$$

Let 'n' be the order of A such that $ng \ mod \ q = 0$, where 'g' denotes the generator of A which is an additive cyclic group under the point addition defined as $P + 0 = P$. The point scalar multiplication over A can be defined as

$$kP = P + \cdots + P(k \ times) \qquad (15.7)$$

Sum of P and Q is point R. The line passing through P and Q interrupts the curve at the point '-R'. The reflection of '-R' is R with respect to the X-axis. This condition is known as point addition as depicted in Figure 15.2.

If two points intersect, i.e., P=Q, then R=P+P and turn out to be a tangent at P, which interconnects the curve at -2P. The image of 2P on the altered sign of the y-coordinate is the outcome of P+P which lies on the

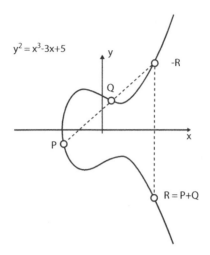

Figure 15.2 Point addition.

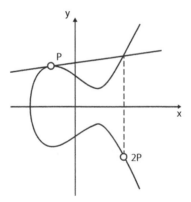

Figure 15.3 Point doubling.

curve E/FP. This is known as point doubling depicted in Figure 15.3 [18]. Figure 15.4 illustrates the ECDH algorithm.

15.4.5 ECDH Key Exchange

The usage of secret key cryptosystem is required for the encryption and decryption of a large amount of information, due to the quicker computation, in compared to the public key cryptosystem. The ECDH key is applied

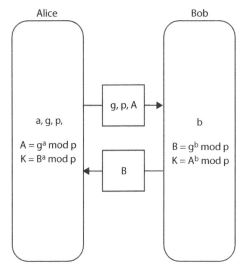

$$K = A^b \bmod p = (g^a \bmod p)^b \bmod p = g^{ab} \bmod p = (g^a \bmod p)^a \bmod p = B^a \bmod p$$

Figure 15.4 ECDH.

to an elliptic curve, for creating a secret key between the clients 'A' and 'B' for single communication session.

Let us assume that the clients correspond on a secret key. 'A' generates a private key '$\mathcal{K}A$' and public key '$\mathcal{P}A = \mathcal{D}A\mathcal{G}$', where $\mathcal{G}$ denotes the elliptic curve generator. 'A' sends the private key to the 'B'. In the same way, 'B' sends the private key '$\mathcal{P}B$' to the 'A'. Upon receiving the message from 'A', 'B' processes $\mathcal{D}B(\mathcal{P}A) = \mathcal{D}A\mathcal{D}B\mathcal{G}$. While receiving the message from 'B', 'A' figures $\mathcal{D}A(\mathcal{P}B) = \mathcal{D}A\mathcal{D}B\mathcal{G}$. At this point, the clients can utilize $\mathcal{D}A\mathcal{D}B\mathcal{G}$, which is a point on the elliptic curve acting as a typical secret key.

15.4.6   DCNN

Convolutional NN (CNN) is a type of specialized multilayer Feedforward (FF) NN. Individual neurons are overlaid in a way such that they respond to the overlying regions in the visual field. The lower layers of the network architecture obtain low-level features while high-level features are obtained in the higher layers. More the number of layers in the network architecture, higher-level features are obtained. CNN uses the backpropagation (BP) algorithm for training the parameters such as weights and biases of each convolutional kernel. The BP algorithm uses its key in the form of parameters. Each kernel is replicated over the input data with the same parameters.

Different features of the input data are extracted by the convolutional operators. Deep CNN (DCNN) with Levenberg-Marquardt (LM) learning is applied for learning the pattern of the input data. The weights are updated depending on the error function with LM learning. Figure 15.1 presents the operation of the CNN. Figure 15.5 depicts the flow diagram of the DCNN. Figure 15.6 shows the DCNN architecture used in this proposed work. The CNN architecture comprises six layers: single input layer, double convolution layers, double subsampling layers and single fully connected layer [20].

The output of the single convolutional layer is estimated through the convolution of the input feature map with the kernel.

$$X_j^k = f\left(\sum_i X_i^{k-1} * W_{ij}^k + B_j^k\right) \tag{15.8}$$

Where X_j^k is the jth output feature map of the kth layer, X_j^k is the weight connecting the ith input feature map to the jth output feature map in the kth layer and B_j^k is the bias factor for the jth output feature map in the kth layer.

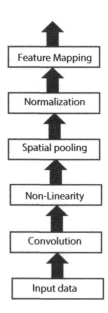

Figure 15.5 Flow diagram of the DCNN.

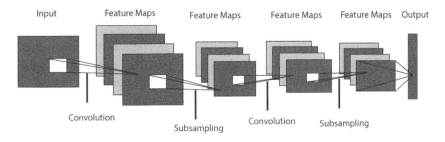

Figure 15.6 Deep CNN model.

In the CNN model, weights are updated based on the LM learning. The change in the weight ΔW is

$$W_{ij} \propto [J^T(W_{ij})J(W_{ij}) + \beta I]^{-1} J^T(W_{ij})\varepsilon(W_{ij}) \qquad (15.9)$$

Where 'J' denotes the Jacobian matrix, 'I' indicates the identity matrix, 'ε' represents the error matrix and 'β' is the combination coefficient [21].

15.4.7   Results

The DCNN produces a population with a high fitness value. This population is the intermediate cipher text used in the encryption of the original message. The ECDH algorithm with ECDH+DCNN+GA achieves

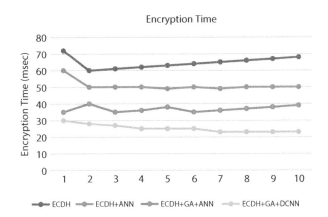

Figure 15.7 Encryption time.

the best interval time when compared to the ECDH [9], ECDH+ANN, ECDH+GA+ANN [18] as the DCNN requires time when applied to the randomness property of the ECDH. Figure 15.7 shows the encryption time and Figure 15.8 presents the decryption time. Figure 15.9 and Figure 15.10 show the encryption and decryption performance of the proposed ECDH+DCNN+GA, ECDH, ECDH+ANN and ECDH+GA+ANN.

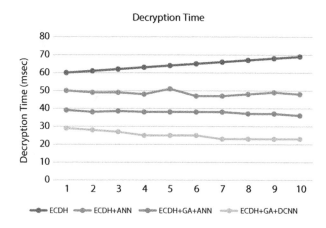

Figure 15.8 Decryption time.

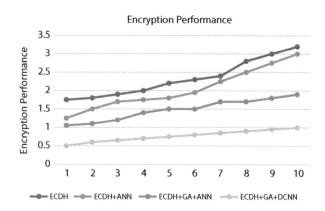

Figure 15.9 Encryption performance.

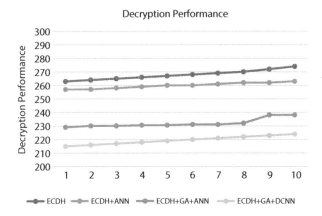

Figure 15.10 Decryption performance.

15.5 Conclusion

This proposed work aimed to achieve secure data communication across the unsecured communication networks and protect sensitive data from the unauthenticated access over the public communication networks. Symmetric cryptography is applied for generating both public and private keys, using ECDH with DCNN for encryption and decryption processes. Using ECDH with DCNN and GA, it achieved data confidentiality, data integrity to prevent manipulations, sender and recipient authentication and prevention of the denial of messages by the recipients or senders. The encryption system is presented based on ECDH with DCNN-GA. An efficient encryption system is constructed through a permanently varying key. Thus, the time consumed is the main metric and the encryption and decryption performance are considered.

References

1. Chen, Y., Trappe, W., Martin, R.P., Detecting and localizing wireless spoofing attacks, in: *2007 4th Annual IEEE Communications Society Conference on Sensor, Mesh and Ad Hoc Communications and Networks*, IEEE, pp. 193–202, 2007.
2. Yılmaz, M.H., Güvenkaya, E., Furqan, H.M., Köse, S., Arslan, H., Cognitive security of wireless communication systems in the physical layer. *Wireless Commun. Mobile Comput.*, 2017, 1–9, 2017.

3. Candes, E. and Donoho, D., Ridglets: The key to high-dimensional intermittency. *Phil. Trans. R. Soc. Lond.*, 357, 2495–2509, 1999.

4. Le Cun, Y. *et al.*, Handwritten digit recognition with a back-propagation network, in: *Proceedings of the 2nd International Conference on Neural Information Processing Systems*, pp. 396–404, 1989.

5. LeCun, Y., Bengio, Y., Hinton, G., Deep learning. *Nature*, 521, 7553, 436–444, 2015.

6. Anselmi, F., Leibo, J.Z., Rosasco, L., Mutch, J., Tacchetti, A., Poggio, T., Unsupervised learning of invariant representations in hierarchical architectures. *arXiv preprint arXiv:1311.4158*, 5, 1–23, 2014.

7. Mallat, S., Understanding deep convolutional networks. *Philos. Trans. R. Soc. A: Math. Phys. Eng. Sci.*, 374, 2065, 20150203, 2016.

8. Quinga-Socasi, F., Zhinin-Vera, L., Chang, O., A deep learning approach for symmetric-key cryptography system, in: *Proceedings of the Future Technologies Conference*, Springer, pp. 539–552, 2020.

9. Tirthani, N. and Ganesan, R., Data security in cloud architecture based on diffie hellman and elliptical curve cryptography. *IACR Cryptol. ePrint Arch.*, vol. 2014, p. 49, 2014.

10. Genkin, D., Pachmanov, L., Pipman, I., Tromer, E., ECDH key-extraction via low-bandwidth electromagnetic attacks on PCs, in: *Cryptographers' Track at the RSA Conference*, Springer, pp. 219–235, 2016.

11. Jogdand, R. and Bisalapur, S.S., Design of an efficient neural key generation. *Int. J. Artif. Intell. Appl. (IJAIA)*, 2, 1, 60–69, 2011.

12. Kinzel, W. and Kanter, I., Neural cryptography, in: *Proceedings of the 9th International Conference on Neural Information Processing, 2002. ICONIP'02*, vol. 3, IEEE, pp. 1351–1354, 2002.

13. Klein, E., Mislovaty, R., Kanter, I., Ruttor, A., Kinzel, W., Synchronization of neural networks by mutual learning and its application to cryptography, in: *NIPS*, pp. 689–696, 2004.

14. Klimov, A., Mityagin, A., Shamir, A., Analysis of neural cryptography, in: *International Conference on the Theory and Application of Cryptology and Information Security*, Springer, pp. 288–298, 2002.

15. Volna, E., Kotyrba, M., Kocian, V., Janosek, M., Cryptography based on neural network, in: *ECMS*, pp. 386–391, 2012.

16. Dong, T. and Huang, T., Neural cryptography based on complex-valued neural network. *IEEE Trans. Neural Networks Learn. Syst.*, 31, 11, 4999–5004, 2019.

17. Shi, J. *et al.*, An approach to cryptography based on continuous-variable quantum neural network. *Sci. Rep.*, 10, 1, 1–13, 2020.

18. Othman, A. and Muniyandi, R., Elliptic curve diffie-hellman random keys using artificial neural network and genetic algorithm for secure data over private cloud. *Inf. Technol. J.*, 15, 77–83, 2016.

19. Brindha, S.A.S. and N.K., G-SRP: Genetic based secured routing protocol for cloud-assisted ad hoc networks in green data centers, in: *Proceedings of Thrid*

International Conference on Computing Paradigms, Integrated Intelligent Research (IIR), 2017.

20. Palm, R.B., Prediction as a candidate for learning deep hierarchical models of data, vol. 5, Technical University of Denmark, 2012.

21. Muthulakshmi, M. and Kavitha, G., Deep CNN with LM learning based myocardial ischemia detection in cardiac magnetic resonance images, in: *2019 41st Annual International Conference of the IEEE Engineering in Medicine and Biology Society (EMBC)*, IEEE, pp. 824–827, 2019.

Part V

AUTOMOTIVE APPLICATIONS

16

Review of Non-Recurrent Neural Networks for State of Charge Estimation of Batteries of Electric Vehicles

R. Arun Chendhuran[1] and J. Senthil Kumar[2*]

[1]*Department of Electronics and Instrumentation, Bannari Amman Institute of Technology, Erode, Sathyamangalam*
[2]*Department of Electrical and Electronics, Bannari Amman Institute of Technology, Erode, Sathyamangalam*

Abstract

Advancements in artificial intelligence and machine learning (ML) has created paradigm-shifts in estimation of state-of-charge of batteries. Machine learning is a sub-set of artificial intelligence that facilitates computers to learn from data through algorithms, without explicitly programming it. Machine learning has evolved to model energy storage devices to determine their state of charge. Accessibility to battery-data and reduced computation time has made data-driven models based on machine learning more attractive. Non-recurrent SoC estimation techniques such as Feed-forward Neural Networks (FNNs), Radial Basis Functions (RBF), Extreme Learning Machine (ELM) and Support Vector Machine (SVM) are reviewed in this paper. It is recommended that SoC Estimation Techniques under comparison should preferably share common data-sets (both training and testing) and learnable parameters, else the comparison may be biased.

Keywords: Battery, SoC, electrochemical, equivalent circuit, impedance

16.1 Introduction

Global warming has demanded electrification of transport in many countries. Electric vehicles have superior performance and efficiency than the

*Corresponding author: senthilkumarj@bitsathy.ac.in

K. Umamaheswari, B. Vinoth Kumar and S. K. Somasundaram (eds.) *Artificial Intelligence for Sustainable Applications*, (267–274) © 2023 Scrivener Publishing LLC

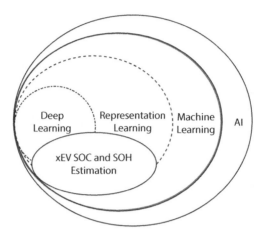

Figure 16.1 Hierarchy of methods of estimation of State-of-Charge and State-of-Health among the sub-sets of AI.

internal-combustion (IC) engine vehicles. However, to identify an optimum efficiency constrained by cost, is highly challenging. The ability of batteries to retain the same performance even after repeated charging and dis-charging cycles, its cost and safety, drive the development of electric vehicles. The demand for high energy density in the batteries of electric vehicles, increase the complexity of battery dynamics and thus create concern for both efficiency and safety. Thus, an efficient battery monitoring system keeps a close watch on the performance of the battery [1]. Battery of the electric vehicle shares a major cost and so accurate estimation of charge inside the battery reduces over-design and increases the overall efficiency [2]. Range anxiety is another challenge to widespread adoption of electric vehicles. Hence, the design of Battery Management System (BMS) which estimates State-of-Charge, is critical. Developments in Artificial Intelligence (AI) have contributed machine-learning based methods, for predicting state-of-charge [3]. Figure 16.1 shows the hierarchy of the sub-sets of AI – (i) Machine-Learning, (ii) Representation-Learning (iii) Deep-Learning and the distribution of SoC and SoH (State-of-Health) prediction methods for electric-vehicles, among these sub-sets.

16.2   Battery State of Charge Prediction Using Non-Recurrent Neural Networks

Prediction of SoC using non-recurrent neural networks is illustrated in this section. While recurrent neural networks have a recurrent connection on the hidden state, non-recurrent neural networks, process inputs only in the forward direction. Popularly referred as Universal Function Approximators, they are capable of learning any non-linear function. Activation function deployed in a non-recurrent neural network helps in learning complex relationships between input and output [4]. State of Charge estimation in a battery operated vehicle is analogous to a fuel-indicator in conventional IC engine vehicles. However, SoC is not measured directly as in a fuel-gauge, instead it is estimated in-directly from physically available signals like current drawn from/fed into the battery, voltage across the terminals and temperature [5]. Nonlinear characteristics inherent to the battery make this task, more challenging. The correctness of State-of-Charge significantly improves vehicle dynamics, safety and reduces the cost of over-sizing the battery-pack. SoC prediction methods based on non-recurrent neural network is illustrated in the following order

i)   Feed Forward Neural Network
ii) Radial Basis Function Neural Network
iii) Extreme Learning Machine
iv) Support Vector Machine

16.2.1   Feed-Forward Neural Network

Input parameters of a system are mapped to its output non-linearly in a Feed-forward Neural Network. It can be applied to any use-case in its simplest form. Each FNN shall be associated with a non-linear activation function. Hyperbolic tangent function mentioned in equation (16.1) is the most preferred non-linear activation function. The hyperbolic tangent function confines the output values to an upper limit of 1 and a lower limit of -1. A rectified linear unit (RELU) represented in (16.2), is an alternative to hyperbolic tangent function, where all negative input values are replaced by zeros.

$$H(t) = \frac{2}{1+e^{-2t}} - 1 \qquad (16.1)$$

$$H(t) = \max(0, t) \qquad (16.2)$$

Learnable parameters of the FNN such as weights W^l_N and bias b are identified iteratively to minimize the loss function. The FNN is trained using back-propagation algorithm [6]. This algorithm differentiates the estimated error partially with respect to weight and bias and in-turn updates them to decrease the error in subsequent iterations. The count of iterations carried-out on the dataset is referred as epoch. The value of epoch limits for the number of training iterations. In-addition to epoch, conditions such as rate of error-reduction may be used to stop the training.

16.2.2 Radial Basis Function Neural Network

A class of Feed-Forward Neural Network containing input layer, hidden layer and output layer (one each), performing linear summation is known as Radial Basis Function (RBF) Neural Network.

$$\varphi_i(x) = G(|| x - w_i ||) = \exp\left(-\frac{|| x_i - w_i ||^2}{\sigma_i^2} \right) \tag{16.3}$$

Instead of using nonlinear activation function which yield a single-value, the neurons in the hidden layer of RBF neural network calculate scaled Euclidean distance, mapped by Gaussian function shown in (16.3). Radial Basis Functions employ centroid vectors to train the neural network instead of determining weight gains. RBF neural networks can be trained faster and can interpolate results better [7]. An extended Kalman Filter (EKF) was used with an RBF neural network for online estimation of State-of-Charge of a lead-acid battery and a Li-ion cell [8] and [9]. Here the battery was modeled using the Radial Basis Function Neural Network, to determine the state-space equations for the extended Kalman Filter, where the state variables are terminal voltage and State-of-Charge, at ambient room temperature. Extended H∞ filter was implemented with RBF neural network in [10]. The same neural network was used with unscented Kalman filter (UKF) in [11].

16.2.3 Extreme Learning Machine

Although the structure of Extreme Learning Machine (ELM) is identical to Feed-Forward Neural Network, it differs in the training algorithm employed. Unlike the FNN which uses back propagation algorithm, the ELM uses Moore-Penrose generalized inverse or pseudo-inverse matrix [12]. Pseudo-inverse matrices are typically used to compute best-fit solution to a set of linear equations which lack a solution. The authors of [13] implemented Extreme Machine Learning on experimental data, to model a Li-ion battery and the SoC was approximated using Kalman Filter. The ELM method has an edge over RBF, characterized by reduced computational demand and smaller SOC estimation error.

This work accounted an ambient temperature of 25°C with 10 neurons for Extreme Learning Machine and 15 neurons for Radial Basis Function. It was observed that the ELM recorded half the estimation time compared to RBF, with lower estimation error. The improvement in estimation accuracy and reduction in computational load is attributed to the use of Adaptive Unscented Kalman Filter than other variants of KFs.

Gravitational Search Algorithm (GSA) was used to identify the optimum count of neurons in an Extreme Learning Machine Model [14]. The neural network consisted of one hidden layer. The network employed two drive cycles namely the US06 and Beijing dynamic stress test (BJDST), at two varied temperatures (25°C and 45°C). The US06 drive cycle is a high-speed, quick acceleration loop, covering 8 miles, lasting for 10 minutes, reaching a top-speed of 130 kph. The dynamic-stress-test simulates the demands of an electric-vehicle battery. But, the ability of the Extreme Learning Machine model to be generalized for electric vehicle applications, was validated using a limited data-set. Besides, the model was trained and validated using the same drive cycle data – Training data, 70% and validation data, 30%. The selection of Machine-Learning structure could be automated using optimization algorithms.

16.2.4   Support Vector Machine

The support vector machine is a class of supervised machine learning algorithm that predominantly solves classification problems. SoC estimation is a regression problem, which requires minimizing the error function. The variant of SVM typically used for regression problems with linearly in-separable data, is referred as Support Vector Regression (SVR). Although, Support Vector Regression (SVR) appears to be similar to Radial Basis Function (RBF) described earlier, SVR parameters are fitted by linear constraints, which are simpler optimization routines. Besides, SVR does not apply cost function penalty to error-fitting, if the error is within a defined-band. This concept of error-tolerance margin provides more stable estimation.

The State-of-Charge of a 60 Ah Lithium Iron Phosphate battery was estimated using SVM in [15]. They used kernels (e.g., RBF) to spot support vectors lying in a hyperspace of multi-dimensions. They identified 903 support vectors responsible for a highly varying profile of voltage across the battery terminals, current drawn from/fed-into the battery, and the surrounding temperature. The research team carried out a similar work on 100 Ah battery too in [16] employing polynomial kernels.

16.3   Evaluation of Charge Prediction Techniques

SoC prediction techniques can be fairly compared only on common-grounds. i.e. when each algorithm is evaluated for the same data, on identical learnable parameters and with uniform training and testing procedures. The strategies given below guide the assessment of state-of-charge estimation methods.

i.   Across all the algorithms under comparison, maintain the same training-dataset and testing-dataset.
ii. Among all the algorithms, maintain equal number of learnable parameters.
iii. Train each model repeatedly.

With reference to the first strategy, datasets available open-source are provided in Table 16.1. These data allow researchers to match their results with others working on the same data. The second strategy allows matching the models for cost of computation and memory utilization, if the models share identical number of training parameters. The third strategy emphasizes multiple trainings. This would reduce the chance of identifying a local minimum. Model-complexity drives the number of epochs required. More the parameters and hidden layers, more number of trainings are required. Through repeated training the model understands the randomness of the training, in-turn reducing the probability of finding a local minimum.

Table 16.1 Open-source data of batteries.

Repository of battery-data	Reference
Li-ion Panasonic NCR 18650 PF	[17]
Li-ion NASA AMCS Prognostics Data Repository	[18]
Li-ion LFP A123 (APR18650 M1A)	[19]
Li-ion LG 18650 HG2	[20]

16.4   Conclusion

The study highlights the significance of data collection and preparation, for training and validating the algorithms. This task is critical to all algorithms driven by data. The process of data-collection can prolong to several months or years, due to the experiments required. In-spite of this cumbersome process, data is generated. The quality of data significantly limits the efficiency of the machine-learning algorithms. Further investigations are necessary to analyze the computation difficulty in the training and deployment of machine-learning models.

References

1. Bilgin, B., Magne, P., Malysz, P., Yang, Y., Pantelic, V., Preindl, M., Korobkine, A., Jiang, W., Lawford, M., Emadi, A., Making the case for electrified transportation. *IEEE Trans. Transp. Electrification*, 1, 1, 4–17, Jun. 2015.
2. Andwari, A.M., Pesiridis, A., Rajoo, S., Martinez-Botas, R., Esfahanian, V., A review of battery electric vehicle technology and readiness levels. *Renew. Sustain. Energy Rev.*, 78, 414–430, Oct. 2017.
3. Zuboff, S., *The age of surveillance capitalism: The fight for a human future at the new frontier of power*, 1st ed., Public Affairs, New York, NY, USA, 2019.
4. Goodfellow, I., Bengio, Y., Courville, A., *Deep learning*, MIT Press, Cambridge, MA, USA, 2016.
5. Hannan, M.A., Lipu, M.S.H., Hussain, A., Mohamed, A., A review of lithium-ion battery state of charge estimation and management system in electric vehicle applications: Challenges and recommendations. *Renew. Sustain. Energy Rev.*, 78, 834854, Oct. 2017.
6. Shrestha, A. and Mahmood, A., Review of deep learning algorithms and architectures. *IEEE Access*, 7, 53040–53065, 2019.
7. Yang, F., Li, W., Li, C., Miao, Q., State-of-charge estimation of lithium ion batteries based on gated recurrent neural network. *Energy*, 175, 66–75, May 2019.
8. Charkhgard, M. and Farrokhi, M., State-of-charge estimation for lithium ion batteries using neural networks and EKF. *IEEE Trans. Ind. Electron.*, 57, 12, 4178–4187, Dec. 2010.
9. Shahriari, M. and Farrokhi, M., Online state-of-health estimation of VRLA batteries using state of charge. *IEEE Trans. Ind. Electron.*, 60, 1, 191–202, Jan. 2012.
10. Alfi, A., Zarif, M.H., Charkhgard, M., Hybrid state of charge estimation for lithium-ion batteries: Design and implementation. *IET Power Electron.*, 7, 11, 2758–2764, Nov. 2014.

11. Gholizade-Narm, H. and Charkhgard, M., Lithium-ion battery state of charge estimation based on square-root unscented Kalman filter. *IET Power Electron.*, 6, 9, 1833–1841, Nov. 2013.

12. Huang, G.-B., Zhu, Q.-Y., Siew, C.-K., Extreme learning machine: Theory and applications. *Neurocomputing*, 70, 1-3, 489–501, Dec. 2006.

13. Du, J., Liu, Z., Wang, Y., State of charge estimation for li-ion battery based on model from extreme learning machine. *Control Eng. Pract.*, 26, 1, 11–19, May 2014.

14. Hossain Lipu, M.S., Hannan, M.A., Hussain, A., Saad, M.H., Ayob, A., Uddin, M.N., Extreme learning machine model for state-of-charge estimation of lithium-ion battery using gravitational search algorithm. *IEEE Trans. Ind. Appl.*, 55, 4, 4225–4234, Jul. 2019.

15. Anton, J.C.A., Nieto, P.J.G., Viejo, C.B., Vilan, J.A.V., Support vector machines used to estimate the battery state of charge. *IEEE Trans. Power Electron.*, 28, 12, 5919–5926, Dec. 2013.

16. Álvarez Antón, J.C., García Nieto, P.J., de Cos Juez, F.J., Sánchez Lasheras, F., González Vega, M., Roqueñí Gutiérrez, M.N., Battery state-of-charge estimator using the SVM technique. *Appl. Math. Modell.*, 37, 9, 6244–6253, May 2013.

17. Panasonic 18650PF li-ion battery data, Accessed: Jan. 20, 2020. [Online]. Available: http://dx.doi.org/10.17632/wykht8y7tg.1#folder-96f196a8-a04d-4e6a-827d-0dc4d61ca97b.

18. Saha, B. and Goebel, K., Battery data set. NASA Ames Prognostics Data Repository, NASA Ames Research Center, Moffett Field, CA, USA. [Online]. Available: http://ti.arc.nasa.gov/project/prognosticdata-repository, 2007.

19. Severson, K.A., Attia, P.M., Jin, N., Perkins, N., Jiang, B., Yang, Z., Chen, M.H., Aykol, M., Herring, P.K., Fraggedakis, D., Bazant, M.Z., Harris, S.J., Chueh, W.C., Braatz, R.D., Data-driven prediction of battery cycle life before capacity degradation. *Nat. Energy*, 4, 5, 383–391, May 2019.

20. Kollmeyer, P., Vidal, C., Naguib, M., Skells, M., LG 18650HG2 li-ion battery data and example deep neural network xEV SOC estimator script, Mendeley Data, 2020.

Driver Drowsiness Detection System

G. Lavanya*, N. Sunand, S. Gokulraj and T.G. Chakaravarthi

Sri Ramakrishna Engineering College, Coimbatore, India

Abstract

Drowsiness is the major problem associated with road accidents. It is necessary to bring a safe technology which helps to improve the mortality rate; most of the accidents occur due to drivers because of mental fatigue and drowsiness. To overcome the problem this chapter introduced a novel system that helps to avoid the accidents. We have chosen two parameters such as eye and mouth that helps to locate the facial landmarks. Based on that we are tracking the eye and mouth aspect ratio that helps us to identify the drowsiness earlier and avoid accidents.

Keywords: Camera, drowsiness, open CV dlib library, eye aspect, mouth aspect ratio

17.1 Introduction

According to the survey, 100,000 accidents occur annually due to driver sleepiness. Fatigue usually occurs due to psychological state of the person. Due to that they lost their control to stop the vehicle.

Due to mental alertness and sleepiness drivers are not able to operate the vehicle properly and safely; due to that there is an increase in risk of accidents. Based on the above conditions, the driver does not focus on the vehicle. To drive safely, driver mental condition should be good. Interaction between the vehicle and driver is always needed to enjoy a safe journey. The main aim is to monitor the driver's eye and mouth, whether

---

Corresponding author: lavanya.gangadharan@srec.ac.in

K. Umamaheswari, B. Vinoth Kumar and S. K. Somasundaram (eds.) Artificial Intelligence for Sustainable Applications, (275–282) © 2023 Scrivener Publishing LLC

it is opened or closed with the help of webcam. By monitoring the above two parameters driver drowsiness was detected earlier. Yawning is another supporting parameter that helps to detect the drowsiness accurately.

Existing solution is classified into various categories such as intrusive and nonintrusive system. In intrusive system they need to wear sensor which is not comfortable to the drivers. Nonintrusive system mainly focused on extracting the facial features that helps to detect the drowsiness.

Our aim is to identify the facial landmarks with the help of that analyzing the Eye and Mouth Aspect Ratio using OpenCV-dlib library. These ratios are compared with the normal values and to alarm the driver based on his eye and mouth position.

17.2   Literature Survey

17.2.1   Reports on Driver's Fatigue Behind the Steering Wheel

Kumari et al. [1] discussed about the drowsiness system and how it affects the people life. Some statistics they revealed that 23% of adults have fallen asleep during driving due to that most of the accidents are occur. Drivers and passenger life was at risk.

17.2.2   Survey on Camera-Based Drowsiness Classification

Anna Liza et al. [2] developed a model that helps to detect drowsiness with parameters such as eye movement and mouth movement with the help of support vector machine (SVM), color spaces such as (RGB, YCbCr and HSV), and algorithms like Random Forest, AdaBoost for monitoring the face detection, and Fuzzy c-means (FCM) for lips segmentation.

Friedrichs et al. [3] proposed and monitored the eye with the help of that they detect the drowsiness They collected dataset of 4 days real time information of road drives and follow the drowsiness. In this paper they were unable to use this method with bad light conditions and persons who are all wearing glass were unable to track the eye drowsiness.

17.2.3   Survey on Ear for Drowsy Detection

Caio et al. [4] in this paper they use various different combinations such as eye localization, threshold was selected to find the whiteness of the eye, and estimate the white region of the eye that disappears based on that drowsiness was identified. Drawbacks of this system use only eye aspect ratio sometimes it may fail to detect.

Yingyu Ji *et al.* [5], in this method they extract eye and mouth features and applied in new algorithms to get better results. In this algorithm they utilized eye map algorithm with the help of that they calculated the contour aspect ratio based on that they determine whether the eye is opened or closed. Based on the above the algorithm provides high accuracy rate and computational efficiency.

Sanam *et al.* [6] in this paper utilized the eye open based on that the status of the driver was classified. In this algorithm they compared with threshold greater than 0.3. If driver threshold level reduced less than 0.3 it automatically counts the frames based on that we have identified that the person has closed their eyes.

Vaibhav Garg *et al.* [7] extracted various physiological data from the driver such as internal heat level and heartbeat rate and also physical data sources includes of yawning and squinting. It further screens Mouth Aspect Ratio (MAR) of the driver up to a fixed number of casings to check the languor and yawning.

17.3 Components and Methodology

17.3.1 Software (Toolkit Used)

OpenCV dlib Library:
It is an open-source computer vision and machine learning software library. In this library they have various algorithms. Those algorithms were very helpful to extract and recognize the various features and also, they help to classify the person action in video camera and also track the drowsiness earlier. With the help of above library, we are able to detect the face landmark; the following figure helps to detect the facial landmarks as shown in Figure 17.1.

17.3.2 Hardware Components

In this work Logitech c20 HD webcam was used to collect the database.

17.3.3 Logitech C270 HD Webcam

It is used as tool to capture images of the person before narrowing it down to the eye region to the mouth. It captures crisp HD 720p/30 fps. It produces high resolution of images. It captures video up to 1280 x 720 pixels.

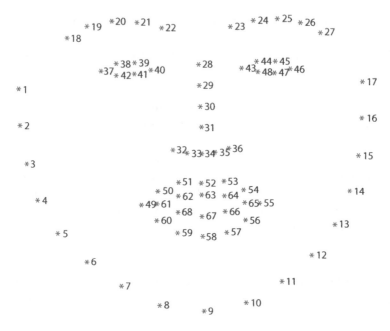

Figure 17.1 Facial landmark model.

17.3.4 Eye Aspect Ratio (EAR)

In this parameter used to calculate two different landmarks horizontal side and vertical side.

Ratio of the distances between horizontal eye and vertical eye landmarks was calculated. They monitor continuously whether the eye is opened or not as shown in Figure 17.2. Calculations was done based on the below formula [10].

$$EAR = \frac{\|p_2 - p_6\| + \|p_3 - p_5\|}{2\|p_2 - p_4\|}$$

Figure 17.2 Eye aspect ratio positions and formula.

$$MAR = \frac{|EF|}{|AB|}$$

Figure 17.3 Mouth aspect ratio position and formula.

17.3.5   Mouth Aspect Ratio (MAR)

Mouth aspect ratio is defined as the ratio of vertical distance of mouth to the horizontal distance of the mouth. When Mouth aspect ratio for yawning person is assumed to greater than 0.43, while the other values of Mouth aspect ratio is less than threshold value that is less than 0.43. The yawn counter is incremented only when the MAR value is greater than the mentioned threshold for more than three frames. Figure 17.3 determines the formula for mouth aspect ratio.

17.3.6   Working Principle

A python file is created named project.py and the code for image acquisition is run. OpenCV and dlib library are downloaded that helps to predict the facial landmarks. This library will help to detect the EAR and MAR. Webcam was employed in the vehicle that helps to record person in real-time. Facial landmarks were extracted from real time video images that will be very helpful to extract features from the image [8]. Use of OpenCV and dlib helps to detect the facial landmarks from the driver. Based on eye blinking, position of driver, head position of the driver, and alignment of face, all the parameters help to estimate the various coordinates that help to detect the drowsiness.

17.3.7   Facial Landmark Detection and Measure Eye Aspect Ratio and Mouth Aspect Ratio

With use of dlib library Eye and mouth localization takes place to localize eye and mouth aspect ratio based on that we can determine whether the person eye is opened or closed. Extraction of eye takes place to localize the geometric coordinates and named them as p1, p2, p3, p4, p5, and p6. Mouth geometrical coordinates are labeled as A, B, C, D, E and F. eye aspect ratio was calculated based on the height and width of the eye [11].

The eye blinking can be eliminated as it is quick reaction and it last for approximately 100-400ms. The N-th frame can be kept as 20 with a time difference of 2 seconds. The threshold value of EAR and MAR is calculated. If the Eye Aspect Ratio threshold value is low and Mouth Aspect Ratio threshold value is high, the driver is alerted.

17.3.8   Results Obtained

In this developed model it automatically detects the both eye and mouth state that helps to detect the drowsiness earlier and avoid accidents. Evaluation of mental state was compared with threshold value. System is also more accurate to find the exact condition of the person [9]. Once the

Figure 17.4 Eye aspect ratio at threshold.

Figure 17.5 Eye aspect ratio below threshold value.

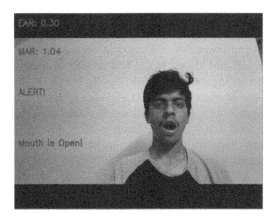

Figure 17.6 Mouth aspect ratio below threshold value.

EAR value becomes less than the threshold value and MAR becomes greater than the threshold value the state will change. Threshold was selected at 0.3 for opening state as shown in Figure 17.4. If the level is reduced below the threshold, it determines the closed state as shown in Figure 17.5.

The number of blinks can be counted as if there is continuous blinking for the driver due to tiredness. The number of frames is set to 15 such that the normal blinking can be eliminated (time difference for each frame is 0.1ms) as shown in Figure 17.6.

17.4 Conclusion

The Driver Drowsiness Detection system helps to avoid accidents. Here they use the combination of webcam and facial landmarks helps to extract the various features from the face based on that driver drowsiness was detected earlier. In future it plans to incorporate pulse oximeter and heart rate sensor to detect the oxygen level and heart rate of the driver.

References

1. Kusuma Kumari, B., Review on drowsy driving: Becoming dangerous problem. *Int. J. Sci. Res.*, 3, 1, 49–51, January 2014.
2. Ramos, A.L.A., Erandio, J.C., Mangilaya, D.H.T., Driver drowsiness detection based on eye movement and yawning using faciallandmark analysis. Institute of Computer Studies, Philippines. *IJSSST*, 20, 1473–8031, 2019.

3. Friedrichs, F. and Yang, B., Camera-based drowsiness reference for driver state classificationunder real driving conditions, Chair of System Theory and Signal Processing University of Stuttgart, Germany.

4. Souto Maior, C.B. and Moura, M.C., Real-time SVM classification for drowsiness detection using eye aspect ratio, September 2018, Probabilistic Safety Assessment and Management PSAM 14, Los Angeles.

5. Ji, Y. and Wang, S., Eye and mouth state detection algorithm-based on contour feature extraction. *J. Electron. Imaging*, 27, 5, 051205, Sep/Oct 2018.

6. Narejo, S. and Soomro, S.S., Development of vehicle driver drowsiness detection system using eye aspect ratio. *PJAEE*, 17, 9, 8957–8971, 2020, Department of Computer Systems Engineering, Mehran University of Engineering & Technology, Jamshoro, Pakistan.

7. Garg, V. and Goel, P., Yawning detection system. *Int. Res. J. Eng. Technol.*, 07, 06, 538–541, June 2020.

8. Bhoyar, A.M. and Sawalkar, S.N., Implementation on visual analysis of eye state using image processing. *Int. Res. J. Eng. Technol.*, 06, 04, 4340–4346, Apr 2019.

9. Gupta, R.K. and Sahu, U.K., Real time face recognition under different conditions. *Int. J. Adv. Res. Comput. Sci. Software Eng.*, 3, 1, 1–18, January 2013.

10. Flores, M.J., Anningll, M., Escalera, A., Real-time warning system for driver drowsiness detection using visual information. *J. Intell. Robot. Syst.*, 59, 2, 10–33, 18 N.2009.

11. Cheng, Q. and Wang, W., Assessment of driver mental fatigue using facial landmarks. IEEE State Key Laboratory of Traffic Control and Safety, 7, 150423–150434, 2019.

Part VI
SECURITY APPLICATIONS

18

An Extensive Study to Devise a Smart Solution for Healthcare IoT Security Using Deep Learning

Arul Treesa Mathew and Prasanna Mani*

School of Information Technology and Engineering, Vellore Institute of Technology, Vellore, India

Abstract

Introduction of IoT Technology had brought in significant changes to the conventional mode of operation in healthcare service sector. The ease of use offered by such IoT-based systems added to its popularity and wide acceptance. Healthcare IoT based systems ranging from self-trackers to wearable assistance devices are used by millions of users in this world today. This has also led to a significant increase in the number of attacks over such systems. The attacks had varying motto like data breach, denial of service, and other malicious intentions. This gives an insight to why the security of healthcare IoT based systems are important. In this paper, we propose a smart solution to this issue, using deep learning based techniques.

Keywords: Healthcare, IoT, deep learning, security

18.1 Introduction

Recent years have marked remarkable improvement in all areas related to our day to day life, through the introduction of IoT and its wide range of applications. Internet of Things, the interconnected deployment of sensing devices, processing and storage units, has taken away the gap between technology and common people. This movement however showed best results in the advancement of healthcare sector. Rather than asking for a

---

Corresponding author: arultreesa.mathew@vit.ac.in; prasanna.m@vit.ac.in

---

K. Umamaheswari, B. Vinoth Kumar and S. K. Somasundaram (eds.) *Artificial Intelligence for Sustainable Applications*, (285–294) © 2023 Scrivener Publishing LLC

medical practitioner's assistance for every single thing, IoT made it easy for the users to keep track of their daily activities and lifestyle on their own, using IoT devices. Self-tracking health applications gained huge popularity among mankind as the users could monitor their daily activities and incorporate necessary changes in their lifestyle as and when required thus ensuring better health.

Healthcare IoT is a new term that is coined to refer to IoT networks that are deployed in healthcare sector. These networks comprise of actuators or sensors for data collection, processing units that perform real time analysis of the observed or collected data, and storage units which are mostly equipped over cloud based systems. In the most common format of healthcare IoT networks, the wearables, sensors employed will be incorporated into a wearable device, equipped with limited computational capacity. Daily activities of the end user like walking, drinking, breath patterns, pulse rate, etc. could be monitored using these wearable devices and a first level yet real time analysis of the sensed data is performed to know whether the vitals are normal. In the implanted versions of healthcare systems, sending out alerts whenever there is a significant drift from the normal behavior, would be an added advantage, as it ensures better support to the patient.

Increased usage and popularity of these smart assistive healthcare devices have also attracted attention of attackers. These IoT based applications, generate a huge amount of data, which are extremely personal and sensitive in nature. This gives out an alert to the security of the contained data. Studies have showed that attacks to such healthcare systems have increased in the recent past. Attacks mostly concentrated on data breach, but cases of data manipulation were also reported which takes the impacts to a higher level. Since the data contained gives out an insight of the user's behavioral patterns, physical strengths and weaknesses, daily routine, etc. getting access to it is of great importance from an attacker perspective.

In this work, we try to perform a detailed study of Healthcare IoT networks, focusing on their strengths, weaknesses, current modes of security, vulnerabilities, and possible countermeasures. Then we also propose a security framework that can enforce better security to healthcare IoT systems, thus protecting the privacy of contained data.

18.2   Related Literature

H.I. Ahmed *et al.* [1] did a survey on various threats and defense mechanisms in IoT Security. They have studied about various security challenges, threats, and defenses that are enforced on the different layers of an IoT environment. Various layers of IoT networks, their functions, vulnerabilities, security requirements, and the current security measures deployed are described in detail. Attacks to various layers are discussed along with suggestions of suitable countermeasures. The heterogeneous nature of IoT network adds more challenge to the security. These challenges include privacy challenges, network infrastructure challenges, big data challenges, and Quality of Service challenges. The authors also have performed an evaluation of IoT Security spanning through various tools, processes, and methodologies.

I. Ahmad *et al.* [2] have also performed an analysis on the security threats to IoT systems. Attack modes like physical attacks, software attacks, network attacks and encryption attacks are discussed in detail. They have also discussed about various applications of IoT based systems. The security enforced to IoT systems using Edge computing and Fog Computing is analyzed along with Block chain enforced security methods.

M. Imdad *et al.* [3] discusses about the security challenges brought in through the wide acceptance and deployment of IoT based systems. The seven basic requirements to enforce security in IoT systems include confidentiality, integrity, availability, authentication, authorization, non-repudiation, and privacy. The possible modes of attacks with reference to these seven security requirements are found out and classifications are done based on their behavior and impacts. They have proposed a secure mechanism which addressed all the listed attacks. The solution is however generic in nature and is expected to be further extended to specific domains.

H. Zakaria *et al.* [4] gives an insight to the possible risks associated with the openness and distributed nature of IoT networks, specifically pointing to its application in the medical sector. The wide acceptance of IoT-based medical assistance systems and their heterogeneous nature of operations have attracted the attention of attackers, who look for possible vulnerabilities thereby launching a successful attack on the systems. The authors have proposed a risk management model to securely use the IoT Systems in the medical care environment. The model devised has made use of COBIT5 (control objectives for information and related technology) as it can easily synergize with other standards. Risk categories like data and application, user change management, security and privacy, physical environment, etc. are used in developing the first phase of the model. HPIA (Hospital Performance Indicators for Accountability) categories like employee satisfaction, customer focus, internal business process, etc. are incorporated to the model later. The model is now under expert review.

The work by D. Sparrell [5], titled Cyber-Safety in Healthcare IoT, discusses the various threats to healthcare IoT systems and also about how the future systems can adapt to the threats and vulnerabilities in real time. Studies have revealed that a good majority of healthcare organizations have been attacked by now. Impacts of these attacks ranged from user data breach to even patient deaths. This gives out an alarm to the necessity of enforcing security to this application of IoT based systems, closely referred as IoHT or Internet of Health Things. Attackers might be either passive or self-motivated, or even experts who are hired as part of a funded campaign being part of a mission. This gives increased responsibility to IoHT designers to enforce security in the systems. Cybersecurity standards like FAIRTM, DoCRA, SBoM, STIXTM, TAXIITM, OpenC2, and CACAO are discussed in the paper.

A. Shepherd *et al.* [6] developed a taxonomy with respect to IoT Medical Security and the perceptions formulated by them in that regard. Basic concerns about security like integrity, availability, authentication, authorization, and audit, are discussed in the user perspective. The proposed taxonomy arranged itself into various classifications like security, users, threats, data, IoT technology, and communication.

M. Algarni *et al.* [7] perform an analytical review on IoT security with respect to enabled application challenges and also recommend some solutions to mitigate these challenges. They overview the applications of IoT like smart homes, smart vehicles, smart cities and healthcare, and also introduces some tools that can be put in place to ensure security of such smart networks. Security protocols like CoAP, IEEE 802.15.4, 6LoWPAN, TLS Protocol, etc. are discussed. In addition, they provide an insight on challenges like security challenges and technological challenges that can pop up in the current research and also some future enhancements.

The works by Obogo Johnson, [8] and [13], consolidated various security and privacy challenges in the healthcare IoT domain. Healthcare IoT has invariably helped in making the disease discovery, treatment, and recovery process easier. The introduction of smart devices at the patient's end and monitoring systems at the medical practitioner's end have made it possible for an expert consultation even discarding the geographical locations of both parties and have many benefits. The key role players in healthcare IoT include the patient or end user, medical practitioner or expert, and healthcare providers. Memory, Energy, and Computation Limitations, dynamic network topology and multi-protocol Network, compromised hardware and software etc. were enlisted as the security challenges. On the other hand, user and device authentication, data modification, eavesdropping, etc. had fallen under the privacy challenges category. The author has also proposed a Physical Unclonable Functions (PUFs) authentication technique as a solution to safeguard from the security and privacy challenges in healthcare IoT.

The solution has two phases, the first stage being the enrolment and deployment of end devices. In the second phase, authentication of these devices is checked.

N. A. Abu Bakar *et al.* [9] in their paper on Security Risk Management in healthcare IoT, describe how IoT technology has transformed healthcare sector. They also point out how the risk management aspects of healthcare IoT are lagging behind when more attention has been diverted to the strategical aspects like architecture, design etc. They propose a model for risk management in healthcare IoT, after performing a detailed study on various challenges to its security. The model proposed is iterative in nature with various phases starting from context establishment, risk assessment, determination phase, and risk treatment if the determination result is risk, or a return to context establishment searching for a new version of context. After the risk treatment is done, a test is conducted to know whether the risk has been treated properly. If it is not, the phase is repeated until the desired level is achieved. This is then followed by a detailed communication and monitoring review.

A. Chacko and T. Hayajneh [10], in their paper discuss the risks associated with the widely accepted IoT based mode of healthcare. The increasing acceptance, ease of use, elimination of geographical barriers etc. are some of the major strengths of this system. Unfortunately, data contained and sensed in the system, is not handled with due importance, with regard to the privacy and security aspects. The healthcare providers are given full access to the user's personal but vital information. However, they fail to ensure the privacy of the user data and also might reuse them according to their commercial requirements and business policies. This becomes an alarming situation when someone with wrong intentions get hold to this data, as a slight modification to the sensed data can result in wrong diagnosis thus even leading to the death of original user. The authors describe how important it is to ensure that the network is capable to run automated work flows, and provide prompt responses to requests for critical information, without breaching its security – strong security policies, malware defenses, activity monitoring etc.

A. MacDermott *et al.* [11] discusses about a multi-faceted approach that can be employed to secure HIoT systems. They have used machine learning techniques that can enforce advanced and persistent level of threat detection and also perform predictive analysis. The authors have brought in a set of monitoring agents being placed very close to the source, of which time criticality is most important. Features related to various activities are considered. A local report about an event with information like event id, timestamp, agent identity, feature affected and the new value, and agent's analysis whether the event is malicious or not, is generated. Consolidating the local reports form the decision about the current security level of the system. The authors of [12, 15, 17], Jurcut, A.D. *et al.*, Gopalan S.S. *et al.*, and Abdullah A. *et al.* have performed a detailed survey on the possibilities of IoT security and challenges. They have given a detailed description on the security concerns to IoT based systems.

F. Hussain *et al.* [14] in their work introduces a framework that can detect malicious traffic in the context of IoT devices used in healthcare sector. An open source tool called IoT Flock is used for data generation. This tool generates use-cases for data corresponding to both normal and malicious behavior of the system. Machine learning techniques are then used on the generated data set to detect any attacks and also to protect the system.

M. A. Al-Garadi *et al.* [16] have performed an analytical survey on using machine learning and deep learning technologies which can be adopted to secure the IoT based systems. Narmatha C [19], in her work performs a comparitive analysis over the advantages and limitations of various cyber-security mechanisms employed to enhance security in modern systems. Odumuyiwa, V. and Chibueze, A. [18], have detailed about an automatic detection system to prevent HTTP based injection attacks. They use deep neural networks to attain this goal. Similarly, Fazeldehkordi, E. *et al.* [20], have performed a case study over various healthcare devices to interpret the importance of securing these IoT systems. The strengths and weaknesses of these techniques are analyzed in the rest of the paper, thus giving ideas to future researches.

The literature analysis can be summarized as follows. The Internet of Things and its wide range of applications have brought in a top to bottom change to the conventional approaches of technology. IoT has narrowed down the gaps between end users and the high end services offered by technology. Given all these, the wide acceptance of IoT based systems has also gained attention of attackers checking for an intrusion into the system with various aims ranging from exposing the vulnerabilities to an attack causing a significant damage to the system and/or disrupting the service. When IoT is used in healthcare sector, such vulnerabilities and attacks might turn even lethal. Hence securing healthcare IoT systems is of great importance. However, the service providers are not either aware of the necessity to secure the systems or are driven away from it due to their business policies. The low computation capacities of IoT end devices and their heterogeneous nature add to the impact of the attacks. Even though there are many frameworks adopted for securing such systems, they fail to address it to the extent where the impacts are minimal or negligible. This opens a new door to research.

18.3   Proposed Model

In this paper, we try to propose a smart system for healthcare IoT which utilizes the capacities of deep learning to provide better surveillance and security to the underlying healthcare IoT network. We try to address three main issues, data breach, data manipulation from unauthorized persons, and unauthorized access to the end devices.

18.3.1   Proposed System Architecture

In general, IoT system will contain three main components: An application that performs the real time analysis of sensed data, hardware components for sensing, analysis and temporary storage, and high end computational or storage systems that are usually fulfilled using cloud service. In our proposed model, we are trying to enhance the application by adding a deep learning capacity to it, so that it can perform a security check on the network along with the real-time analysis of sensed data.

A schematic architecture diagram of the proposed model is shown in Figure 18.1. As mentioned above, we are using deep learning approach to secure the system from unwanted and malicious access thus offering a better privacy to user's sensitive information.

There are three parts to this system. As mentioned in Figure 18.1, the physical layer of this system still remains to contain the sensory devices and related hardware. This layer is responsible for sensing the relevant vital signs from the user on a consistent basis. There can be one or more sensors in this layer each one of them doing a specific but distinct task.

The android-based application is the main topic of discussion in the proposed secure system. In addition to its normal role of conducting the primary analysis of the sensed information, we propose to add an additional module to it with which the same application can be made use of for sensing the network traffic, monitoring it for any unauthorized access trials. The deep learning methods first are trained on the patterns of data access that occurs from authorized sources. This information will contain potential IP addresses, MAC addresses of authenticated devices, log patterns to be expected from authorized resources etc. It will perform a network scan frequently to know whether there is a potential vulnerability that could be exploited by an attacker. If found, it sends out alerts to the system administrator for resolving the issue. Similarly, if a malicious attacker successfully gets hold of a system, the application learns it during the scanning phase and immediately initiates alerts to cease the network traffic to that IP, thus protecting the information.

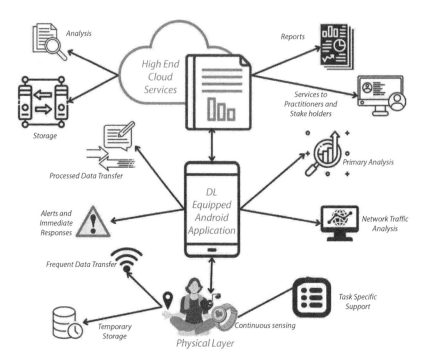

Figure 18.1 Schematic architecture diagram.

The high-end services are realized using the cloud-based system, which offers an extra security to the stored data through its own security mechanisms.

18.4 Conclusions and Future Works

Healthcare sector has undergone tremendous changes through the introduction of IoT based solutions. Benefits of such systems are enormous that it could bring components of healthcare industry together discarding their geographical separations and other differences. But this has also attracted the attention of persons with malicious intentions to search for vulnerabilities of the system thus exploiting it for their personal gains. However, attacks to healthcare systems cannot be treated light as it involves potential risks to the users' lives. The malicious interventions can modify the device settings thus denying the original service which may even lead to death of the person. The person behind this act still remains unaffected, as this incident would be treated as a hardware malfunction in the first place. This shows how important it is to secure the healthcare IoT based systems. Here, we propose a smart solution that employs deep learning to enhance the security. The enhancement is done on an android based application which is primarily used for the first line analysis of the sensed data. The application also performs frequent network scans to detect any unauthorized access trials and sends out alerts so that it is mitigated.

The system is in its implementation phase; data collection is progressing. Testing and training data will be segregated and the system will then be trained to meet the desired goals. Then the system has to be submitted for testing, expert reviews, refinements and final analysis. Future works include enhancing the performance of the system with timely changes so that it can be made compatible with the healthcare systems of future.

References

1. Ahmed, H.I., Nasr, A.A., Abdel-Mageid, S., Aslan, H.K., A survey of IoT security threats and defenses. *Int. J. Adv. Comput. Res.*, 9, 45, 325–350, 2019, https://doi.org/10.19101/ijacr.2019.940116.
2. Ahmad, I., Niazy, M.S., Ziar, R.A., Khan, S., Survey on IoT: Security threats and applications. *J. Robot. Control (JRC)*, 2, 1, 42–46, 2021, https://doi.org/10.18196/jrc.2150.
3. Imdad, M., Jacob, D.W., Mahdin, H., Baharum, Z., Shaharudin, S.M., Azmi, M.S., Internet of Things: Security requirements, attacks and counter measures. *Indones. J. Electr. Eng. Comput. Sci.*, 18, 3, 1520, 2020, https://doi.org/10.11591/ijeecs.v18.i3.pp1520-1530.
4. Zakaria, H., Abu Bakar, N.A., Hassan, N.H., Yaacob, S., IoT security risk management model for secured practice in healthcare environment. *Proc. Comput. Sci.*, 161, 1241–1248, 2019, https://doi.org/10.1016/j.procs.2019.11.238.
5. Sparrell, D., Cyber-safety in healthcare IoT. *2019 ITU Kaleidoscope: ICT for Health: Networks, Standards and Innovation (ITU K)*, 2019, https://doi.org/10.23919/ituk48006.2019.8996148.
6. Shepherd, A., Cooper, J., Kesa, C., Internet of Things (IoT) medical security: Taxonomy and perception. *Issues Inf. Syst.*, 21, 3, 227–235, 2020, https://doi.org/https://doi.org/10.48009/3_iis_2020_227-235.
7. Algarni, M., Alkhelaiwi, M., Karrar, A., Internet of Things security: A review of enabled application challenges and solutions. *Int. J. Adv. Comput. Sci. Appl.*, 12, 3, 2021, https://doi.org/10.14569/ijacsa.2021.0120325.
8. Obogo, J., Security and privacy challenges in healthcare IoT devices for patient treatment and monitoring, 2020, doi: https://doi.org/10.13140/RG.2.2.13613.31206.
9. Abu Bakar, N.A., Wan Ramli, W.M., Hassan, N.H., The Internet of Things in healthcare: An overview, challenges and model plan for security risks

management process. *Indones. J. Electr. Eng. Comput. Sci.*, 15, 1, 414, 2019, https://doi.org/10.11591/ijeecs.v15.i1.pp414-420.

10. Chacko, A. and Hayajneh, T., Security and privacy issues with IoT in healthcare. *EAI Endorsed Trans. Pervasive Health Technol.*, 4, 14, 155079, 2018, https://doi.org/10.4108/eai.13-7-2018.155079.

11. MacDermott, A., Kendrick, P., Idowu, I., Ashall, M., Shi, Q., Securing things in the healthcare Internet of Things. *2019 Global IoT Summit (GIoTS)*, 2019, https://doi.org/10.1109/giots.2019.8766383.

12. Jurcut, A.D., Ranaweera, P., Xu, L., Introduction to IoT security, in: *IoT Security*, pp. 27–64, 2019, https://doi.org/10.1002/9781119527978.ch2.

13. Obogo, J., A security and privacy architecture for healthcare IoT devices, 2020, https://doi.org/10.13140/RG.2.2.24485.22243.

14. Hussain, F., Abbas, S.G., Shah, G.A., Pires, I.M., Fayyaz, U.U., Shahzad, F., Garcia, N.M., Zdravevski, E., A framework for malicious traffic detection in IoT healthcare environment. *Sensors*, 21, 9, 3025, 2021, https://doi.org/10.3390/s21093025.

15. Gopalan, S.S., Raza, A., Almobaideen, W., IoT security in healthcare using AI: A survey. *2020 International Conference on Communications, Signal Processing, and their Applications (ICCSPA)*, pp. 1–6, 2021.

16. Al-Garadi, M.A., Mohamed, A., Al-Ali, A.K., Du, X., Ali, I., Guizani, M., A survey of machine and deep learning methods for Internet of Things (IoT) security. *IEEE Commun. Surv. Tutor.*, 22, 3, 1646–1685, third quarter 2020, https://doi.org/10.1109/COMST.2020.2988293.

17. Abdullah, A., Hamad, R., Abdulrahman, M., Moala, H., Elkhediri, S., CyberSecurity: A review of Internet of Things (IoT) security issues, challenges and techniques. *2019 2nd International Conference on Computer Applications & Information Security (ICCAIS)*, pp. 1–6, 2019, https://doi.org/10.1109/CAIS.2019.8769560.

18. Odumuyiwa, V. and Chibueze, A., Automatic detection of HTTP injection attacks using convolutional neural network and deep neural network. *J. Cyber Secur. Mobil.*, 9, 489–514, 2020, https://doi.org/10.13052/jcsm2245-1439.941.

19. Narmatha, C., Advancements, merits & demerits of cyber security: A critical study. In *2020 International Conference on Computing and Information Technology (ICCIT-1441)*, pp. 1–6, IEEE, 2020, September.

20. Fazeldehkordi, E., Owe, O., Noll, J., Security and privacy in IoT systems: A case study of healthcare products. *2019 13th International Symposium on Medical Information and Communication Technology (ISMICT)*, pp. 1–8, 2019.

19

A Research on Lattice-Based Homomorphic Encryption Schemes

Anitha Kumari K.[1]*, Prakaashini S.[1] and Suresh Shanmugasundaram[2]

[1]Department of IT, PSG College of Technology, Coimbatore, Tamil Nadu, India
[2]Department of Engineering, Botho University, Botswana, Africa

Abstract

With the large amount of data growing these days, every individual, companies, domains and many more are in the need for a proper and more secure system. All though there are already many ways to protect our data and secure them, there is still something missing in them. Every intruder trying to steal our personal data and information comes up with various ideas to break into the security system which is protecting our data. But in the recent days homomorphic encryption plays a significant role in protecting the data by performing encryption on the cipher text itself. A much more secured way for securing our data than usual homomorphic encryption is lattice-based homomorphic encryption. This paper aims to give a detailed and a very clear view on how this lattice-based homomorphic encryption works and its uses. In addition, this paper also aims to discuss the applications which use lattice-based homomorphic encryption and their significance in the recent growing domains of protecting or securing large amount of data from unauthorized break-in and destruction.

Keywords: Homomorphic encryption, lattice, quantum attacks, hard problems

19.1 Introduction

This chapter outlines lattice-based homomorphic encryptions that are needed to secure our data. Many cryptographic algorithms and methods are created every day and many of them are being used in present. But

---

*Corresponding author: kak.it@psgtech.ac.in

K. Umamaheswari, B. Vinoth Kumar and S. K. Somasundaram (eds.) *Artificial Intelligence for Sustainable Applications*, (295–310) © 2023 Scrivener Publishing LLC

all of them have some default cons in them which allow the intruders to break through the algorithm and gain access to our secure data. In order to overcome this security issue experimenters came up with another method called homomorphic technology. This homomorphic encryption technique is merged with many other growing technologies such as the fog computing and edge computing and was proven to be one of the safest security algorithms [17].

This paper describes a new approach called lattice-based homomorphic encryption which has the ability to overcome any types of attacks and provide highest security better than any other cryptographic algorithms and techniques. Most of the data breaching takes place when the data is added to the cloud. In order to prevent this breach experimenters came up with a solution of encrypting the data on the cloud. So, when the data is in a cipher text it will be difficult for any hacker or intruder to break in and decipher it.

Performing computations on the encrypted data without decrypting it was the best way chosen in order to protect and secure data. Companies holding large amount of data started adapting to this encryption method. But like the other cryptographic mechanisms the homomorphic encryption technique also had its own defect. It was prone to quantum attacks.

These quantum attacks were performed through quantum computers which have the capability to perform hard computations and with its capability it could solve any type of problems and crack every cryptographic technique which is found previously. To stop these quantum attacks a security mechanism called the post quantum cryptography emerged. Since it could overcome quantum attacks it was mainly termed and addressed as quantum resistant. One such post quantum cryptography mechanism is the lattice-based homomorphic encryption. This paper will discuss every detail about this lattice-based homomorphic encryption. Through this security mechanism we can protect our data anywhere at all times. It could be on the systems or cloud; it will be protected irrespective of what the intruding technique is. It may be through a normal email, a malicious cloud injection or even a high computational quantum computer, the data will remain clear and protected.

19.2   Overview of Lattice-Based HE

A lattice is basically a set of linear independent vectors. It can be defined as, let n and d be two positive integers. Let b1 $\cdots$ bd $\in$ R n be 'd' linearly independent vectors. The lattice L generated by (b1 $\cdots$ bd) is the set

$L = X d i = 1 Zbi = (X d i = 1 xibi \mid xi \in Z)$. The vectors $b1 \cdots bd$ are called a vector basis of L. The lattice rank is n and the lattice dimension is d. If n = d then L is called a full rank lattice.

The lattice-based homomorphic encryption is said to be very secure because the vectors which are taken for the encryption are never in the same dimension. For every round of encryption, the vectors considered are of different dimensions. They need not have to be at the same diagonal nor adjacent to the previous lattices considered. Because of this property, the encryption key considered for every round differs and hence makes it difficult to decrypt. This lattice-based homomorphic encryption is proven to satisfy three properties,

- Highly secure
- Resistant to quantum attacks
- Capable of processing large data

A) Highly secure

No matter how large the data is, it should have a secure space to be stored at and must not be exposed to unauthorized person. It tops the hierarchy of all security mechanisms and cryptographic technique in protecting and securing the data [4]. It works on any platform irrespective of the backend that the system is running on. With networks being a tunnel to penetrate and gain illegal access, lattice-based homomorphic encryption provides the utmost security.

B) Resistant to quantum attacks

The computers which have high GPU and computational power can be used to crack any kind of algorithm. The special kind of computers recently which are used to break the most well-known algorithms is called the quantum computers. The lattice-based homomorphic encryption proves to be immune to any kind of attacks including these quantum attacks performed by these high computational quantum computers [26].

C) Capable of processing large data

With every organization and sector growing, there is definitely an increase in the large fast-growing data. In order to process and maintain these data, technologies and techniques such as the big data and data science are devised. But it lacks security. Researchers say there is still no high-level security in the big data processing technologies. The lattice-based homomorphic technique processes large amount of data and also provides high amount of security to the data to be protected.

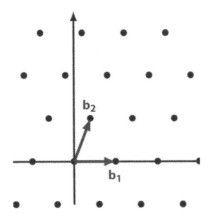

Figure 19.1 Structure of lattice dimensions.

In Figure 19.1, we can see the different dimension of vectors in the lattice and how they are considered.

Table 19.1 shows various crypto-systems that are in use. Namely RSA, Diffie-Hellman, Elliptic curve, NTRU and Lattice-based encryption. RSA (Rivest–Shamir–Adleman) algorithm is an algorithm which uses two keys in order to perform encryption and decryption on the modern computers. Although the algorithm is very strong asymmetric cryptographic system it is still prone to attacks.

Diffie-Hellman is another asymmetric algorithm that is primarily for meant for key exchange. And this algorithm also was broken and left secured less. Followed by the Elliptic curve cryptography, which was also had a security break down. Among all the other asymmetric cryptographic methods the elliptic curve was found to be very complex and hard to be penetrated through. Since all these major cryptographic

Table 19.1 Security status of various crypto-systems.

Cryptosystem	Broken by quantum
RSA	Broken
Diffie-Hellman	Broken
Elliptic Curve	Broken
NTRU	Not broken yet
Lattice-based	Not broken yet

algorithms were broken, experimenters had to come up with a much-secured algorithm.

This led to the growth of newer cryptographic algorithms such as NTRU and lattice-based homomorphic encryption. Lattice-based cryptography can be made to build cryptographic schemes such as NTRU, GGH, LWE and many more [18–24, 25]. Till date it is proved that these lattice-based cryptography and these schemes have not been broken and provide almost security to any amount of data. The lattice-based homomorphic encryption can also be used to build fully homomorphic encryption. The applications of lattice-based homomorphic encryption is very vast. It can be used in other algorithms using hash functions. It can be used to provide high security in legal authorization techniques such as digital signature. These can also be used in identity-based encryption systems.

19.3   Applications of Lattice HE

Lattice-based homomorphic encryption is growing day by day being proved to be one of the most secured algorithms. Many applications and software are working on it as their primary security algorithm. A few of its applications are

- Cloud applications
- Digital signatures
- Improving security and transparency

In Figure 19.2, we can see the process of how lattice-based homomorphic encryption takes place in cloud. AWS, and many more, although they are very secure compared to attacks happening on a physical system, the attacks taking place on the cloud is very high. When we look at the transactions happening over the cloud, they are prone to two kinds of attacks. One is the active attack and another the passive attack. Through active attack the intruder may get access to the transaction being performed on the cloud and modify it. Whereas the passive attack is when the intruder gets every access to the transaction but only eavesdrop them and not modify it. In both these kinds of attacks the vulnerability faced is the key exchange and data being sent. To overcome these kinds of attacks we go for lattice-based homomorphic encryption. Where the DO (data owner sends the cloud service provider the encrypted data and a re-encryption key. Simultaneously, the data owner will also send

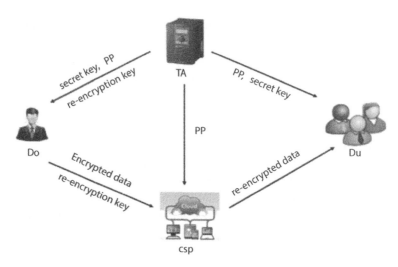

Figure 19.2 Lattice-based HE on cloud.

the secret public key and re-encryption key to the TA (trusted authority). The trusted authority and the cloud service provider now have the only public key sent by the data owner. Finally, the DU (data users) get access to the cloud through the public shared across the system by the data owner and the data here get re-encrypted. This makes it possible for the data user to decrypt the re-encrypted data using the public key. With the above process we can see the significance lattice-based homomorphic encryption plays in the cloud applications.

Digital signatures are used provide authentic access over digital messages to the authorized users. This digital signature plays a vital role in providing authenticity over digital data as well as it can also be misused. In order to overcome any disruption or frauds in these digital signatures, experimenters have come up with various algorithms and schemes. One such algorithm is the DSA (digital signature algorithm) which was used in many applications to provide high confidentiality and a proper authenticity to the authorized users alone. But intruders could easily break down this algorithm in many applications. In such cases lattice-based homomorphic encryption can play a vital role. While using lattice-based homomorphic encryption the security achieved was very high. The key generated for the mechanism was based on different linear combinations of vectors. The vector diagonals were never the same and key generated differ every time. Through this there were no sequential access and quest attacks was also prevented.

Improved security and transparency were quite a problem in many other cryptographic algorithms. With linear vectors of different dimensions chosen for every round of key generation, the lattice-based homomorphic encryption provides a high security. The transparency between the data owner and the data user is very clear and highly transparent. It works on the worst-case lattice problem which later let to the evolvement of many other scheme such as NTRU, Ring LWE and GGH encryption scheme. Most of the schemes provide high security and transparency. They all used the same concept of lattice-based homomorphic encryption with different genres. The three schemes are now playing their significant role in various domains such as the healthcare domain, banking sector and many more.

19.4 NTRU Scheme

The NTRU is a public key crypto system which replaced the RSA and ECC crypto systems by being resistant to all quantum attacks. It had a vast crypto strength and is much faster than the RSA algorithm. The NTRU algorithm consists of two other algorithms, NTRUEncrypt and NTRUSign. Each one of them have a different purpose to perform and which is done in a very clear manner. The NTRUEncrypt algorithm is used mainly for encryption and the NTRUSign algorithm is used for digital signatures. The have few steps in the encryption and decryption process which is shown in the Figure 19.3.

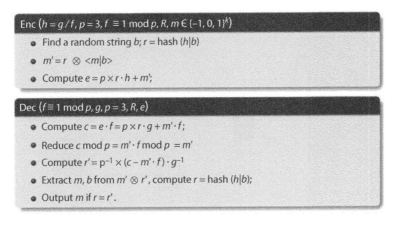

Figure 19.3 Encryption and decryption in NTRU.

In the NTRU algorithm there is no limitations on the size of the input taken or considered. With the above-mentioned encryption and decryption technique, we will be able to provide a secure path of communication between the sender and the receiver. All the operations that take place in the NTRU algorithm are done through a convolution multiplication. The NTRUEncrypt was mainly created to perform a secure encryption and to solve the SVP (shortest vector problem) easily. The NTRUSign was initially said to be a polynomial authentication and signature scheme (PASS). It was built based on the GGH signature scheme.

The NTRUEncrypt and NTRUSign are used in many domains nowadays. One such important domain is the healthcare domain. Where there is huge transaction of the patient's data and records, there is a high need for those data of the patients to be secured and prevent the any kind of unauthorized access. The Figure 19.4 shows the process of medical transaction and storage in the cloud and how they are accessed. Initially the patient provides all his/her details through a CCU. The data or record processing here uses the NTRU algorithm and homomorphically encrypted data which gets saved in the cloud-based server. This encryption is done through a private key. Later the data in the cloud is accessed by the healthcare professional using the public key. The decryption process is done through this key, thus the chances of breaking this system is very hard.

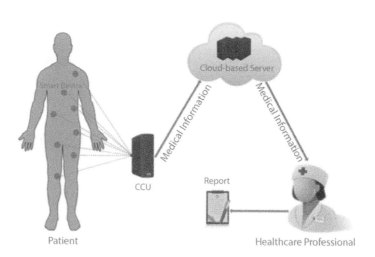

Figure 19.4 NTRU in healthcare domain.

19.5   GGH Signature Scheme

The GGH (Goldreich-Goldwasser-Halevi) signature scheme was built in order to solve the closest vector problem (CVP). To solve this closest vector problem the sender has to take a good basis from the lattice. This point would represent a specific message and the verifier would take a bad basis from the lattice and check if that point is anywhere close to the good basis point. If so, then it will get verified. But there were few defects in this algorithm as, while the verifier is considering a point which is nearby or close to the good Basis lattice point, it may result in an error. So, they had to come up with another much better signature scheme. By having the GGH signature scheme, experimenters were able to build a much secure and faster digital signature algorithm known as the NTRUSign.

In Figure 19.5, we can see how the verifier can use bad basis point in the lattice to find if it is anywhere near to the good basis lattice point which is representing a particular message. Although the point to be considered can be anywhere near the good basis lattice point, the senders could not take any dimensions of the lattice because it led to increase of noise in the message and caused errors.

The mathematical exposure of the NTRU algorithm might seem very complex but it also exhibits high speed and efficiency compared to the other algorithms. Initially in order to perform the key generation, we have to consider two prime numbers such as p and q and also two other polynomials say F and G satisfying certain properties. The coefficients of these polynomials can be either [-1,0,1]. Now the key can be generated using the key generation formula. Later we need to perform the encryption. But before encryption we have to convert the message to a binary format since it accepts polynomials only with coefficients [-1,0,1]. Later once its

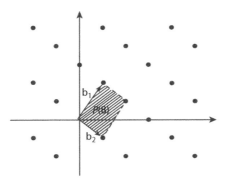

Figure 19.5 Lattice points in GGH scheme.

encrypted we can decrypt it using the decryption formula. The NTRU is said to be really secure because at every stage it considers polynomials and they cannot be backtracked.

19.6   Related Work

Various research works on Lattice-based homomorphic encryption are discussed in the following section:

A. Lattice-Based Homomorphic Encryption of Vector Spaces [1]
In this paper Carlos Aguilar Melchor, *et al.* discusses the different probabilistic crypto-systems. We know based on the vector spaces only we will be able to consider the good base point to identify and re-identify the message interpreted in a specific lattice position. In this paper they also discuss the different encryption and decryption technique that takes places based on the vector spaces. Consideration of these vector spaces matters the post in the processing of the data.

B. Accelerating NTRU-Based Homomorphic Encryption Using GPUs [2]
In this paper, Dai, *et al.* [2], discuss the different cryptographic algorithms which are used to perform a perfect homomorphic encryption using the GPUs. When we look at the latest improvised versions of latest GPUs, most of them use the Chinese reminder algorithm (CRA) in them. The graphical processing unit plays a significant role nowadays in the upcoming systems and PCs. Every operating system gets adapted to a different graphical processing unit and since it is widely used the security in it shown to be very vulnerable and prone to a space where any unauthorized person or a hacker can miss use it. In order to protect data on the network and through the GPU although there are many other cryptographic algorithms, we go for this NTRU based homomorphic based encryption. We know NTRU has two other algorithmic segments in it namely for the encryption and the digital signature verification. The speed and security can be increased in a high pace when we are able to accelerate the NTRU based homomorphic encryption using the GPUs.

C. A Lightweight Lattice-Based Homomorphic Privacy-Preserving Data Aggregation Scheme for Smart Grid [3]
In this work, Asmaa Abdallah, *et al.* [3] addresses a new power consumption aggregation scheme that exploits light-weight lattice-primarily based totally homomorphic crypto system. It is totally light-weight,

privatives-keeping. We know that now a days the consumers in the smart grid are growing vastly. We know that the smart grid can compute, automate, control and access all the electrical applications with technology evolving pretty fast. When such a technology is growing so fast, definitely the amount of security needed is high. In this paper, the authors have proposed a data aggregation scheme which will be much secured and protect the consumers information. It will also provide privacy to the consumers and preserve them until the next authorized access. In order to this kind of privacy and preserving data aggregation scheme for the smart grid, they have induced the homomorphic encryption technique in the smart grid. Through this the data that is present in the smart grid will not be just in an encrypted form but all homomorphically encrypted, which means performing encryption on the encrypted text itself. Through this the privacy of the data and the security in the smart grid will be increased.

D. At the Cross Roads of Lattice-Based and Homomorphic Encryption to Secure Data Aggregation in Smart Grid [6]
The primary objective of the proposed work by Rihem Ben Romdhane, *et al.* [6] is to create a very clever home equipment which will be report correctly on the data used and aggregated in the smart grid. There are many other privacy preserving and data aggregation schemes introduced in smart grid previously, but this one is much clever than the others because it communicates through signals inside the house itself. Through this there will not be any cross connections or disruptions in between. Home appliance with proper communication signals can be connected to the smart grid and computed on. When this is done, the privacy also comes as a second factor it. There is a need to protect this smart grid privacy used at one house from the neighboring smart grids being used and prevent them from cross lines. Thus, in this paper they have a discussed the possible ways to create a lattice-based homomorphic encryption to secure data aggregation in smart grids.

E. Analysis of Partially and Fully Homomorphic Encryption [7]
In this work, Liam Morris [7] aims to provide theoretical perspective on homomorphic encryption. Homomorphic encryption is way to protect the data over any digital domain or platform. There are many people nowadays who have found various schemes and techniques to break through the secured crypto systems and algorithms protecting the private ads secured data. In order to prevent them from intruding and increase the security of these crypto systems, experimenters have come up with

the advances solution of homomorphic encryption. Homomorphic encryption is a way to protect the data by performing encryption on the encrypted data. Under homomorphic encryption there are two types of encryptions which can be future divided into many other schemes and algorithm. The two homomorphic encryption can be named as the partially homomorphic encryption and fully homomorphic encryption. Fully homomorphic encryption can be done on any kind of data and perform all kind of arithmetic operations and schemes at a time. It can perform the addition and multiplication operations at the same encryption standard. Partially homomorphic encryption can be done on any kind of and perform certain kinds of arithmetic operations and schemes on the data to be secured. Like the fully homographic encryption, the partially homomorphic encryption cannot perform both the addition and multiplication operations, it is limited to work only on either of them. Either addition or multiplication. In this paper they have further discussed all the schemes which all under these two fully homomorphic encryption and partially homomorphic encryption.

F. Accelerating LTV-Based Homomorphic Encryption in Reconfigurable Hardware [8]
The work done by Berk Sunar, *et al.* [8] portrays the homomorphic encryption scheme that has created its widespread usage in academia and industry. Despite speedy advances within 6 years, FHE schemes are nonetheless now no longer equipped for deployment because of a performance bottleneck [5, 12–16]. Here we introduce a custom hardware accelerator optimized for a category of reconfigurable common sense to deliver LTV primarily based totally really homomorphic encryption schemes one step in the direction of deployment in real-lifestyles applications. The accelerator is attached through a quick PCI interface to a CPU platform to offer homomorphic assessment offerings to any application that desires to aid blinded computations. Specifically, we introduce a number of theoretical remodel primarily based totally multiplier structure capable of effectively coping with very huge polynomials. When synthesized for the Xilinx Vertex 7 own circle of relatives the provided structure can compute the manufactured from huge polynomials in below 6.25m sec making it the quickest multiplier layout of its type presently to be had within side the literature and is extra than 102 instances quicker than a software program implementation. Using this multiplier, we are able to compute a re-linearization operation in 526 msec. When used as an accelerator, for instance, to assess the AES block cipher, we estimate a in step with block homomorphic assessment overall performance of

442 msec yielding overall performance profits of 28.5 and 17 instances over comparable CPU and GPU implementations, respectively. Many crypto systems with homomorphic properties are performing quite good. For example, RSA, Paillier, and ElGamal are partly homomorphic. It turned into idea that a completely homomorphic crypto system turned into feasible, even though no person had but carried out. In 2009 the primary completely homomorphic crypto system was developed by Craig Gentry. Rather than the use of easy modular mathematics, Gentry's crypto system is lattice-based totally.

G. A Practical Homomorphic Encryption: A Survey [10]
In this research work Ciara Moore, *et al.* [10] have discussed on how homomorphic encryption is practically used in various applications. We know that the best way to store data now a days is to store it on the cloud based on its various advantages and security mechanisms. The cloud paves a way to both advantages and disadvantages. Since everyone is adapting to cloud it also comes with some cons. The security is definitely high in it, but when it comes for comparison of physical storage systems the security in it is low [9]. In this paper, they have provided a detailed survey on the application on this homomorphic encryption on the cloud. The reasons behind why people trust the cloud services and cloud platform is detailed in this paper. The various types of homomorphic encryption and decryption techniques which are implemented in the cloud are discussed. They have even taken few real time cloud platforms and experimented on the homomorphic encryption techniques in it.

H. Toward Basing Fully Homomorphic Encryption on Worst-Case Hardness [11]
Gentry proposed a totally homomorphic public key encryption scheme that makes use of perfect lattices. The safety of his scheme is based on the hardness of problems: an average-case selection hassle over perfect lattices, and the sparse (or "low-weight") subset sum hassle (SSSP).We offer a key era set of rules for Gentry's scheme that generates perfect lattices in step with a "nice" average-case distribution. Then, the authors discussed about worst-case/average-case connection that bases Gentry's scheme (in part) at the quantum hardness of the shortest unbiased vector hassle (SIVP) over perfect lattices within side the worst-case. Worst-case/average-case connection is the primary in which the average-case lattice is a perfect lattice, which appears to be vital to assist the safety of Gentry's scheme.

19.7 Conclusion

The recent statistics from several researches' states that the lattice-based homomorphic encryption is one of the most secured and transparent security algorithms to be adapted in recent days. The lattice-based homomorphic encryption having the capability to provide a security mechanism which can be resistant to any kind of attacks including the major quantum attacks. Using the technique of generating different linear combination of lattice vectors at each round, the lattice homomorphic encryption is able to provides highest security. Having many more schemes under this algorithm such as the NTRU algorithm as NTRUEncrypt and NTRUSign in it, and the GGH signature scheme, lattice-based homomorphic mechanism is growing and plays a vital role in very growing domains and sectors. This lattice-based homomorphic encryption is mainly used in the medical healthcare sector, e-commerce sector and the banking systems. According to researchers the healthcare domain is the domain which uses this lattice-based homomorphic encryption the most. With the current pandemic caused by covid-19, there have been many patients being admitted in the hospital every day and many even contact the doctors through the online platform. In such a scenario, there is large amount of data being processed and they need a higher end security mechanisms and algorithms to maintain the privacy of the patients. The GGH signature scheme also has become a very important scheme used for reviewing Digital message through the access of digital signature. Through this survey we have discussed all the applications of lattice-based homomorphic encryption and all the other schemes and algorithms falling under the lattice-based homomorphic encryption.

References

1. Wew Melchor, C.A., Castagnos, G., Gaborit, P., Lattice-based homomorphic encryption of vector spaces, in: *2008 IEEE International Symposium on Information Theory*, 2008, July, IEEE, pp. 1858–1862.
2. Dai, W., Doröz, Y., Sunar, B., Accelerating NTRU based homomorphic encryption using GPUs, in: *2014 IEEE High Performance Extreme Computing Conference (HPEC)*, 2014, September, IEEE, pp. 1–6.
3. Abdallah, A. and Shen, X.S., A lightweight lattice-based homomorphic privacy-preserving data aggregation scheme for smart grid. *IEEE Trans. Smart Grid*, 9, 1, 396–405, 2016.

4. Gentry, C., Fully homomorphic encryption using ideal lattices, in: *Proceedings of the Forty-First Annual ACM Symposium on Theory of Computing*, 2009, May, pp. 169–178.

5. Brakerski, Z. and Vaikuntanathan, V., Lattice-based FHE as secure as PKE, in: *Proceedings of the 5th Conference on Innovations in Theoretical Computer Science*, 2014, January, pp. 1–12.

6. Romdhane, R.B., Hammami, H., Hamdi, M., Kim, T.H., At the cross roads of lattice-based and homomorphic encryption to secure data aggregation in smart grid, in: *2019 15th International Wireless Communications & Mobile Computing Conference (IWCMC)*, 2019, June, IEEE, pp. 1067–1072.

7. Morris, L., Analysis of partially and fully homomorphic encryption, Rochester Institute of Technology, pp. 1–5, 2013.

8. Doröz, Y., Öztürk, E., Savaş, E., Sunar, B., Accelerating LTV based homomorphic encryption in reconfigurable hardware, in: *International Workshop on Cryptographic Hardware and Embedded Systems*, 2015, September, Springer, Berlin, Heidelberg, pp. 185–204.

9. Ma, C., Li, J., Ouyang, W., Lattice-based identity-based homomorphic conditional proxy re-encryption for secure big data computing in cloud environment. *Int. J. Found. Comput. Sci.*, 28, 06, 645–660, 2017.

10. Moore, C., O'Neill, M., O'Sullivan, E., Doröz, Y., Sunar, B., Practical homomorphic encryption: A survey, in: *2014 IEEE International Symposium on Circuits and Systems (ISCAS)*, IEEE, pp. 2792–2795, 2014.

11. Gentry, C., Toward basing fully homomorphic encryption on worst-case hardness, in: *Annual Cryptology Conference*, 2010, August, Springer, Berlin, Heidelberg, pp. 116–137.

12. Stehlé, D. and Steinfeld, R., Faster fully homomorphic encryption, in: *International Conference on the Theory and Application of Cryptology and Information Security*, 2010, December, Springer, Berlin, Heidelberg, pp. 377–394.

13. Van Dijk, M., Gentry, C., Halevi, S., Vaikuntanathan, V., Fully homomorphic encryption over the integers, in: *Annual International Conference on the Theory and Applications of Cryptographic Techniques*, 2010, May, Springer, Berlin, Heidelberg, pp. 24–43.

14. Brakerski, Z. and Vaikuntanathan, V., Fully homomorphic encryption from ring-LWE and security for key dependent messages, in: *Annual Cryptology Conference*, 2011, August, Springer, Berlin, Heidelberg, pp. 505–524.

15. Gentry, C. and Halevi, S., Implementing gentry's fully-homomorphic encryption scheme, in: *Annual International Conference on the Theory and Applications of Cryptographic Techniques*, 2011, May, Springer, Berlin, Heidelberg, pp. 129–148.

16. Bos, J.W., Lauter, K., Loftus, J., Naehrig, M., Improved security for a ring-based fully homomorphic encryption scheme, in: *IMA International Conference on Cryptography and Coding*, 2013, December, Springer, Berlin, Heidelberg, pp. 45–64.

17. Fan, J. and Vercauteren, F., Somewhat practical fully homomorphic encryption. *IACR Cryptol. ePrint Arch., 2012*, p. 144, 2012.
18. Hoffstein, J., Pipher, J., Silverman, J.H., NSS: An NTRU lattice-based signature scheme, in: *International Conference on the Theory and Applications of Cryptographic Techniques*, 2001, May, Springer, Berlin, Heidelberg, pp. 211–228.
19. Lei, X. and Liao, X., NTRU-KE: A lattice-based public key exchange protocol. *IACR Cryptol. ePrint Arch., 2013*, p. 718, 2013.
20. Valluri, M.R., Cryptanalysis of Xinyu *et al.*, NTRU lattice-based key exchange protocol. *J. Inf. Optim. Sci.*, 39, 2, 475–479, 2018.
21. Xu, Z., He, D., Vijayakumar, P., Choo, K.K.R., Li, L., Efficient NTRU lattice-based certificateless signature scheme for medical cyber-physical systems. *J. Med. Syst.*, 44, 5, 1–8, 2020.
22. Ducas, L., Lyubashevsky, V., Prest, T., Efficient identity-based encryption over NTRU lattices, in: *International Conference on the Theory and Application of Cryptology and Information Security*, 2014, December, Springer, Berlin, Heidelberg, pp. 22–41.
23. Hoffstein, J., Howgrave-Graham, N., Pipher, J., Whyte, W., Practical lattice-based cryptography: NTRUEncrypt and NTRUSign, in: *The LLL Algorithm*, pp. 349–390, Springer, Berlin, Heidelberg, 2009.
24. Bernstein, D.J., Chuengsatiansup, C., Lange, T., van Vredendaal, C., NTRU prime: Reducing attack surface at low cost, in: *International Conference on Selected Areas in Cryptography*, 2017, August, Springer, Cham, pp. 235–260.
25. Santhiya, B. and Anitha Kumari, K., Analysis on DGHV and NTRU fully homomorphic encryption schemes, in: *Proceedings of International Conference on Artificial Intelligence, Smart Grid and Smart City Applications. AISGSC 2019 2019*, L. Kumar, L. Jayashree, R. Manimegalai (Eds.), Springer, Cham, 2020, https://doi.org/10.1007/978-3-030-24051-6_61.
26. Khalid, A., McCarthy, S., O'Neill, M., Liu, W., Lattice-based cryptography for IoT in a quantum world: Are we ready?, in: *2019 IEEE 8th International Workshop on Advances in Sensors and Interfaces (IWASI)*, 2019, June, IEEE, pp. 194–199.

Biometrics with Blockchain: A Better Secure Solution for Template Protection

P. Jayapriya[1]*, K. Umamaheswari[2] and S. Sathish Kumar[3]

[1]Centre for Future Networks and Digital Twin, Department of Computer Science and Engineering, Sri Eshwar College of Engineering, Coimbatore, Tamil Nadu, India
[2]Department of IT, PSG College of Technology, Coimbatore, Tamil Nadu, India
[3]Research Institute Mississippi State University, Starkville, MS, USA

Abstract

Biometrics, with its own uniqueness to each individual, has indeed been adopted as a secure authentication factor by several domains. The biometric trait features are extracted and stored in database. The stored biometric template databases are under the control of a central authority. Biometric templates are vulnerable to attacks such as forgery, modification, and deletion. Blockchain technologies offer outstanding designs and useful tools for protecting and preserving private data stored in biometric templates, but at a price. With a focus on biometric template storage and preservation, a significant issue in biometrics that is mostly unresolved, the advantages and challenges of merging blockchain with biometrics are discussed in this paper. The suggested approach demonstrates that merging biometrics with blockchain improves template protection.

Keywords: Biometric, finger knuckle, feature extraction, nodes, security, template

20.1 Introduction

Blockchain is a new emerging technology that ensures the strong data security. The blockchain database is decentralized which is relatively protected by cryptographic technique. The individual who owns the data has

---

Corresponding author: jayapriy@gmail.com

K. Umamaheswari, B. Vinoth Kumar and S. K. Somasundaram (eds.) Artificial Intelligence for Sustainable Applications, (311–328) © 2023 Scrivener Publishing LLC

authority over who has access to it in the decentralized system, and they can choose to share it as they see fit [1, 2]. This means that sensitive information, whether from private companies or the government, does not have to transit via data storage aggregators. Researchers are interested in a new biometric called Finger Knuckle because it is user-friendly, contactless, and inexpensive. Old ways of securing one's privacy, like as passwords, tokens, and key codes, have been increasingly phased out since the introduction of how unique and secure the biometric recognition is with each individual [3]. Biometrics is a unique feature, and once stolen, there is no substitute source to reproduce it, thus it should be protected [4]. When the template is kept in a centralized database, there are hazards related to biometrics such as spoofing, data manipulation, identity theft, and channel interception. By combining this revolutionary technology with biometrics, new and more secure channels for authentication and authorization may be widened. It could be a useful tool for avoiding cyber fraud, eavesdropping, and hacking, all of which are growing more common in today's linked society [5, 6].

The majority of previous research has been on the secure preservation of biometric templates to minimize attacks [7–9]. The raw biometric data is extracted, pre-defined features are blended with hash values, and a template is saved. The database contains both the encrypted template and the security measures for the template that use cryptography and cancellable methods. Despite the fact that templates prevent direct data leaking, if a template is compromised, reverse engineering can be used to determine the actual data [4, 5].

To overcome issues in existing techniques, integrating blockchain with biometrics could have a lot of benefits. As first approximations, blockchain technology [10] may be able to enable biometric systems with important properties such as robustness, traceability, accessibility, or universal access. Such characteristics made possible by blockchain technology could be particularly valuable in biometrics, for example, in securing biometric templates [11] and ensuring confidentiality in biometric systems [12].

We built Biometric Template protection with blockchain technology to tackle the aforementioned issues and inadequacies of conventional techniques. When biometrics and blockchain are combined, it results in decentralized biometric authentication, improved performance accuracy, and protected template storage. Blockchain transactions are verified and documented. As a result, the transactions can be tracked indefinitely.

In this study the theoretical frame work is given to secure the biometric authentication from the enrolment of the finger knuckle image to storing in the database. The proposed framework may then be applied to a network architecture that is decentralized and consists of access points and diverse nodes without a central hub; blockchain technology enables us to use decentralized criteria for the establishment of authentication. The sections of the paper are organized as follows: Section 20.2, Blockchain Technology; Section 20.3, Biometric architecture; Section 20.4, Blockchain in Biometrics; Section 20.5, Conclusion.

20.2 Blockchain Technology

Blockchain is a decentralized public ledger that contains all previous data and transactions for the system. Such transactions be present as documented in blocks, which are generated in addition stored in a sequential order on the blockchain (immutable) [13]. Blockchain technology, which was intended as the core technology of the Bitcoin protocol, is used in the secure transmission of crypto currency (coins and tokens) without the need for a central financial institution. It has had a lot of success, and it has gotten the attention of tech companies that are doing research on the technology.

A blockchain is governed by a worldwide peer-to-peer (P2P) network of nodes that uses consensus method to verify new blocks. All nodes in the network retain the very same data replica, obviating the need for a trusted centralized power to govern data. The evolution in the blockchain includes from version 1.0 to version 4.0. Blockchain version 1.0 is based on crypto currencies, smart contracts in version 2.0, version 3.0 handled both decentralized storage and communication. Finally the current 4.0 proposes a new approach which can be implement the blockchain technology in medicine, vehicle parking system, voting, financial and banking systems [14–18].

A. Distributed Ledger
The term "blockchain" refers to distributed ledger technology (DLT), which have quickly gained popularity as a new way of storing and regulate data. Distributed ledger technology is divided into two categories. The ledger is regarded as a public ledger if that can be accessed by anybody (like the one used in Bitcoin and Ethereum). A ledger could also be private if only a limited number of authorized nodes have access to all the data and are able to take part in consensus.

B. Blockchain Architecture
The blockchain was first introduced in 1991. A group of experts devised a method for time stamping digitalized documents without causing them to change. Additionally, Satoshi Nakamoto changed and improved the

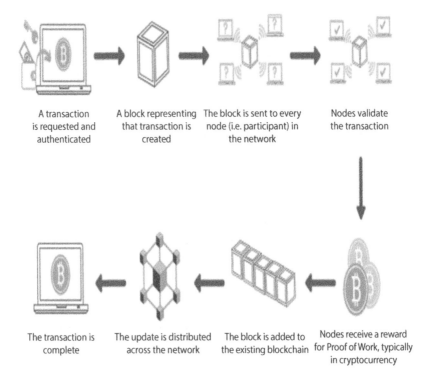

Figure 20.1 Blockchain architecture.

method. In 2008, Nakamoto launched the first crypto currency, Bitcoin, a blockchain-based endeavor [19]. Figure 20.1 shows the architecture of the blockchain.

Basic Components of Architecture

- **Node** – is a represents user or computer within the blockchain architecture and each node contain the entire replica of the ledger.
- **Transaction** – is minimum block which contains the records, information of the transactions.
- **Block** – a database structure for discrete transaction data across all network nodes.
- **Chain** – a collection of blocks placed in a predetermined arrangement.
- **Miners** – specialized nodes that examine blocks before incorporating them into a blockchain framework.

- **Consensus (consensus protocol)** – a collection of rules and agreement that control the execution of blockchain transactions.

A. Authentication

Although the blockchain was created without the need for a central authority, transactions must still be verified. This is accomplished through the use of cryptographic keys, a string of data (similar to a password) that uniquely recognizes a user besides grants access to their "account" or "wallet" of value on the system. Each user has a private key as well as a public key that everybody can view. Combining them creates a safe digital identity that may be used to 'unlock' transactions and authenticate individuals via digital signatures [20].

B. Authorization

The users must approve a transaction before it can be included in a block of the chain. Consensus is used to add transactions to the chain, which requires the acceptance of a majority of nodes. The vendors of the network's computers are rewarded for confirming transactions. This is referred to as "proof of work."

C. Proof of Work

People who own computers in the network must solve a difficult mathematical challenge in order to add a block to the chain using Proof of Work. The act of "mining" entails the resolution of a problem, and miners are typically paid in bitcoin. But mining is a challenging job. Only trial and error can solve the mathematical problem, and even then, there is only a 1 in 5.9 trillion chance of success.

D. Proof of Stake

Later blockchain networks adopted "Proof of Stake" validation consensus procedures, where users are only allowed to choose, verify, and validate transactions if they have a stake in the blockchain, which is often achieved by possessing some form of crypto currency. This saves a large amount of processing power because no mining is required. Furthermore, "Smart Contracts" that instantaneously complete transactions when certain conditions are met are now a part of blockchain technology.

Key Characteristics of Blockchain Architecture Blockchain architecture possesses a lot of benefits for businesses [1]. Here are several embedded characteristics:

- Cryptography
- Immutability
- Decentralization
- Anonymity
- Transparency
- Provenance

Types of Blockchain

Blockchain is classified into four types: permission less public blockchain, permissioned private blockchain, consortium blockchain and hybrid of two private and public [21]. All types offer protection against fraudulent and erroneous ledger users. Figure 20.2 shows the characteristics of each of the four types of blockchain.

Public blockchain: A public blockchain design assures that anyone interested in participating can examine the data and use the network (e.g. Bitcoin, Ethereum, and Lite coin blockchain systems are public). It is more secure than a private network, which provides less privacy and needs a large amount of processing power.

Private blockchain: The private system, in contrast to the public blockchain design, is only controlled by users from a single organization or by approved users who have been asked to participate. It is more secure than the public but has fewer computational capabilities.

Consortium blockchain: This blockchain structure could be made up of several entities. Procedures in a consortium are established and regulated by the users who have been pre-assigned. These architectures are allowed

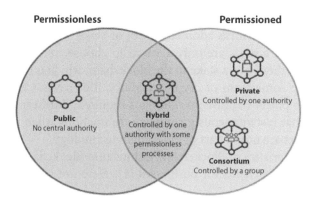

Figure 20.2 Types of blockchain.

to access, partly private, and semi-decentralized, and are particularly suitable for business and financial organizations with a limited group of participants.

Hybrid blockchain: A hybrid blockchain is one that is run by a single entity but also draws some authority from the public blockchain, which is required to carry out some transaction validations. A hybrid blockchain is demonstrated by IBM Food Trust.

20.3   Biometric Architecture

Personal-identification technologies which are both reliable and convenient are required for building secure and effective access controls. Hand-based biometrics makes use of various internal and exterior characteristics that are unique to each person. Hand-based biometric systems have a high level of user acceptability, and with the advent of touch less imaging, they are becoming simpler and easily accessible [22].

The finger knuckle print (FKP) is a type of biometric that may be employed for person identity. There are various advantages to using finger-knuckle image. First, unlike fingerprints, user approval of external surface

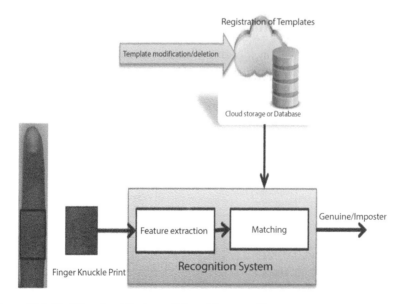

Figure 20.3 Traditional architecture of biometric recognition system.

image is quite high because there is no stigma of prospective criminal inquiry in existing evaluation [23]. Spoofing, data corruption, identity fraud, and network interception are all risks associated with storing the finger knuckle biometric template in a centralized database.

Researchers have suggested numerous ways to overcome this problem for decades, in order to make the system more safe and secured. The traditional finger knuckle biometric recognition system is shown in the Figure 20.3 [3].

Biometric Attacks

Xiao [24] performs an attack analysis to determine the strengths and weaknesses of biometric authentication, and also an effort is being made to counter spoofing attacks in order to improve the security in biometric systems. Biometric systems are vulnerable to external attacks, according to Ratha *et al.* [25]. They identified image acquisition, feature extraction, matching, and decision stages as attack/vulnerability levels in a conventional biometrics recognition system. Figure 20.4 depicts the fundamental biometrics recognition system as well as the locations where attacks can be carried out.

Challenges and Limitations

According to the research, merging blockchain and biometrics provides greater benefits and new opportunities. However, there are several restrictions with present blockchain technology that prevent this from being done directly and the issues are depicts in Figure 20.5 [5].

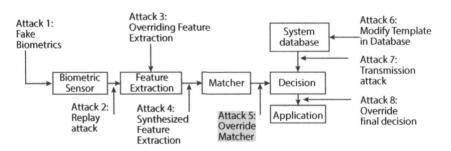

Figure 20.4 Various attacks.

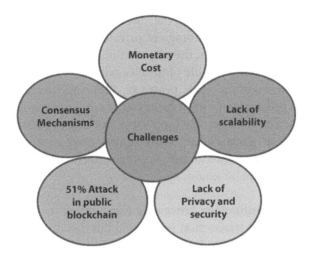

Figure 20.5 Various types of challenges in blockchain.

Limitations

Its ability to handle transactions at this time is quite limited, i.e. ten transactions per second.

1) Its real design necessitates the storage of all system transactions, causing the storage space required for its management to rapidly expand.
2) Its resistance to various forms of attacks has not yet been thoroughly investigated.

• **Monetary Cost in Executing Smart Contracts**: Toexecute the smart contract in blockchain such as Ethereum need to reward each node as fee for executing the instructions in crypto currency called gas. For example simple instructions it cost 1 gas where for encryption calculation it costs nearly 20k gas which is very expensive. The first research problem is to reduce the cost of embedding the biometric system in blockchain.

   • **Privacy:** All participating nodes are aware of the operations if they are conducted in a public network The usage of cryptographic keys in this situation is appropriate because they limit the potential applications. The layer of blockchain privacy is composed of participants, words, and data.

- **Participants:** Through the use of cryptographic tools including off-chain storage of private data, ring signatures, and stealth addresses, the players should remain anonymous both inside and outside of the blockchain.
- **Terms:** By using range proofs or Pedersen commitments, term privacy keeps the logic of smart contracts hidden.
- **Data:** The data privacy layer's last and most crucial objective is to always keep transactions, smart contracts, and other data, such biometric number plates, encrypted, both on-chain and off-chain.

• **Processing Capability:** The processing capability of the blockchain is to execute thousands of transaction per second but this is not suitable for all the circumstances. And also it takes considerable amount of time for confirmation which delays the biometric authentication systems in different blockchain.

• **Scalability:** This is main noticeable downside in the blockchain technology. Hypothetically, the nodes in the blockchain network will be stored in all the node of the blockchain network. This will increase the size of the blockchain quickly and now available size of Bitcoin and Ethereum are 200GB and currently 300GB [26]. And this scalability arise an issue in some of the applications such as IoT.

- **Security:** The blockchain security depiction is still under construction. If an attacker discovers that the computational capacity of any private or public blockchain exceeds 50%, an attack based on transactions modification is possible [27]. This attack can be used against blockchain that use non-proof-of-work consensus algorithms, such as PoS or PoA, which are commonly used in private or consortium topologies. . The main security problem related to blockchain is programming errors. For example the DAO attack which create the whole Ethereum network in risk [28].

20.4   Blockchain in Biometrics

This section provides a review of blockchain applications in biometrics. Here the existing solutions are reviewed and discussed. The general architecture of biometric with blockchain is shown in Figure 20.6.

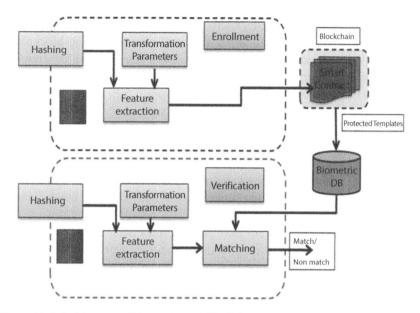

Figure 20.6 Architecture of biometrics with blockchain.

Lee and Yang [29] suggested using blockchain to secure the template with a nail biometric identification. The features are extracted using a histogram of oriented gradients and local binary patterns. With the aid of random forest trees and support vector machines, classification accuracy is calculated. The proposed nail biometric authentication leverages blockchain technology to secure the data so that it can be traced and recoded when the template is modified or deleted.

The idea of using the "side chain" of data processing to integrate user data, such as the fingerprint template and other user data, and save it there is discussed by the author in [30]. This data will then be validated against the "Aadhar card number" on the "main chain." Congestion can be reduced effectively with this tactic. The Ethereum network is used to compare data to verify a user's identity.

Patients are verified by storing encrypted hybrid patterns of the patient on the blockchain network [31]. The RFID and the patient's finger-vein feature are analyzed and hashed using the MD5 and AES algorithms in this hybrid pattern. As a result, attacks like brute force and spoofing are nearly impossible. If a patient enlists, the processed data is delivered from the accessing node to the blockchain, where it is recorded and then authenticated.

To address the vicious attack on the existing system, [32] suggested the biometric e-ID system to verify the voting by employing blockchain technology. Butchman *et al.* [33] have recommended using blockchain to secure breeder documentation. The breeder document saves the user's biometric data, and a block with the document's hash function is created and added to the blockchain.

The deployment of a concept termed biometrics token has been proposed by Nandakumar *et al.* [34]. The token can only be used once, and the blockchain hash mechanism prevents deduplication and multiple uses of the token. The biometrics-blockchain hybrid is still in its infancy. Gracia [35] had shown the feasibility of merging bio metrics using blockchain in a distributed system.

Delgado-Mohatar *et al.* [36] have also offered a perspective on how biometrics and blockchain are integrated to enhance the performance of each other. Zhou *et al.* [37] developed a simple, traceability technique for fingerprint-based system authentication. Various recent studies have proposed the idea of combining these technologies for improved security.

Aside from the integration of biometrics and blockchain, blockchain has proven certain advantages in several domains such as healthcare [38], intelligent products [39] and smart energy [40, 41].

20.4.1 Template Storage Techniques

Biometric template protection is classified into two such as i) biometric cryptosystems and ii) cancellable biometric. Here the template is protected based on blockchain technique using smart contract. The template storage in blockchain is costly than the computational cost. Full on-chain storage, data hashing, and linked data structures are some of the various storage schemes utilized for template storage [42].

Full on-chain Storage: The templates are directly stored in the blockchain based on smart contract. It is very expensive and ineffective. Ethereum cost of storing 1kb of data is $170 for 1ETH [43].

Data hashing: The data is stored in the offline mode. It is efficient when compared with full on-chain storage because it stores the hash value of the biometric template using smart contract of the blockchain instead of storing the full template. The template can be stored in other external device such as public cloud or in concern servers. In any scenario, distributed database systems like IPFS [44] would be preferable in this scenario to preserve the distributed spirit, resilience to control, and high availability and accessibility blockchain. It can also employ any cryptographic algorithm, like the SHA3 series, to generate outputs ranging from 224 to 512 bits long. One disadvantage of this method is that it still requires ensuring the data availability stored outside of the blockchain technology. If such data were lost or tampered with, even if the change was never noticed, the system's viability would be jeopardized.

Linked Data Structure: By arranging the hash values in a linked data structure, the data hashing is improved. Merkle trees [45], for example, are used in database integrity verification, P2P networks, and blockchain [46]. Each Merkle tree node stores the cryptographic hash information of the concerned children node. Because it is recursive, the root contains statistical information about the entire tree's total number of nodes. As a result, any modification or update to any node in the tree will have an impact on the root node.

Pros of Pairing Biometrics with Blockchain Technology

- Biometric Authentication systems can be transformed by leveraging the blockchain's potential to make them substantially more secure.
- Blockchain technology employs data encryption methods to keep data secure in decentralized ledgers which could only be read by others in authority or someone who has been allowed access by the authorized individuals.
- When comparing to centralized databases, blockchain eliminates the need for intermediaries, simplifying complex transactions and lowering operational expenses.
- By integrating the two technologies, tech behemoths will be able to create flawless solutions for authentication and authorization and authentication that preserve biometric data safe in a distributed ledger system, granting consumers complete control.
- Biometric data is saved in distributed ledgers with blockchain, which means that data from many users is not maintained together. This signifies that this system has no single point of failure. As a result, thieves are less incentivized to trawl through multiple ledgers for individual identifying data. Government organizations, financial institutions, and corporate firms can all benefit from these technologies that enable self-sovereign identity management.

20.5 Conclusion

Identity systems that are usable, safe, flexible, confidentiality, and keep the individual in control seem to be in high demand for both the public and private sectors. However, distributed ledger technologies have been beginning to overcome some of the scaling issues that have kept them from being used in more advanced applications such as biometrics. Both of these aspects, we expect, will pique industry enthusiasm in how distributed ledger technology might be applied to biometrics.

Moreover, considering the decentralized and immutable structure of blockchain-stored biometric data, it is critical that such systems provide privacy, security, and scalability by design. We hope that this article will inspire future conversation on this fascinating topic, as well as contribute in some little way to defining the critical design principles required to develop an architecture that meets these security, scalability, and privacy needs.

References

1. Makhdoom, I., Abolhasan, M., Abbas, H., Ni, W., Blockchain's adoption in IoT: The challenges, and a way forward. *J. Netw. Comput. Appl.*, 125, 251–279, 2018.
2. Yli-Huumo, J., Ko, D., Choi, S., Park, S., Smolander, K., Where is current research on blockchain technology?—A systematic review. *PLoS One*, 11, 10, e0163477, 1–27, 2016.
3. Zhou, B., Xie, Z., Ye, F., Multi-modal face authentication using deep visual and acoustic features. *IEEE International Conference on Communications (ICC)*, pp. 1–6, 2019.
4. Jain, A.K., Nandakumar, K., Nagar, A., Biometric template security. *EURASIP J. Adv. Signal Process.*, 1, 113, 1–17, 2008.
5. Ratha, N.K., Connell, J.H., Bolle, R.M., Enhancing security and privacy in biometrics-based authentication systems. *IBM Syst. J.*, 40, 3, 614–634, 2001.
6. Matyáš, V. and Říha, Z., Biometric authentication—Security and usability, in: *Advanced Communications and Multimedia Security*, pp. 227–239, 2002.
7. Mehmood, R. and Selwal, A., Fingerprint biometric template security schemes: Attacks and countermeasures, in: *Proceedings of ICRIC 2019*, Springer, Cham, pp. 455–467, 2020.
8. Sarkar, A. and Singh, B.K., A review on performance,security and various biometric template protection schemes for biometric authentication systems. *Multimed. Tools Appl.*, 79, 27721–27776, 2020.

9. Yang, W., Wang, S., Hu, J., Zheng, G., Chaudhry, J., Adi, E., Valli, C., Securing mobile healthcare data: A smart card based cancelable finger-vein bio-cryptosystem. *IEEE Access*, 6, 36939–36947, 2018.

10. Zhang, W., Yuan, Y., Hu, Y., Nandakumar, K., Chopra, A., Sim, S., De Caro, A., Blockchain-based distributed compliance in multinational corporations cross-border intercompany transactions, in: *Advances in Information and Communication Networks*, pp. 304–320, Springer International Publishing, Springer, 2019.

11. Nandakumar, K. and Jain, A.K., Biometric template protection: Bridging the performance gap between theory and practice. *IEEE Signal Process. Mag.*, 32, 5, 88–100, 2015.

12. Bringer, J., Chabanne, H., Patey, A., Privacy-preserving biometric identification using secure multiparty computation: An overview and recent trends. *IEEE Signal Process. Mag.*, 30, 2, 42–52, 2013.

13. Crosby, M. *et al.*, *BlockChain technology: Beyond bitcoin*, Sutardja Center for Entrepreneurship & Technology Technical Report, University of California, Berkeley, 2015.

14. Jaikaran, C., *Blockchain: Background and policy issues*, Congressional Research Service, Washington DC, 2018.

15. Mazonka, O. *et al.*, Blockchain: Simple explanation. *Journal of Reference*, vol. 29, pp. 1–3, 2016.

16. Radziwill, N., Blockchain revolution: How the technology behind Bitcoin is changing money, business, and the world. *Qual. Manage. J.*, 25, 1, 64–65, 2018.

17. Saito, K. and Yamada, H., What's so different about blockchain? Blockchain is a probabilistic state machine. *IEEE 36th International Conference on Distributed Computing Systems Workshops*, Nara, Japan, pp. 168–175, 2016.

18. Raval, S., *Decentralized applications: Harnessing Bitcoin's blockchain technology*, O'Reilly Media, Inc., 2016.

19. Tasca, P. and Tessone, C., A taxonomy of blockchain technologies: Principles of identification and classification. *Ledger*, 4, 1:43, 2019.

20. Nakamoto, S., Bitcoin: A peer-to-peer electronic cash system. Decentralized Business Review, p. 21260, 2008.

21. Fernández-Caramés, T. and Fraga-Lamas, P., A review on the use of blockchain for the Internet of Things. *IEEE Access*, 6, 32979–33001, 2018.

22. Kumar, A. and Ravikanth, C., Personal authentication using finger knuckle surface. *IEEE Trans. Inf. Forensics Secur.*, 4, 1, 98–110, 2009.

23. Kumar, A., Personal identification using finger knuckle imaging. IITD Techn. Rep. IITD-BRL-07-2, 2007.

24. Xiao, Q., Security issues in biometric authentication. *Proceedings from the Sixth Annual IEEE Systems, Man and Cybernetics (SMC) Information Assurance Workshop*, West Point, NY, USA, pp. 8–13, 2005.

25. Ratha, N.K., Connell, J.H., Bolle, R.M., Enhancing security and privacy in biometrics-based authentication systems. *IBM Syst. J.*, 40, 614–634, 2001.

26. Dannen, C., *Introducing ethereum and solidit*, vol. 1, Springer, Berlin/ Heidelberg, Germany, 2017.

27. Eyal, I. and Sirer, E.G., Majority is not enough: Bitcoin mining is vulnerable. *Lect. Notes Comput. Sci.*, 8437, 436–454, 2014.

28. Atzei, N. *et al.*, A survey of attacks on Ethereum smart contracts SoK, in: *Proc. Intl. Conf. on Principles of Security and Trust*, Springer, 2017.

29. Lee, S.H. and Yang, C.S., Fingernail analysis management system using microscopy sensor and blockchain technology. *Int. J. Distrib. Sens. Netw.*, 14, 550147718767044, 2019.

30. Pawade, D., Sakhapara, A., Andrade, M., Badgujar, A., Adepu, D., Implementation of fingerprint-based authentication system using blockchain, in: *Soft Computing and Signal Processing*, pp. 233–242, Springer, Berlin/Heidelberg, Germany, 2019.

31. Mohsin, A., Zaidan, A., Zaidan, B., Albahri, O., Albahri, A., Alsalem, M., Mohammed, K., Based Blockchain-PSO-AES techniques in finger vein biometrics: A novel verification secure framework for patient authentication. *Comput. Stand. Interfaces*, 66, 103343, 2019.

32. Páez, R., Pérez, M., Ramírez, G., Montes, J., Bouvarel, L., Architecture for biometric electronic identification document system based on blockchain. *Future Internet*, 12, 2020.

33. Buchmann, N., Rathgeb, C., Baier, H., Busch, C., Margraf, M., Enhancing breeder document long-term security using blockchain technology, in: *IEEE Annual Computer Software and Applications Conference*, vol. 2, pp. 744–748, 2017.

34. Nandakumar, K., Ratha, N., Pankanti, S., Darnell, S., Secure one-time biometric tokens for non-repudiable multiparty transactions, in: *IEEE Workshop on Information Forensics and Security*, pp. 1–6, 2017.

35. Garcia, P., Biometrics on the blockchain. *Biom. Technol. Today*, 5, 5–7, 2018.

36. Delgado-Mohatar, O., Fierrez, J., Tolosana, R., VeraRodriguez, R., Blockchain and biometrics: A first look into opportunities and challenges, arXiv:1903.05496, 2020.

37. Zhou, X., Hafedh, Y., Wang, Y., Jesus, V., A simple auditable fingerprint authentication scheme using smartcontracts, in: *International Conference on Smart Blockchain*, Springer, pp. 86–92, 2018.

38. Gordon, W.J. and Catalini, C., Blockchain technology for healthcare: Facilitating the transition to patient-driven interoperability. *Comput. Struct. Biotechnol.*, 16, 224–230, 2018.

39. Stokkink, Q. and Pouwelse, J., Deployment of a blockchain-based self-sovereign identity, arXiv preprint arXiv:1806.01926, 2018.

40. Aggarwal, S., Chaudhary, R., Aujla, G.S., Jindal, A., Dua, A., Kumar, N., Energy chain: Enabling energy trading for smart homes using blockchains in smart grid ecosystem, in: *ACM MobiHoc Workshop on Networking and Cybersecurity for Smart Cities*, p. 1, 2018.

41. Magnani, A., Calderoni, L., Palmieri, P., Feather forking as a positive force: Incentivising green energy production in a blockchain-based smart grid, in: *ACM Workshop on Cryptocurrencies and Blockchains for Distributed Systems*, pp. 99–104, 2018.

42. Gomez-Barrero, M. *et al.*, Multi-biometric template protection based on homomorphic encryption. *Pattern Recognit.*, 67, 149–163, July 2017.

43. Delgado-Mohatar, O., Fierrez, J., Tolosana, R., Vera-Rodriguez, R., Blockchain meets biometrics: Concepts, application to template protection, and trends, arXiv preprint arXiv:2003.09262, 2020.

44. Ozyilmaz, K.R. and Yurdakul, A., Designing a blockchain-based IoT infrastructure with ethereum, swarm and: The software solution to create high availability with minimal security risks. *IEEE Consum. Electron. Mag.*, 8, 2, 28–34, 2019.

45. Merkle, R.C., A digital signature based on a conventional encryption function, in: *Conf. on the Theory and Applications of Cryptographic Techniques on Advances in Cryptology (CRYPTO)*, Springer, London, UK, pp. 369–378, 1988.

46. Dannen, C., *Introducing ethereum and solidity: Foundations of cryptocurrency and blockchain programming for beginners*, A Press, Berkeley, CA, USA, 2017.

Index

Also of Interest

Check out these published and forthcoming titles in the "Artificial Intelligence and Soft Computing for Industrial Transformation" series from Scrivener Publishing

Artificial Intelligence for Sustainable Applications
Edited By K. Umamaheswari, B. Vinoth Kumar and S. K. Somasundaram
Published 2023. ISBN 978-1-394-17458-4

Cognitive Intelligence and Big Data in Healthcare
Edited by D. Sumathi, T. Poongodi, B. Balamurugan and Lakshmana Kumar Ramasamy
Published 2022. ISBN 978-1-119-76888-3

Convergence of Deep Learning in Cyber-IoT Systems and Security
Edited by Rajdeep Chakraborty, Anupam Ghosh, Jyotsna Kumar Mandal and S. Balamurugan
Published 2023. ISBN 978-1-119-85721-1

The New Advanced Society
Artificial Intelligence and Industrial Internet of Things Paradigm
Edited by Sandeep Kumar Panda, Ramesh Kumar Mohapatra, Subhrakanta Panda and S. Balamurugan
Published 2022. ISBN 978-1-119-82447-3

Digitization of Healthcare Data Using Blockchain
Edited by T. Poongodi, D. Sumathi, B. Balamurugan and K. S. Savita
Published 2022. ISBN 978-1-119-79185-0

Tele-Healthcare
Applications of Artificial Intelligence and Soft Computing Techniques
Edited by R. Nidhya, Manish Kumar and S. Balamurugan
Published 2022. ISBN 978-1-119-84176-0

Impact of Artificial Intelligence on Organizational Transformation
Edited by S. Balamurugan, Sonal Pathak, Anupriya Jain, Sachin Gupta, and
Sachin Sharma and Sonia Duggal
Published 2022. ISBN 978-1-119-71017-2

Artificial Intelligence for Renewable Energy Systems
Edited by Ajay Kumar Vyas, S. Balamurugan, Kamal Kant Hiran Harsh S.
Dhiman
Published 2022. ISBN 978-1-119-76169-3

Artificial Intelligence Techniques for Wireless Communication and Networking
Edited by Kanthavel R., K. Ananthajothi, S. Balamurugan and R. Karthik
Ganesh
Published 2022. ISBN 978-1-119-82127 4

Advanced Healthcare Systems
Empowering Physicians with IoT-Enabled Technologies
Edited by Rohit Tanwar, S. Balamurugan, R. K. Saini, Vishal Bharti and
Premkumar Chithaluru
Published 2022. ISBN 978-1-119-76886-9

Smart Systems for Industrial Applications
Edited by C. Venkatesh, N. Rengarajan, P. Ponmurugan and S. Balamurugan
Published 2022. ISBN 978-1-119-76200-3

Intelligent Renewable Energy Systems
Edited by Neeraj Priyadarshi, Akash Kumar Bhoi, Sanjeevikumar
Padmanabam, S.Balamurugan, and Jens Bo Holm-Nielson
Published 2022. ISBN 978-1-119-78627-6

Human Technology Communication
Internet of Robotic Things and Ubiquitous Computing
Edited by R. Anandan. G. Suseendran, S. Balamurugan, Ashish Mishra
and D. Balaganesh
Published 2021. ISBN 978-1-119-75059-8

Nature-Inspired Algorithms Applications
Edited by S. Balamurugan, Anupriya Jain, Sachin Sharma, Dinesh Goyal,
Sonia Duggal and Seema Sharma
Published 2021. ISBN 978-1-119-68174-8

Computation in Bioinformatics
Multidisciplinary Applications
Edited by S. Balamurugan, Anand Krishnan, Dinesh Goyal, Balakumar Chandrasekaran and Boomi Pandi
Published 2021. ISBN 978-1-119-65471-1

Fuzzy Intelligent Systems
Methodologies, Techniques, and Applications
Edited by E. Chandrasekaran, R. Anandan, G. Suseendran, S. Balamurugan and Hanaa Hachimi
Published 2021. ISBN 978-1-119-76045-0

Biomedical Data Mining for Information Retrieval
Methodologies, Techniques and Applications
Edited by Sujata Dash, Subhendu Kumar Pani, S. Balamurugan and Ajith Abraham
Published 2021. ISBN 978-1-119-71124-7

Design and Analysis of Security Protocols for Communication
Edited by Dinesh Goyal, S. Balamurugan, Sheng-Lung Peng and O.P. Verma
Published 2020. ISBN 978-1-119-55564-3

www.scrivenerpublishing.com

Printed and bound by CPI Group (UK) Ltd, Croydon, CR0 4YY

27/10/2024

14580131-0003